MW00680636

STUDENT LEARNING GUIDE

to accompany

MANAGEMENT FOR PRODUCTIVITY

JOHN R. SCHERMERHORN, Jr.
Southern Illinois University at Carbondale

Prepared by
PATRICK KROLL
University of Minnesota at Minneapolis

JOHN WILEY & SONS
NEW YORK CHICHESTER
BRISBANE TORONTO
SINGAPORE

Permissions

The following articles are reprinted with permission:

1. "Management Blamed for U.S. Auto Lag," *Minneapolis Star and Tribune,* July 27, 1982. Reprinted by permission of AP Newsfeatures.

2. "Munsingwear Aims at Increased Sales," *Minneapolis Star and Tribune,* May 1, 1983. Reprinted with permission from the *Minneapolis Star and Tribune.*

3. "Teamwork in Business," *The Royal Bank Letter,* Vol. 63, No. 1, Jan./Feb. 1982. © The Royal Bank of Canada 1982. Reprinted by permission.

4. "Leadership, Management and the Seven Keys," by Craig M. Watson. From *Business Horizons,* March/April 1983, pp. 8-13. Copyright 1983 by the Foundation for the School of Business at Indiana University. Reprinted by permission.

5. "Surviving the Second Industrial Revolution," by John Diebold. Reprinted by permission of the publisher from "Surviving the Second Industrial Revolution," by John Diebold, from *Management Reveiw,* March 1983, pp. 8-15. © 1983 by AMACOM, a division of American Management Associations. All rights reserved.

6. "The Productivity Value of Environment," by Michael Maas. Reprinted by permission of the publisher from "The Productivity Value of Environment," by Michael Maas, from *Management Reveiw,* March 1983, pp. 16-20. © 1983 by AMACOM, a division of American Management Associations. All rights reserved.

7. "The Social Readjustment Rating Scale," by T.H. Holmes and R.H. Rahe. From *Journal of Psychosomatic Research 11,* pp. 213-218, 1967. Copyright 1967 by *Journal of Psychosomatic Research 11.* Reprinted by permission.

Reproduction and adaptation of employment questionnaire from "The Employment Interview: A Summary and Review of Recent Research," by Richard O. Avery and James E. Campion, *Personnel Psychology,* Vol. 35, 1982, with permission.

Time Wasters adapted from *The Time Trap* by Alec R. MacKinzie, McGraw Hill Book Company, 1975, with permission.

Comparative indicators table and findings adapted from "Where We Stand: The U.S. Vis-a-Vis Everyone Else," by Andrew Cross, *Business Horizons,* March/April 1983, with permission.

Job application questionnaire and comparison adapted from "A Survey of the Chief Personnel Officers in the 500 Largest Corporations in the United States to Determine Their Preference in Job Application Letters and Personal Resumes," by Barron Wells, Nelda Spinks, and Janice Hargrave, *The ABCA Bulletin*, June 1981, with permission.

Copyright © 1983 by John Wiley & Sons, Inc.

All rights reserved.

Reproduction or translation of any part of this work
beyond that permitted by Sections 107 or 108 of
the 1976 United States Copyright Act
without the permission of the copyright owner is unlawful.

Requests for permission or further information
should be addressed to the
Permissions Department, John Wiley & Sons, Inc.

ISBN 0 471 88609 2

Printed in the United States of America

10 9 8 7 6 5 4 3 2 1

CONTENTS

HOW TO USE THE LEARNING GUIDE

This student learning guide is closely coordinated with your textbook *Management for Productivity* by John Schermerhorn. By using the learning guide you should save considerable study time and facilitate your learning. There are several features used throughout this guide that should help you master the text content:

1. Learning objectives for each chapter
2. Chapter highlights or overviews
3. Terms and concepts
4. Exam items to test your comprehension of material
5. Individual learning exercises to help apply what you have learned

A special feature of this learning guide is the chapter-by-chapter programmed learning exercise. That is, each chapter is greatly condensed into what educators call programmed format. Key terms and concepts are to be recalled by you in order to finish short, incomplete sentences from the text. The key learning principle incorporated into the programmed material is reinforcement. By reading the text and then filling in blanks in the programmed study section, you are challenging yourself to recall key concepts and then reinforcing learning as you verify accuracy of your recall from the text. As a result you should retain material more readily than through simply reading and highlighting, and you should retain material longer. Answers for the programmed material are in the back of this guide.

Throw away the messy highlighters. No need to laboriously underline material within the text. The programmed learning material allows you to eliminate the highlighting. By eliminating the high-lighting habit, you should improve your reading rate instead of slowing it down through the tedious underlining process. You will find that with rapid, intensive reading you will become more efficient in your learning and raise your own interest level.

Learning Guide Format

The learning guide is comprised of 21 chapters divided into 7 separate parts paralleling the text format. Part 1, for example, has both a format depicting the 3 chapters and a Part 1 theme, as well as a chapter-by-chapter outline. Each of the 7 learning guide parts is comprised of:

1. Highlights
2. Chapter titles
3. Career perspective
4. Learning activities including:
   a. A reprinted journal article to provide the student extra resources for discussion.
   b. Exercises which provide a variety of short learning applications based upon chapter content and made directly relevant to students' needs.
   c. A section called "matching wits with the experts" which allows the student to compare his/her views with those of authority in a particular field.
   d. An experiential learning exercise such as a business simulation in which the student must deal in comprehensive fashion with a business/management problem.
5. "A look back and a look ahead" section that helps link parts together.

Chapter Format

Each chapter within each major part of this guide includes:

1. Chapter title
2. Learning objectives to be mastered
3. Chapter overview or "highlights"
4. Programmed learning exercise
5. "Testing Your Knowledge," a section of sample test items

PART I
INTRODUCTION

INTRODUCTION — PART 1

(Chapters 1 — 3)

<u>Highlights</u>

Part 1, Chapters 1—3 of the text, introduces managers and management activities existing in a dynamic world of change and competition. Early in Chapter 1, for example, the author raises the issue of falling U.S. productivity in contrast to the high and rising rates of productivity being achieved by the Japanese managers and workers. Why is the U.S. faltering in productivity?

Each of the first three chapters provides important perspectives regarding the importance of management in the quest for greater organizational effectiveness—productivity. Chapter 1, for example, reminds us that in the United States we have become a society of institutions—that we do not operate on the job simply as individuals, but as members of this group or that group. We are constantly being required to interact with other members of departments in which we work and with other individuals and subgroups in the organization as a whole.

To make the chapter more personalized, you should think about how well you believe that you operate in the group setting. What knowledge and skills do you have now to help you function in organizational settings, and what additional ones do you need?

Historically speaking, in what differing ways was management organization structure and productivity viewed? Was management's understanding of the nature of work and workers significantly different in the early 1900s compared with today? Chapter 2 helps provide the historical perspective regarding evolving management theory and practice.

Chapter 3 ties the question of how to improve productivity—a recurring theme in our text—to fundamental managerial skills including decision making and problem solving. Again, you should try to identify personally with the chapter material by asking yourself questions related to key points in the chapter:

1. Do I have a set of steps to use when faced with complex problems?
2. Could I be an effective manager considering the demands made on managers in the organizational, problem-solving setting?
3. How might I improve my own problem-solving techniques?

<u>Chapter Titles for Part 1</u>

Chapter 1 — Managers, Management, and Productivity
Chapter 2 — Historical Perspectives on Management
Chapter 3 — The Manager as Decision Maker and Problem Solver

CAREER PERSPECTIVE — PART 1

To begin each major part of the learning guide, a "Career Perspective" activity will be presented to help you develop one or more interests or skills in respect to entering and advancing in a career.

Write Your Own Resumé

Based upon the author's format under the career perspective at the end of Chapter 1 of the text, you are to design and write your own resumé or you may use the sample resumé below. Once written to your satisfaction, get it professionally typed.

Compare your own resumé to that of Terry Lee, the person created by the author of the text. Then answer certain critical career-related questions: What should you be doing to establish or expand your credentials by the time you graduate? In other words, what strengths can you build on and what weaknesses can you overcome?

Sample Resumé Format

Identification
Name

Address

Phone

Career Objective

Education

Employment Experience

Volunteer Experience

Summary
Strengths:

Limitations:

References

Write Your Own Cover Letter

Resumes are not always solicited by companies, but instead are sent without request by the applicant. However, the unsolicited resume usually needs some form of introduction, and this introduction is usually done through a cover letter.

You are to write a one-page letter of self-introduction to accompany your resume. You must decide both the content of the letter and the style and tone. Do you want to sound assertive, for example? In charge? Hard working? How will you present yourself overall? Ask a classmate or a faculty adviser to read and respond to both your letter and resumé.

Use the exercise, "Matching Wits with the Experts" at the end of Part 1 as a guide to see what professional personnel administrators prefer in terms of content and style of both the resume and the cover letter.

1 Managers, Management, and Productivity

STUDENT LEARNING OBJECTIVES

After completing the chapter material you should be able to:

1. Define management and describe the environment in which managers operate.
2. Define organizations and the importance of organizations, and list the three "key" organization ingredients.
3. Explain different managerial levels and types of management positions and the respective responsibilities associated with each.
4. Relate management "success" to its contribution to productivity.
5. List and briefly explain management processes, functions, and roles.
6. Distinguish among the three different essential managerial skills.

CHAPTER HIGHLIGHTS

Managers
Organizations
Managers in organizations
Productivity and the manager's role
The management process
The nature of managerial work
Managerial skills
The study of management

PROGRAMMED LEARNING

The following statements are drawn from actual textbook content in abbreviated form. The blanks within the statements are numbered to correspond with the answer blanks at the left. By duplicating spaces at the left, we hope this will speed up your review of material later on.

Work and the manager

1. _____

An activity that produces value for other people is called _____(1).

2. _____
3. _____

A person in an organization who is responsible for the _____(2) performance of one or more people is a _____(3).

4. _____

People are a basic _____(4) of organizations.

5. _____

_____(5) resources such as information, equipment, and facilities are used to produce a good or service.

6. _____
7. _____
8. _____

The manager's job is to help the organization achieve a high level of _____(6) through the utilization of its _____(7) and _____(8) resources.

9. _____

The basic task of every manager is to help organizations get things done through _____(9).

10. _____

No job is more vital to our society than that of _____(10).

Organizations: The manager's work setting

11. _____

Managers work in _____(11).

12. _____
13. _____
14. _____

An organization is a collection of _____(12) working together in a division of _____(13) to achieve a common _____(14).

15. _____

Managers are universal in that they are _____(15) to organizations.

16. _____

Organizations perform tasks that are beyond _____(16) capabilities alone.

17. _____

Organizations begin with _____(17).

18. _____
19. _____
20. _____

The three ingredients involved in organizations are: common _____(18), division of _____(19), and hierarchy of _____(20).

21. _____
22. _____

The purpose of an organization is to produce a _____(21) or _____(22).

23. _____

One way to analyze any organization is to view it as an _____(23) system.

24. _____

The final good or service produced from the resource transformation process represents the organization's _____(24).

25. _____

The production of this good or service is made possible by the direct interaction of the organization with its _____(25).

Division of labor and authority

26. _____

The essence of organization is coordinated _____(26).

27. _____

A combination of the work of many people is what allows organizations to overcome the _____(27) limitations of their members.

28. _____   _____(28) of labor is the process of breaking the work into smaller components and allocating them to individuals.

29. _____   Formal _____(29) is one way in which a manager coordinates the division of labor.

30. _____   Formal authority permits one the right to _____(30).

31. _____   _____(31) is an important basis for managerial action, and some managers are better at using it than others.

32. _____   Persons at the highest levels of management ensure that _____(32) are set and accomplished.

33. _____   _____(33) and _____(34) guidelines for subordinates at lower
34. _____   levels are interpreted by middle managers.

35. _____   _____(35) managers constitute the second or third level in the hierarchy of authority.

36. _____   Middle managers are _____(36) through which information flows upward in the hierarchy.

37. _____   First line managers _____(37) the plans and directions of middle and upper managers on a day-to-day basis.

38. _____   The situations in which lower level managers operate are high in potential
39. _____   conflict and demand considerable _____(38) and _____(39) skill on the manager's part.

Types of managers

40. _____   _____(40) managers have responsibility for work which makes a direct contribution to production of the organization.

41. _____   _____(41) managers support the production of efforts of the line personnel.

42. _____   _____(42) managers are responsible for more complex organizational subunits.

43. _____   _____(43) are managers who work in public or nonprofit organizations.

44. _____   Most managers are simultaneously _____(44) and _____(45).
45. _____

46. _____   Managers are also held accountable by their superiors for _____(46) of their work units.

47. _____   In order to achieve satisfactory performance, managers depend upon the efforts of their _____(47).

Productivity and the manager

48. _____   The ultimate criterion of managerial success is the _____(48) of the group of people reporting to the manager.

49. _____   The summary measure of the quality of work performance with resource utilization included is called _____(49).

50. _____   The basic performance responsibility of all managers includes maintaining a highly productive work unit over _____(50).

51. _____   Two criteria that measure a manager's success in the quest for productivity
52. _____   are performance _____(51) and performance _____(52).

53. _____	Effectiveness is an output measure of task or goal _____(53).
54. _____	Efficiency is a measure of the _____(54) realized versus _____(55)
55. _____	consumed.

The management process

56. _____	_____(56) is defined as the process of planning, organizing, leading, and controlling resources.
57. _____	Management is also a noun that represents a field of _____(57)
58. _____	_____(58) based upon scientific foundations.
59. _____	Time spent on _____(59) is proportionately greater at lower management levels than in higher levels.
60. _____	Time spent on _____(60) is relatively the same at each management level.
61. _____	Overall, managerial work is well characterized as involving _____(61),
62. _____	_____(62), _____(63), and controlling.
63. _____	

Developing managerial skills

64. _____	A _____(64) is an ability to translate knowledge into action that results in the desired performance.
65. _____	_____(65) skills are more important at lower management levels where supervisors are dealing with concrete problems.
66. _____	_____(66) skills are more important at higher levels of management.
67. _____	_____(67) is any change in behavior that occurs as a result of experience.

TESTING YOUR KNOWLEDGE

True and False Self Test

Directions: Circle the letter (T or F) of the correct response for each of the following statements.

T F   1. Besides using people, organizations also involve combinations of machinery, equipment, raw materials, facilities, and money.

T F   2. By giving some managers formal authority over other managers, a hierarchy of authority is created.

T F   3. Tactile direction of the enterprise requires a manager to monitor the environment to identify potential problems and opportunities associated with this direction.

T F   4. Titles common to staff managers are legal counsel, personnel manager, and quality control manager.

T F   5. Management is defined as delegating and controlling lower level subordinates.

T F   6. The management process requires a capability to make decisions, solve problems, and take action.

T F   7. Management has two basic functions only—leading and controlling.

T F   8. In the modern management era, planning and organizing are quite frequently delegated to the lower level managers.

T F   9. There is only one characteristic to measure managers' success—efficiency.

T F   10. Productivity indices exclude such things as output per person hour, clients served and student credit hours taught per faculty.

Multiple Choice Self Test

Directions: Circle the letter of the response that best completes each of the following statements.

1. An activity that produces value for other people is called:
    a. work
    b. working
    c. production
    d. productivity

2. An organization is not complete without:
    a. collection of people
    b. division of labor
    c. common purpose
    d. all of the above

3. Organizations begin with:
    a. money
    b. machines
    c. people
    d. customers

4. The level of management that is responsible for strategic direction of the organization is:
    a. top
    b. middle
    c. lower
    d. all of the above

5. An example of staff management would be:
    a. director of operations
    b. manager of production
    c. foreperson over the ditch digging crew
    d. quality control manager

6. The ultimate criterion of management success is his/her:
    a. popularity with subordinates
    b. longevity in the position and organization
    c. effect on productivity
    d. level of earnings
    e. depends on whose perspective we might consider

7. If productivity were the ultimate measure of managerial success, then the means employed to achieve it is called management:
    a. politics
    b. policies
    c. process
    d. none of the above

8. The higher the management level, the greater the time allocated to:
    a. planning
    b. organizing
    c. controlling
    d. leading
    e. both a and b are correct

9. Managerial roles include:
    a. interpersonal relationships
    b. information processing
    c. decision making
    d. all of the above

10. Regarding technical skills deployed in management, they are relatively more important at which level?
     a. upper
     b. middle
     c. lower
     d. each level uses technical skills about as often as the other

Matching Self Test

Directions: Write the letter of the description that best fits each numbered item in the blank provided.

_____ 1. Henry Mintzberg

_____ 2. Skill

_____ 3. Robert Katz

_____ 4. Administrator

_____ 5. Middle manager

_____ 6. Formal authority

_____ 7. First line manager

_____ 8. Hierarchy of authority

_____ 9. Management functions

_____ 10. Conceptual skill

a. Classified essential skills of managers into 3 categories.

b. Managers who work in nonprofit organizations are ɔeled this.

c. Views managerial work as being interpersonal, informational, and decision-making.

d. Dean, department head, and district comptroller are examples of this.

e. Having the ability to view the organization as a whole.

f. Coordinated division of labor.

g. Coordination at different levels of management.

h. Planning, organizing, leading, and controlling.

i. Learning.

j. Implements plans and directives of middle and upper management.

2 Historical Perspectives on Management

STUDENT LEARNING OBJECTIVES

After completing the chapter you should be able to:

1. Compare and contrast management as an art and a science.
2. Define management in terms of a profession.
3. List sources of some of the earliest systematic thinking about management.
4. Define classical management and explain the three branches of classical management.
5. Define behavioral management and explain major research contributions from Hawthorne and that era to more recent contributors to management theory and application.
6. Explain the common elements of quantitative analysis, management science, and operations research in defining management.
7. List and explain the four chatacteristics of the quantitative management approach.
8. Identify and compare the two modern approaches to management and describe how the author incorporates the modern approach into the text.

CHAPTER HIGHLIGHTS

Perspectives on management
The evolution of management thought
Classical approaches to management
Behavioral approaches to management
Quantitative approaches to management
Modern approaches to management

PROGRAMMED LEARNING

The following statements are drawn from actual textbook content in abbreviated form. The blanks within the statements are numbered to correspond with the answer blanks at the left.

Management foundation

1. _____ A _____(1) is a set of concepts and ideas that systematically explains and predicts physical and social phenomena.

2. _____ The term used to predict the behaviors of organizations and their members is called _____(2) theory.

3. _____ In order to make good problem-solving decisions in their day to day efforts, managers must use good _____(3).

Perspectives on management practice

4. _____ J. Paul Getty feels that experience alone is not a good indicator of _____(4) ability.

5. _____ Management can be defined as both an _____(5) and _____(6).
6. _____

7. _____ Something a person practices based on skills to achieve a desired result is called an _____(7).

8. _____ A _____(8) is a body of knowledge systematically created via the scientific method.

9. _____ Management as a science provides managers with a vocabulary of terms and concepts to allow work experiences to be clearly_____(9) shared and discussed.

10. _____ With concepts specified, managers can _____(10) their impressions of work and share them with others.

11. _____ All organized activities depend upon a _____(11).

12. _____ Management as a science provides managers with _____(12) for dealing with many of the work-setting problems.

13. _____ Management has been referred to as a _____(13) and managers as
14. _____ _____(14).

15. _____ _____(15) and _____(16) are the essence of any profession.
16. _____

17. _____ Being a manager clearly satisfies some but not all the basic criteria of _____(17).

18. _____ Management is enhanced by the presence of a basic body of _____(18)
19. _____ or _____(19) foundation.

Evolution of management thought

20. _____ Management principles which we know as _____(20) and division of
21. _____ _____(21) were established by Adam Smith.

22. _____ Smith's ideas ushered in the _____(22) Revolution.

23. _____ The Industrial Revolution was practiced by Henry Ford who made _____(23) production a modern reality.

24. _____ The classical approach to management assumes that people are
25. _____ _____(24) and _____(25) in their orientation to work.

26. _____
27. _____
28. _____

The three branches of the classical approach to management are scientific _____(26), _____(27) principles, and _____(28) organization.

29. _____
30. _____

Fred Taylor emphasized that management objectives should be stated to secure maximum _____(29) for the employer and maximum _____(30) for the employee.

31. _____
32. _____
33. _____
34. _____

Fred Taylor offered four principles of scientific management: develop a _____(31) for every job; select workers with the right _____(32) for the job; offer proper _____(33) to employees who cooperate; and support workers by _____(34) their work and smoothing the way for them.

35. _____

Frank and Lillian Gilbreth are the acclaimed pioneers of _____(35) study in industry.

36. _____
37. _____
38. _____

The Gilbreths' work established the foundations for later advances in the areas of job _____(36), work _____(37), and _____(38) wage plans.

39. _____
40. _____
41. _____

The work of Fayol, Follett, Mooney, and Urwick has allowed the management theory to derive its emphasis on four processes: planning, _____(39), _____(40), _____(41).

42. _____

Max Weber is considered the father of _____(42).

43. _____

Managers using general principles of management will achieve _____(43).

44. _____

Managers using proper organizational _____(44) will achieve productivity.

45. _____

_____(45) was the ideal organizational form for Weber.

Behavioral approaches to management

46. _____

Classical theorists developed rather _____(46) approaches to management.

47. _____
48. _____
49. _____

Taylor, Fayol, Weber, and others assumed that if given proper job _____(47) and _____(48) practices and _____(49) structures, people would likely be productive.

50. _____
51. _____

The various branches of the behavioral approach to management generally reflect a shared belief in people's _____(50) and _____(51) nature.

52. _____
53. _____

Elton Mayo established two facts as having special importance in increasing worker productivity: positive group _____(52) and _____(53) management.

54. _____
55. _____
56. _____
57. _____

The Hawthorne Studies shifted attention of managers away from _____(54) and _____(55) aspects of work to _____(56) and _____(57) behavior factors as further keys to output.

58. _____
59. _____
60. _____

Maslow's theory states that individual _____(58) cause tensions which affect worker _____(59) and _____(60).

61. _____

Maslow's deficit principle states that a _____(61) need is not a motivator of behavior.

62. _____   Maslow's _____(62) principle states that people have a hierarchy of
63. _____   _____(63).

64. _____   A deprived need causes a _____(64) that dominates individual at-
65. _____   tention and determines individual _____(65).

66. _____   Maslow implies that a manager who satisfies human needs will achieve
                       _____(66).

67. _____   McGregor advocated that managers must shift from a very negative Theory
68. _____   _____(67) attitude toward employees to a more open trustworthy
                       Theory _____(68) attitude.

69. _____   A Theory X manager assumes that subordinates by their nature
                       _____(69) work.

70. _____   Theory X style management can cause managers to be very directive, nar-
                       row, and _____(70) oriented.

71. _____   Theory Y management encourages the allowing to subordinates more
72. _____   _____(71), _____(72), and _____(73) in their work.
73. _____

74. _____   In order to accomodate the mature personality, Chris Argyris advises
75. _____   managers to expand on: job _____(74), task _____(75), and re-
                       sponsibility and more participation.

Quantitative approaches to management

76. _____   When a problem is encountered via quantitative approach to management,
77. _____   it is _____(76) analyzed; appropriate _____(77) computations are
78. _____   made; and an _____(78) solution is selected as a result.

79. _____   The essence of any quantitative management approach is found in the
80. _____   following characteristics: primary focus on _____(79) making, based
81. _____   upon _____(80)decision criteria, use of formal _____(81) models,
82. _____   and frequent use of electronic _____(82).

83. _____   According to QA approaches managers using QA techniques will achieve
                       _____(83).

84. _____   Success in the application of quantitative techniques depends on both
85. _____   the _____(84) expertise of the scientist and the willingness of other
                       persons to _____(85) the recommended problem solutions.

Modern approaches to management

86. _____   The current newer approaches to modern management require a need for
                       managers to know what will work best in any given _____(86).

87. _____   Modern management approaches try to balance the _____/_____(87)
88. _____   assumptions of the classical school with the _____/_____(88) assump-
                       tions of the behavioralists.

89. _____   The modern approaches of management build from a base of _____(89).

90. _____   Modern management assumes that people are _____(90) and
91. _____   _____(91).

92. _____   Modern managers attend to the multiple and varied _____(92) of
                       employees.

93. _____   Modern managers _____(93) the patterns of needs, action tendencies
94. _____   and desires over time and respond to a wide variety of organizational
95. _____   _____(94) and managerial _____(95).

96. _____   According to Barnard, the essence of any organization is _____(96) among people.

97. _____   Barnard claims that a "_____"(97) will be the result of the willingness to serve and allow people to accomplish the task together.

98. _____   The general systems theory brings the _____(98) into visability as a critical management issue.

99. _____   The contingency approach to management emphasizes _____(99) differences and the need for managers to respond to them.

100. _____   The main point behind the contingency perspective is to help managers analyze and understand _____(100) differences and choose responses that best facilitate productivity.

101. _____
102. _____
103. _____   Depending upon such things as _____(101) demands, _____(102) factors, and group _____(103), the managers' actions will vary from one situation to the next.

The approach of this book

104. _____
105. _____   The author's goal is to help you the student understand management _____(104) and the nature of the contemporary work _____(105) so that your managerial decisions and actions will always be sound and successful.

TESTING YOUR KNOWLEDGE

True and False Self Test

Directions: Circle the letter (T or F) of the correct response for each of the following statements.

T   F   1. Management theory suggests that the best managers are usually X style in their assumptions.

T   F   2. Adam Smith is known as the father of scientific management.

T   F   3. Management functions are planning, organizing, leading, and controlling.

T   F   4. Theory Y managers are directive and control oriented.

T   F   5. Chris Argyris suggests that managers using responses to mature personalities will achieve high productivity.

T   F   6. The Quantitative approach to management emphasizes environmental differences and the need for managers to respond to them.

T   F   7. Productivity is usually not a high goal of management.

T   F   8. Management can be defined as both an art and a science.

T   F   9. J. Paul Getty emphasized that a college degree will almost certainly guarantee success as a manager.

T   F   10. Motion study is the science of measuring effects of automation on human feelings.

Multiple Choice Self Test

Directions: Circle the letter of the response that best completes each of the following statements.

1. An example of an application of classical approach to management is:
    a.   administrative principles
    b.   scientific method
    c.   bureaucratic organization
    d.   all of the above
    e.   none of the above

2. In particular, the lessons of scientific management relate to:
    a.   the role of compensation as an incentive to increase employee productivity
    b.   the design of jobs
    c.   proper selection of people for jobs
    d.   training people to perform particular tasks
    e.   all of the above

3. The human relations school of management attempts to improve productivity of employees by:
    a.   manipulating economic factors
    b.   adjusting physical or environmental factors
    c.   effecting social and human factors
    d.   none of the above

4. If employees are satisfied in terms of needs, they are not likely to be:
    a.   motivated
    b.   productive
    c.   friendly
    d.   cooperative

5. Managers who view employees as lazy, irresponsible, and resistant to change are labeled by McGregor as theory:
    a.   X
    b.   Y
    c.   Z
    d.   0, as in zero

6. Regarding employees in the U.S. in general, what is probably an accurate generalization to make:
    a.   Very few employees fit Theory X designation.
    b.   Most are Y-type employees.
    c.   X and Y employees probably don't exist side by side in the same department since they are so different.
    d.   Whether employees are X or Y depends upon a variety of circumstances so that it is best not to generalize.

7. Chris Argyris believes that in practicing scientific or classical management styles, that:
    a.   self-actualizing opportunities for employees may be hurt when such styles are used
    b.   dependency relations can develop
    c.   psychological failure may occur as a result of people being over directed
    d.   all of the above

8. Modern contingency approaches to management eliminate the belief that:
    a.   people want to be self-directed
    b.   there is one best way to do things
    c.   money can serve to improve people's interest in productivity
    d.   employees can be self-directed in their work

9. If the ultimate goal of managers is productivity, then the way to achieve this is to:
    a. push for productivity as an ongoing management mandate
    b. organize for high worker and job specialization
    c. set up all jobs so that financial rewards are for piece rates or other output measures
    d. consider all variables in the situation and proceed on that basis

10. If the manager pushes productivity as his/her major interest, the employees:
    a. will likely rebel
    b. demand a percent of the output results
    c. get sick of this goal
    d. can't say without seeing the actual situation

Matching Self Test

Directions: Write the letter of the description that best fits each numbered item in the blank provided.

_____ 1. Hawthorne study

_____ 2. Max Weber

_____ 3. Theory X managers believe

_____ 4. Classical approach to management

_____ 5. Frederick Taylor

_____ 6. A characteristic of the Weberian bureaucracy

_____ 7. Specialization and division of labor

_____ 8. Quantitative management

_____ 9. Maslow's Theory

_____ 10. Management theory

a. Believed that the object of management was to share maximum prosperity for employer and employee.

b. Division of labor.

c. Predicts and explains behaviors of organizations and their members.

d. Shifted attention of managers from purely physical and technical aspects of work to social and human factors.

e. Hierarchy of needs.

f. Shares a common assumption that people are rational and economic.

g. Revolutionized the world of work.

h. Father of bureaucracy.

i. Electronic computers, economic decisions, and math models.

j. People prefer to be led, not to lead.

3 The Manager as a Decision Maker and Problem Solver

STUDENT LEARNING OBJECTIVES

After completing this material you should be able to:

1. Define choice making, decision making and problem solving, and distinguish differences among them.
2. List and explain managerial problem-solving skills and styles.
3. List and explain problem-solving steps.
4. Explain different types of managerial problems.
5. Repeat the text examples of barriers to problem solving and how to deal with these barriers.
6. Formulate and analyze ways to generate alternative solutions to problems via creative, innovative methods.
7. Discuss relative merits of group versus individual approaches to problem solving.

CHAPTER HIGHLIGHTS

Choice making, decision making, and problem solving
Managerial problem solving
The problem-solving process
Finding and identifying problems
Formulating and analyzing alternative solutions
Choosing among alternative solutions: making the decision
Implementing solutions and evaluating results

PROGRAMMED LEARNING

The following statements are drawn from actual textbook content in abbreviated form. The blanks within the statements are numbered to correspond with the answer blanks at the left.

Problem-solving environment

1. _____   Good managers don't simply solve problems, they solve the _____(1) problems.

2. _____   The process of evaluating and selecting among alternative potential solutions to a problem is _____(2) making.

3. _____   _____(3) _____(4) is the process of identifying a discrepancy be-
4. _____   tween an actual and desired state of affairs and then taking action to resolve the discrepancy.

Managerial problem solving

5. _____   A problem exists whenever there is a difference between an actual situation and a _____(5) situation.

6. _____   Problem seekers are forward-thinking managers who _____(6) prob-
7. _____   lems and opportunities and take appropriate _____(7).

8. _____   A systematic thinker approaches problems in a _____(8) and
9. _____   _____(9) fashion.

10. _____   An _____(10) thinker is more flexible and spontaneous.

11. _____   _____(11) problem solving tends to be quick and simple.

12. _____   _____(12) problem solving tends to be thorough and more balanced, and the ideas of many people are taken into account.

13. _____   Finding and identifying the _____(13) is the first stage of the problem-solving process.

14. _____   Once a problem is recognized it is possible to formulate one or more alternative _____(14).

15. _____   Given the alternatives along with the pros and cons of each, a manager can
16. _____   then choose a preferred _____(15) of _____(16).

17. _____   Given the preferred solution, appropriate _____(17) plans can be established.

18. _____   The problem-solving process remains incomplete unless the manager
19. _____   checks to insure that after the intended actions are taken, the _____(18) and _____(19) situations are finally one and the same.

Finding and identifying problems

20. _____   Problem finding involves identifying gaps between _____(20) and
21. _____   _____(21) states and determining causes.

22. _____   Routine problems arise on a regular basis and can be addressed through
23. _____   standard responses called _____(22) _____(23).

24. _____   _____(24) problems are ones that are anticipated as situations which will require decisions in the future.

25. _____   Higher level managers generally spend a greater proportion of their time
26. _____   on _____(25) and _____(26) problems.

27. _____   Some problems need to be considered vis-a-vis the possibility of doing _____(27).

Formulating and analyzing alternative solutions

28. _____   An application of ingenuity and imagination which results in a novel approach or unique solution to a problem is called _____(28).

29. _____   A block to creativity characterized by confusion of important and insignificant data is called a _____(29) block.

30. _____   A block to creativity based on taboos and traditions is called a _____(30) block.

31. _____   _____(31) is a group technique for identifying alternatives.

32. _____   _____(32) grouping is a group technique for identifying and evaluating alternatives.

33. _____   _____(33) exists in the decision environment when information is sufficient to predict the results of each alternative.

34. _____   _____(34) involves a lack of complete certainty of outcomes in making decisions.

35. _____   When managers are unable to even assign probabilities to the outcomes attached to various problem-solving alternatives, _____(35) exists.

36. _____   Uncertainty forces managers to rely heavily on individual and group _____(36) to succeed in problem solving.

37. _____   An _____(37) of alternatives lists each alternative and summarizes time requirements, costs, favorable and unfavorable points of each.

38. _____   A _____(38) tree graphically illustrates the alternatives available to a manager attempting to solve a problem.

39. _____
40. _____   Once alternatives are formulated and analyzed, a final choice of alternatives must be made. At this point in the problem-solving process, a manager
41. _____   must answer three questions: Is a _____(39) really required? How should the choice be _____(40)? _____(41) should be involved in the choice?

42. _____
43. _____   When presented with a problem, it is recommended that managers ask themselves the following questions: Is the problem _____(42) to
44. _____   deal with? Might the problem _____(43) itself? Is this my _____(44) to make?

Choosing among alternatives: Making and implementing the decision

45. _____   _____(45) decision theory views the manager as acting in a world of complete certainty.

46. _____   Behavioral decisions theory assumes that people act only in terms of what they _____(46) about a given situation.

47. _____
48. _____   Rather than facing a world of complete certainty, the behavioral decision maker acts under _____(47) and with limited _____(48).

49. _____
50. _____   _____(49) decision making is difficult to reach, but it is also the most _____(50) of the three decision methods.

51. _____   The final challenges in the problem-solving process are to _____(51)
52. _____   the chosen solution and _____(52) results.

TESTING YOUR KNOWLEDGE

True and False Self Test

Directions: Circle the letter (T or F) of the correct response for each of the following statements.

T   F   1. The three categories of action into which managers fall are problem avoiders, problem solvers, and problem seekers.

T   F   2. Three questions to ask in the problem-solving process include "What is the actual situation?" "What is the desired situation?" and "Whom can we blame?"

T   F   3. Problem finding involves identifying gaps that represent deficiencies or unexploited opportunities.

T   F   4. Nonroutine problems call for programmed decisions.

T   F   5. By defining a problem too broadly or narrowly you focus on symptoms rather than causes.

T   F   6. A group technique for identifying alternatives is called creativity.

T   F   7. Risk and uncertainty can be eliminated by the assistance of a decision matrix or payoff table.

T   F   8. The "satisficing" style of decision making means facilitating the use of the decision matrix.

T   F   9. The actual choice of a particular problem solution can be arrived at through individual, consultative, or group consensus methods.

T   F   10. Acceptance will always be greater if the group is involved in the decision-making process.

Multiple Choice Self Test

Directions: Circle the letter of the response that best completes each of the following statements.

1. The process of evaluating and selecting among alternative potential solutions is:
   a. choice making
   b. decision making
   c. problem solving
   d. problem implementation

2. The process of identifying a discrepancy between an actual and desired state of affairs is a major part of:
   a. monitoring
   b. coordinating
   c. problem solving
   d. decision making

3. Intuitive thinking compared to systematic thinking:
   a. has no place in managerial problem solving.
   b. is a thing that women do better than men.
   c. results from the right hemisphere of the brain.
   d. is OK for a game of poker, but not helpful in business.

4. The problem-solving process is not complete until there is reconciliation of:
   a. hard feelings that may have developed among employees in working on a problem.
   b. desired and actual situations.
   c. goals between different departments involved.
   d. all of the above.

5. Identifying problems is done by determining:
   a. deviations from past experience
   b. deviations from plans
   c. other people's views
   d. performance of the competition
   e. all of the above

6. A good alternative to problem solving which too often gets overlooked is:
   a. increasing the budget
   b. improving human relations
   c. doing nothing
   d. determining what the boss would be pleased with

7. A source of error in problem identification is that the problem is defined:
   a. too broadly
   b. too narrowly
   c. via symptoms
   d. all of the above

8. Persons who have a tendency to define problems from their own limited viewpoints are described as using:
   a. prejudice
   b. distortion
   c. selective perception
   d. rose colored glasses

9. Creativity blocks in problem solving include:
   a. perceptual
   b. cultural
   c. emotional
   d. intellectual
   e. all of the above

10. Criteria for determining when a situation is a problem include:
    a. budgetary
    b. human relations
    c. productivity
    d. all of the above

Matching Self Test

Directions: Write the letter of the description that best fits each numbered item in the blank provided.

_____ 1. Consensus

_____ 2. Decision tree

_____ 3. Choice making

_____ 4. Analytical

_____ 5. Problem solving

_____ 6. Placing a student on academic probation

_____ 7. Intuitive thinker

_____ 8. Nonroutine problems

_____ 9. Nominal grouping

_____ 10. Problem finding

a. Process of evaluating and selecting among alternative potential solutions.

b. Process of identifying a discrepancy between an actual and desired state of affairs and taking action.

c. A systematic thinker.

d. A situation that calls for nonprogrammed decisions.

e. Involves identifying gaps between actual and desired states and determining their causes.

f. Graphically illustrates the alternatives available to a manager trying to solve problems.

g. Most participative of decision methods.

h. Flexible and spontaneous.

i. A programmed decision.

j. When participants work alone and respond in writing with an alternative solution to a problem.

LEARNING ACTIVITIES — PART 1

In this section, and in each subsequent major part section of the learning guide, you will have a chance to get away from the text, and be more involved with management material in a direct sense. You will find chances to relax a bit, be creative, and try your hand at applying the material.

Number 1 — Supplemental Reading and Discussion

Directions: Read the following reprinted business journal article and write short responses to the questions that follow.

MANAGEMENT BLAMED FOR U.S. AUTO LAG

Auto makers in the United States can match the Japanese in advanced technology, but fall behind because of poor management and use of labor that is only beginning to be corrected, a new study concluded Monday.

The two-year study said that the American manufacturers must face "something close to a cultural revolution" in the way management deals with workers if the industry is to compete with foreign companies.

The study was conducted by a 12-member panel that included representatives from the auto companies, labor, and management experts from a number of universities and research groups.

In recent years the Japanese have accounted for more than a fourth of the auto sales in the United States.

The study said the cost of producing a Japanese car ranges from $750 to $1,500 below that of producing an American car because of increased productivity and a cheaper labor force. Since Japanese cars are sold at prices comparable to U.S. autos, the Japanese companies have a higher profit margin.

"Despite a popular image of Japanese superiority in advanced technology, explanation of the Japanese productivity advantage seems to be more a matter of differences in management . . . than superior automation or faster work pace," the study concluded.

William Abernathy, a Harvard professor and management expert who headed the study group, said the U.S. industry has begun changing its attitudes toward workers, is trying to improve management philosophies and has shown to be "fairly innovative" in terms of making changes.

"But they have a lot (farther) to go," he said in an interview. "If you look at the best plants in the industry they've made major strides, but there's a host of worst plants in the industry in which there's a lot of change yet to come down."

And some barriers between management and workers will be difficult to erase, he added.

The study, conducted by the National Academy of Engineers, declines to predict the future of the U.S. auto industry, although it outlines one scenario that would have American companies move substantial operations abroad. In this case two-thirds of every car sold in the United States may one day be built in a foreign country, the study said.

But another scenario has the U.S. manufacturers undergoing a "Fundamental structural change" that would result in American companies recouping their world market share with a performance-oriented line of cars.

But survival will require fundamental changes, the study said.

"In the case of productivity, product quality and the role of the work force, we are talking about something close to a cultural revolution, about fundamental changes in the way the business is managed and the way people at all levels participate in the enterprise," it said.

Source: *Associated Press* and the *Minneapolis Star and Tribune*, Tuesday, July 27, 1982.

Questions Regarding the Article

1. Do you agree that in hopes of improving worker productivity in the United States, management is faced with a cultural revolution? Or is this an exaggeration? Explain what you would characterize as a cultural revolution and how it would affect employees — attitudes and productivity.

2. Much of the falling off of productivity in the U.S. is laid on management. Is this accurate? What other factors in recent years have hurt U.S. productivity?

Number 2 — Exercise: Determine Your Own Productivity!

A major theme throughout this text is productivity of managers as well as that of employees in general. Since productivity is a very individual matter, it is appropriate to determine your own productivity at this time in your life. To do this, please complete the following productivity questionnaire:

Productivity Questionnaire

Directions: Circle **yes** or **no** for each of the following questions and then at the end determine your score or rating in terms of productivity.

Yes   No   1.   For each class that I take I average no more than one late or missed assignment per quarter.

Yes   No   2.   I regularly plan what to do and when to do it.

Yes   No   3.   I have regular, scheduled blocks of time for this and other classes.

Yes   No   4.   When studying or doing other things that require high levels of concentration, I am able to avoid interruptions.

Yes   No   5.   While in a typical class, I am able to concentrate on the subject matter at least 80% of the time.

Yes   No   6.   When carrying a full academic load or the equivalent (if employed for example and part time) I am able to maintain a B or better grade average.

Yes   No   7.   In preparing for exams I seldom cram via last minute or late night marathon sessions since I have kept up along the way.

Yes   No   8.   I have long-term (1 to 5 year) plans made.

Yes   No   9.   I write a daily "to do" list, a laundry list of activities and priorities.

Yes   No   10. I use my time effectively overall.

Productivity activity scoring: For each "yes" answer that you circled, give yourself five points, and add the 5s to get a total:

Points	Productivity rating
50	Perfect
45	Exceptional
40	Very good
35	Good
30	Fair
25 or less	Needs improvement

Number 3 — Exercise: Daily Planning Activity

Successful managers have one thing in common (besides excellent secretaries); they plan both short-term objectives and long-range gaols. On a short-term and/or daily basis, managers often use what is called a "to do" list to set objectives and establish priorities.

Directions: For the three busiest days of your week write a "to do" list by first randomly listing objectives or activities for each day. Next prioritize with the A, B, C method, making the As your high priority items. Place an X in the A column for each to do item that merits high priority.

	To Do List	*Priority determination*		
		A	*B*	*C*
1.				
2.				
3.				
4.				
5.				
6.				
7.				
8.				
9.				
10.				

Discussion of "to do" activity (after three days):

1. Did you use your time better as a result of the to do list, and setting priorities?

2. How does this activity relate to corporate planning? Productivity?

3. What merit does this activity have for avoiding certain time waster problems such as procrastination or allowing yourself to be interrupted?

Number 4 — Matching Wits with the Experts
(preferences on job application letters and personal resumes)

Directions: To start Part I of the Learning Guide you were instructed to write a resume and cover letter to assist you in pursuing employment. The following questionnaire should help you evaluate the content of your own resume and cover letter. This questionnaire was completed by 175 chief personnel officers employed in the 500 largest corporations in the U.S.

Complete the questionnaire, and then compare your responses with those of the experts. As a result of the experts' opinions, you may find that you will need to make some changes on your resume. Response choices are arranged from 1 to 5: 1=strong agreement; 2=moderate agreement; 3=undecided; 4=moderate disagreement; 5=strong disagreement.

Answer choices					*Question*
					Initial contact
1	2	3	4	5	1. The initial contact with a job applicant should be a personal interview.
1	2	3	4	5	2. Written information about the applicant is preferred for the initial contact with the job applicant.
1	2	3	4	5	3. If the initial contact with the job applicant is to be in writing, a resume only is preferred.
1	2	3	4	5	4. Both a cover letter and a resume must be obtained from a job applicant for a personnel director to have all the necessary information.
1	2	3	4	5	5. Handwritten cover letters and resumes are acceptable.
					Regarding the applicant's cover letter
1	2	3	4	5	6. Letters of application are welcomed even though there are no job openings.
1	2	3	4	5	7. Letters of application should include a reason why the job applicant is interested in the job.

1	2	3	4	5	8.	An attention-getting first sentence will stimulate interest in a particular applicant's letter of application.
1	2	3	4	5	9.	The tone of the letter of application is important.
1	2	3	4	5	10.	Good grammar and spelling are essential.
1	2	3	4	5	11.	A job applicant should state his understanding of the requirements of the position.
1	2	3	4	5	12.	The letter should show how the applicant's education and experience fit the job requirements.
1	2	3	4	5	13.	A potential employee should ask for a personal interview in his letter of application.

Regarding the applicant's resume

1	2	3	4	5	14.	A one-page resume is the preferred length.
1	2	3	4	5	15.	Keeping a resume neat is essential.
1	2	3	4	5	16.	A photograph included with the cover letter is desirable.
1	2	3	4	5	17.	Commendations of the job applicant should be listed in the resume.
1	2	3	4	5	18.	One reference is adequate in the resume.
1	2	3	4	5	19.	The types of persons listed as references in the resume are important.
1	2	3	4	5	20.	Military service of the applicant should be included in the resume.
1	2	3	4	5	21.	Personal information such as date of birth, phone, address, marital status, dependents, etc., should be included in the resume.
1	2	3	4	5	22.	A resume should contain an applicant's physical and health status.
1	2	3	4	5	23.	General as well as specific educational qualifications—such as majors, minors, and degrees—should be included.
1	2	3	4	5	24.	Willingness to relocate should be included in the resume.
1	2	3	4	5	25.	A list of scholarships, awards, and honors should be included.
1	2	3	4	5	26.	The resume should contain previous work experience concerning jobs held, dates of employment, company addresses, and reasons for leaving.
1	2	3	4	5	27.	Special aptitudes should be listed in the resume.
1	2	3	4	5	28.	A list of grades in major or minor subjects in college should be included in the resume.
1	2	3	4	5	29.	The major source of a person's financing while in college should be included.
1	2	3	4	5	30.	A resume should contain the salary requirements of a job applicant.
1	2	3	4	5	31.	The traditional order in which information is presented in a resume is desirable (personal information, education, experience, references).
1	2	3	4	5	32.	The applicant's strongest points (education, work experience, etc.) should be listed first in the resume without regard to traditional order.

Summary Comparison of Resume Questionnaire

After completing the questionnaire, you may find it interesting to compare notes with responses of the experts. There were 175 survey responses, but for simplicity we lumped the two "agree" columns together and also the two disagreement columns. Undecided and nonresponses are not included. If you are interested in the entire study, see reference below.

Scoring:

Item	No. agree	No. disagree	Item	No. agree	No. disagree
1	22	77	17	53	27
2	93	4	18	10	61
3	32	58	19	54	29
4	61	29	20	87	4
5	35	49	21	61	19
6	89	6	22	55	30
7	81	8	23	95	2
8	41	31	24	91	2
9	90	5	25	90	3
10	97	0	26	98	2
11	43	25	27	80	6
12	78	13	28	41	40
13	69	13	29	52	23
14	67	11	30	57	24
15	96	3	31	71	16
16	20	60	32	59	31

Source: Wells, Barron; Spinks, Nelda; Hargrave, Janice. "A Survey of the Chief Personnel Officers in the 500 Largest Corporations in the United States to Determine Their Preference in Job Application Letters and Personal Resumes." *The ABCA Bulletin*, June 1981, pp. 3-7.

Number 5 — Experiential Learning

Each part of this learning guide will include at least one experiential learning opportunity. Ideally, this should be done in small groups and preferably in class. However, if time does not permit, you may still benefit from this hands on applied learning experience.

Is There A Problem?

With all the talk in the text about problem-solving, is it clear when a "problem" is a problem? Read the following situation and discuss with classmates whether or not there is a problem.

You have become supervisor of 10 employees who seem to be a stable group and respectful of each other. You notice during a regularly scheduled coffee break that Ted, a 40-year-old married man, and Allyce, a 25-year-old single woman, are absent from their usual places in the coffee group.

Being curious, you walk down the hall searching, even though they are not required to attend coffee break in the lunch room. They can, for example, leave the building if they choose.

In an open supply room you find them embracing in a seemingly passionate way. They see you. They seem momentarily frozen in their surprised looks, but then they continue as if you aren't present. To your knowledge they are not violating any written rules in your rule and policy book.

As their supervisor what should you do?

1. Nothing, but leave quietly.
2. Say, "Excuse me; we'll see you back on the job, I trust!"
3. Give them a verbal reprimand on the spot, and get them to stop it.
4. Calmly ask them to go back to the coffee room, but say nothing else.

5. Tell them that they are not to report back to work, but rather to see you in your office immediately.
6. Fire both on the spot.
7. Say nothing now, but go call Ted's wife to let her know and take care of it.

Discussion of the scenario, "Is There a Problem?"

1. Is there a problem? If you say yes, then write it down. If you say no, explain why you say no.

2. How do organizations decide when a situation is a problem? That is, what criteria do you feel they might use? Discuss this with classmates. How important, for example, is productivity and related terms in the quest to determine when a problem exists?

3. To what extent do personal values and attitudes enter into the determination of whether or not there is a problem? Should a manager's personal values enter in?

4. What actions by a manager should be done here—if any?

LOOKING BACK; LOOKING AHEAD

Part 1 of the text and this learning guide has introduced you to the dynamic world of management. An underlying theme, productivity, was highlighted and will serve as an on-going theme throughout this text. You might want to explore the issue of productivity a bit more by asking:

1. Is the emphasis on productivity overdone in our society?
2. Does the pursuit of productivity by managers have negative side effects?
3. What other missions or purposes should organizations concern themselves with?

Part 2 deals with a key management function—planning. It is through planning that organizations set in motion a variety of other functions and worker activities that help achieve its goals.

Not everyone wants to become a manager. We realize this. However, we hope that through each unit you will find some of the concepts useful in terms of an improved self-managed life style. In Part 2, for example, you may want to adapt some of the planning ideas to your own setting.

PART II
PLANNING FOR PRODUCTIVITY

INTRODUCTION — PART 2

(Chapters 4 and 5)

Highlights

Part 2, Chapters 4 and 5 of the text, introduces the first and probably most important management function—planning. In Chapter 4, for example, the importance of planning is stressed in terms of managers being able to assess the future and make provision for it. The author stresses that "to become effective as a manager requires that you become a good planner."

Chapter 4 also emphasizes the "primary principle of planning" that states through planning the other managerial functions—organizing, leading, and controlling—can be more effectively carried out. In Chapter 4 you will learn the planning process and benefits and limitations of planning.

Through Chapter 5 reading you will learn about more comprehensive planning entitled strategy. Strategies set the direction for organizations and guide the allocation of resources. The author carefully explains the major elements in strategic planning.

Throughout this part you should examine your own planning activities at this time in your life. Granted, collegiate life to a certain extent is already planned for you. Majors are prescribed, classes are scheduled by colleges and universities, and responsibilities in terms of term papers and exams are set up by professors. In effect, others have planned your life, and this can be detrimental to your own skill development in planning.

You may want to develop or improve upon your own short- and long-range planning skills as they are introduced by the author.

Chapter Titles for Part 2

Chapter 4 — Fundamentals of Planning
Chapter 5 — Strategic Planning and Organizational Objectives

CAREER PERSPECTIVE — PART 2

Mapping Your Employment Strategy

In the Part 1 Career Perspective exercise you were instructed to write your own resumé and letter of application for employment. Of course there is more to job hunting than preparing a resumé and writing a letter of introduction. You need to learn about management career areas that might be right for you. Do you prefer, for example, a large, medium, or small company? Public or private? Service or manufacturing? Retail, wholesale or producer type businesses? Do you have a geographic preference?

Planning is the subject of this section, and you can get a stronger orientation to planning by doing some planning on your own behalf. This career exercise should be done by you with careful introspection.

Directions

For each variable on the left, write a brief reaction after checking whether it is a positive, negative, or neutral factor in terms of your employment and career interests.

Employment/Career Mapping

	Personal reaction			
Variable	*Negative*	*Positive*	*Neutral*	*Personal notes or comments*

1. Geographic Location
   Foreign Country
   U.S.:
   - Northeast
   - Southeast
   - Midwest
   - South
   - Southwest
   - West
   - Northwest
   - Other (list yourself)

2. Locale
   - Large metro area
   - Suburban
   - Smaller city
   - Rural area

3. Business/Organization Type
   - Public, nonprofit
   - Private, profit making
   - Large
   - Medium
   - Small
   - Retail
   - Wholesale
   - Producer

4. Product/Service Preference
   You list preferences and nonpreferences:

	Personal reaction			
Variable	*Negative*	*Positive*	*Neutral*	*Personal notes or comments*

5. Management Tradition or Philosophy
    Classical/bureaucratic
    Human relations oriented
    Contingency oriented and participatory

6. Department within an Organization
    Human Resources
    Marketing
    Production/Service
    Finance
    Quality Control
    Research
    Other (list)

Summary: Summarize what appear to be your preferences in employment based upon the above exercise.

4 Fundamentals of Planning

STUDENT LEARNING OBJECTIVES

After completing the chapter material you should be able to:

1. Explain the importance of planning as the first and underlying management function.
2. Define planning and its dimensions.
3. Distinguish between strategic and tactical plans.
4. List and explain steps in formal planning, the planning process.
5. Contrast some of the author's "different approaches" to planning.
6. Define forecasting and explain its role in overall organizational planning.
7. List and explain different forecasting techniques.
8. Summarize benefits of planning as well as limits.

CHAPTER HIGHLIGHTS

Do managers really plan?
Planning as a management function
The planning process
Forecasting
Benefits of planning
Making planning effective

PROGRAMMED LEARNING

The following statements are drawn from actual textbook content in abbreviated form. The blanks within the statements are numbered to correspond with the answer blanks at the left.

The planning environment

1. _____
2. _____

The first of the four basic managerial functions, _____(1), is the way in which managers assess the _____(2).

3. _____

Planning is formally defined as a process of setting _____(3).

4. _____
5. _____
6. _____

Planning is _____(4) in nature, requires a system of _____(5), and is focused on desired future _____(6).

7. _____

Mintzberg argues that managers are too busy to _____(7).

Planning as a management function

8. _____
9. _____
10. _____

It is through planning that managers set the stage for further decisions on how to _____(8), _____(9), and _____(10).

11. _____

An intended means for accomplishing a desired result is called a _____(11).

12. _____

A process of thinking before taking action is called _____(12).

13. _____
14. _____
15. _____
16. _____

Because a plan describes an intended course of action, it should answer questions of what, _____(13), _____(14), _____(15), and by _____(16).

17. _____

The desired future state or end result to be accomplished through implementation of the plan is called the planning _____(17).

Dimensions of plans

18. _____

Plans that are comprehensive are called _____(18).

19. _____
20. _____

Plans more limited in scope and which address those activities and resources required to implement the master or strategic plan are called _____(19) or _____(20).

21. _____

Plans designed to meet the needs of a unique situation are called _____-use(21) plans.

22. _____

Top level managers spend greater proportions of their time on longer-term and _____(22) planning.

23. _____

A plan that is comprehensive in scope and establishes the action framework through which an organization intends to survive is called _____(23).

Tactical and strategic plans

24. _____
25. _____

Operational plans can be divided into those of _____(24) use such as policies and procedures, and _____(25) use such as budgets.

26. _____

A broad guideline for making decisions and taking action is called a _____(26).

27. _____
28. _____

Policies commit managers to general action _____(27) or _____(28).

29. _____
30. _____

Standing-use plans which very precisely describe what actions are to be taken in specific situations are called _____(29) and _____(30).

31. _____
32. _____

Procedures and rules are meant to specify _____(31) and permit little or no individual _____(32).

33. _____
34. _____

Single-use plans developed for a specific circumstance or time frame are called _____(33) and _____(34).

35. _____

A budget that allocates resources to a project, unit or individual based on a single estimate of cost is labeled _____(35).

36. _____

The intent of _____-based(36) budgeting is for managers to reconsider their priorities, objectives and activities with each new cycle.

37. _____

Single-use plans that tie activities to specific time frames or targets are called _____(37).

The planning process

38. _____

As a process, planning involves deciding in advance of action what, when, how and by _____(38) something is to be done.

39. _____
40. _____
41. _____
42. _____
43. _____

The five steps in formal planning include: defining your _____(39), determining where you stand relative to the _____(40), developing your _____(41) regarding future conditions, identifying and choosing among _____(42) courses of action, and _____(43) the plan.

44. _____

Planning that focuses efforts and energies on doing what you already do, but trying to do it as best you can is called _____ _____(44).

45. _____

Planning that analyzes the external environment and makes the internal adjustments necessary to exploit opportunities and minimize problems is called _____ _____(45).

46. _____

When you want to do what you and/or others are already doing, but want to do it better, you should use _____-_____(46) planning.

47. _____

Plans developed at lower levels without constraints and sequentially passed up the hierarchy to top management are called _____-_____(47) planning.

48. _____

Bottom-up planning may fail to result in integrated overall _____(48).

49. _____
50. _____

Top-down planning may at times fail to meet the needs of _____(49) level employees to _____(50) in planning.

51. _____
52. _____
53. _____
54. _____

Managers are advised to combine the best elements of both the top-down and bottom-up planning approaches by communicating to all concerned the basic planning _____(51), seeking _____(52) from others, laying out various _____(53), but letting all levels comment, and working hard all along the way to get _____(54).

Forecasting

55. _____

The responsibility for the measurement and evaluation of action results, and the reformation of plans where appropriate is called _____(55).

56. _____

Without control, planning lacks _____ _____(56).

57. _____

An attempt to predict outcomes which will happen in the future is called _____(57).

58. _____

A forecast is a vision or perspective on the future which managers use as a planning _____(58).

59. _____   A forecasting technique which uses expert opinions to predict the future is called _____(59).

60. _____   A sophisticated qualitative way of gathering and synthesizing the expert opinions of many persons is the _____(60) technique.

61. _____   A forecasting technique that uses statistical analysis and mathematics to predict future events is called _____(61).

62. _____   A forecasting method that makes predictions by projecting trends of the past and present into the future is called _____-_____(62) analysis.

63. _____   _____(63) Modeling is a forecasting technique that builds complex computer models to simulate the future.

64. _____   A way to predict consumer tastes, employee preferences and political choices for the future is called a _____(64) survey.

65. _____   In the final analysis, forecasting always relies on _____(65) judgment.

66. _____   Forecasts are subject to _____(66).

Benefits and limitations of planning

67. _____   In terms of benefits of planning, planning promotes _____(67),
68. _____   _____(68), and _____(69).
69. _____

70. _____   Planning that is done in the sense of anticipating events which may occur in the future is called _____(70) planning.

71. _____   The purpose of planning is to keep management the master of the organization's _____(71).

72. _____   Planning also clarifies _____-_____(72) chains.

73. _____   A means-ends chain links work efforts of individuals and groups at various levels of the organization to a common _____(73).

74. _____   Planning facilitates performance by focusing manager's attention on
75. _____   _____(74), setting _____(75), emphasizing _____(76)
76. _____   strengths, coping with ever-changing _____(77) environments, and
77. _____   facilitating _____(78).
78. _____

79. _____   Plans may fail for a variety of reasons. Some from the text are: top man-
80. _____   agement failing to incorporate _____(79) into the organization's
81. _____   routines; poor _____(80) is used as the basis for planning; there is a
82. _____   lack of necessary _____(81) support for plans; _____(82) to change.

TESTING YOUR KNOWLEDGE

True and False Self Test

Directions: Circle the letter (T or F) of the correct response for each of the following statements.

T F 1. Planning is formally defined as a process of setting objectives.

T F 2. Mintzberg argues that planning should not be the number one objective of management.

T F 3. An intended means for accomplishing a desired result is called a managerial activity.

T F 4. Plans that are comprehensive and long-term are called "tactile."

T F 5. Middle managers spend a greater proportion of their time on long-term and strategic planning than do top managers.

T F   6. A broad guideline for making decisions and taking action is called a policy.

T F   7. Procedures and rules specify actions to support policies.

T F   8. The intent of zero-based budgeting is for managers to reconsider their priorities, objectives, and activities with each new budget cycle.

T F   9. The first step in planning is to analyze economic conditions and determine how they relate to your organization at that time.

T F 10. Forecasting is an attempt to predict outcomes which will happen in the future.

Multiple Choice Self Test

Directions: Circle the letter of the response that best completes each of the following statements.

1. The first and underlying management function is:
   a. planning
   b. organizing
   c. staffing
   d. controlling

2. A characteristic of planning which presents a special challenge to management is:
   a. its anticipatory nature
   b. its systems character
   c. its role in creating desired future states
   d. all of the above
   e. none of the above

3. Which of the following is labeled by your text as a strategic planning:
   a. production planning
   b. financial planning
   c. marketing planning
   d. personnel planning
   e. none of the above

4. An example of a standing use plan is:
   a. policies
   b. procedures
   c. rules
   d. budgets
   e. all but **d** of the above

5. Policies are valuable to organizations if they help:
   a. coordinate activities
   b. improve efficiency
   c. stabilize the firm
   d. decision making without losing flexibility
   e. all of the above

6. An example of a single-use plan is:
   a. budgeting
   b. scheduling
   c. financing
   d. setting policies
   e. both **a** and **b**

7. Zero-based budgeting refers to a budgeting technique which assumes:
   a. the company is broke
   b. the project to be budgeted will recover costs and break even within the first year of startup
   c. a project is budgeted as if it were to be newly initiated even though it might be old
   d. none of the above is accurate

8. The steps in the planning process include all the following except:
   a. what
   b. why
   c. when
   d. by when
   e. how

9. In formal planning the step in which you develop premises is:
   a. step one
   b. step two
   c. step three
   d. step four
   e. step five

10. Planning as a function should be done by:
   a. only top management
   b. top and middle management
   c. all management levels
   d. all management and nonmanagement employees

Matching Self Test

Directions: Write the letter of the description that best fits each numbered item in the blank provided.

_____ 1. Delphi Technique

_____ 2. Policies

_____ 3. Strategic

_____ 4. Bottom-up

_____ 5. Econometric Modeling

_____ 6. Time analysis

_____ 7. Quantitative

_____ 8. Planning

_____ 9. Contingency planning

_____ 10. Statistical survey

a. A forecasting method that makes predictions by projecting trends of the past and present into the future.

b. A forecasting technique which uses the future.

c. A plan that is comprehensive in scope and establishes the action framework through which an organization intends to survive and prosper.

d. A guideline that commits managers to making decisions and taking action.

e. Plans developed at lower levels that could lack cohesion in overall direction.

f. An activity that sets the stage for further decisions on how to organize, lead, and control.

g. A forecasting technique that builds complex computer models to simulate future events.

h. A sophisticated qualitative way of gathering and synthesizing the expert opinions of many people.

i. The opinion poll from a newspaper survey.

j. A plan that is done in the sense of anticipating events which may occur in the future.

5 Strategic Planning and Organizational Objectives

STUDENT LEARNING OBJECTIVES

After completing the chapter material you should be able to:

1. Define strategy as a planning concept, and list types of strategies.
2. Explain the relationship between strategies and organizational objectives.
3. Explain how objectives serve the five basic organizational purposes.
4. List and explain the purposes and steps of strategic planning.
5. Identify the four major elements in strategic planning.
6. Identify and explain the author's list of strategic planning principles.
7. Relate the manager's role to strategic planning.

CHAPTER HIGHLIGHTS

The concept of strategy
Organizational objectives
Strategic planning and organizational objectives
Major elements in strategic planning
Strategic planning and the manager

PROGRAMMED LEARNING

The following statements are drawn from actual textbook content in abbreviated form. The blanks within the statements are numbered to correspond with the answer blanks at the left.

The concept of strategy

1. _____ A comprehensive plan or action orientation that sets critical direction and guides the allocation of resources for an organization is called a _____(1).

2. _____ A focus for decision-making and action which represents a "best guess" regarding what must be done to insure longer-run prosperity for the organization is called a _____(2).

3. _____ Any strategy begins with _____-_____(3).

4. _____ Every strategy has the capability to guide _____(4) direction of an organization.

5. _____ Strategy defines the _____(5) in which an organization intends to
6. _____ move, and establishes the _____(6) for action to get there.

Types of strategies

7. _____ Maintaining the present course of action is called a _____(7) strategy.

8. _____ A strategy that implies a decision to slow down, cut back, and seek performance improvement is called _____(8).

9. _____ Growth is necessary for long-run _____(9).

10. _____ Growth is equated with _____(10).

11. _____ Growth is thought to benefit not only the organization, but also _____(11).

12. _____ Growth helps attract quality _____(12).

Organizational objectives

13. _____ Simply put, a good strategy helps achieve organizational _____(13).

14. _____ Those ends which the organization seeks to achieve by its existence and operations are called _____(14) objectives.

15. _____ The means through which these ends are pursued at any given point in time are called _____(15).

16. _____ Objectives that constitute the organization's formal purpose or mission such as would be stated in a report to shareholders are called _____(16).

17. _____ The specific ends toward which organizational resources are actually allocated are called _____(17) objectives.

18. _____ Official objectives help organizations achieve: _____ion(18),
19. _____ _____ion(19), _____ion(20), _____ion(21), and
20. _____ _____ion(22).
21. _____
22. _____

23. _____ A series of objectives linked to one another at the various levels of management such that each higher level objective is supported by one or more lower level one(s) is called a _____(23) of objectives.

Strategic planning and organizational objectives

24. _____   A plan that is comprehensive in scope and reflects the overall direction of the total organization or one of its subunits is called _____(24).

25. _____   The process of determining the major objectives of an organization and defining the strategies that will govern use of resources is called _____(25) planning.

26. _____
27. _____   Strategic planning helps clarify for organization members and outsiders: the _____(26) or _____(27) the organization intends to provide; the _____(28) it will use to produce them; and, the performance _____(29) underlying these efforts as a whole.
28. _____
29. _____

30. _____
31. _____   The essence of strategic planning is to seriously assess current _____(30), examine future _____(31) and threats in the environ-ment, assess these opportunities and threats against the organization's internal strengths and _____(32), identify several strategic _____(33), evaluate the alternative strategies vis-a-vis organiza-tional objectives, select a _____(34) and then implement it through medium or short-term _____(35) plans.
32. _____
33. _____
34. _____
35. _____

Major elements of strategic planning

36. _____
37. _____   Four major elements in the appraisal stage of strategic planning include analysis of: the organization's _____(36) and _____(37), threats and _____(38) in the external environment, managerial _____(39) and the corporate _____(40), and internal strengths and _____(41) of the organization.
38. _____
39. _____
40. _____
41. _____

Strategic planning principles

42. _____   The first strategic planning principle states that strategy and objectives must direct effort toward accomplishment of the organization's basic _____(42).

43. _____   The next strategic planning element is analysis of threats and _____(43).

44. _____
45. _____   Strategic objective number two states that strategy and objectives should target effort on specific _____(44) which will solve key _____(45) and exploit key _____(46) in the organization's external environment.
46. _____

47. _____   Through analysis of the external environment, managers gain _____(47) on what the organization's strategy might be.

48. _____
49. _____   An internal appraisal of an organization clarifies actual organizational _____(48), and establishes a realistic basis for _____(49) planning.

50. _____   Some important areas of strategic planning questions should be addressed including: _____(50) resources, technology, and systems.

51. _____
52. _____   Strategic planning principle number three states that strategy and objectives should build upon _____(51) and minimize _____(52) in the orga-nization.

53. _____   A manager's decisions and actions will always be affected in part by his personal _____(53).

54. _____   Organizations benefit when _____(54) culture is properly matched with strategy.

55. _____
56. _____   Strategic planning principle number four states that strategy and objectives should be consistent with prevailing managerial _____(55) and cor-porate _____(56).

Strategic management vs. operating management

57. _____ The managerial responsibility of formulating and implementing strategies that lead to longer-term organizational success is called _____(57) management.

58. _____ Strategic management sets the _____(58) or action framework for operating management.

59. _____ Operating management, in turn, uses resources to do the things necessary to _____(59) strategy.

60. _____ Henry Mintzberg argues that actual planning in the manager's work-a-day world may become planning via_____(60).

61. _____ Another emerging view of strategic planning that complements the work of Mintzberg to some extent is the concept of strategic planning through logical _____(61).

62. _____ Logical incrementalism views strategies emerging over time as a series of incremental _____(62) to existing patterns of behavior.

63. _____
64. _____ Strategic planning failures fall into two categories, failures of _____(63) and failures of _____(64).

65. _____ Failures that reflect poor handling of the activities through which the elements were addressed are called failures of _____(65).

66. _____
67. _____
68. _____
69. _____
70. _____
71. _____

A set of basic guidelines on how to make strategic planning effective include the following: use a _____(66) for minimizing errors of substance; get the right _____(67) involved; don't be afraid to conclude that an existing strategy is _____(68); approach strategic planning with responsibility for the total _____(69); use strategic planning as a stepping _____(70) for success in other functions; remember that a good strategy alone will not insure organizational _____(71).

TESTING YOUR KNOWLEDGE

True and False Self Test

Directions: Circle the letter (T or F) of the correct response for each of the following statements.

T F 1. The specific ends towards which organizational resources are actually allocated are called resource funds.

T F 2. The existence of a hierarchy of objectives is important only to larger organizations.

T F 3. Strategy is an organization's way of maintaining a positive relationship with its internal environment.

T F 4. The first strategic planning element is analysis of threats and opportunities.

T F 5. An internal appraisal of an organization clarifies actual capabilities and establishes a realistic basis for strategic planning.

T F 6. Organizations benefit when corporate culture is properly matched with strategy.

T F 7. Strategic management uses resources to do the things necessary to implement strategy and realize its impact on organization objectives.

T F 8. Good strategy will insure organizational success.

T F 9. Simultaneous use of more than one of the other strategies is called combination strategy.

T F 10. Through analysis of the external environment, managers gain perspective on what the organization's strategy might be.

Multiple Choice Self Test

Directions: Circle the letter of the response that best completes each of the following statements.

1. Any strategy begins with:
    a. budget assessment
    b. problem solving
    c. decision making
    d. behavior assessment

2. The direction in which an organization intends to move is called:
    a. tactic
    b. goals
    c. strategy
    d. objectives

3. Uncertain environments lend themselves to what type of strategies:
    a. programmed
    b. semi-programmed
    c. flexible
    d. contingency

4. A growth strategy, according to Glueck, can be done for what reason:
    a. long-run survival
    b. organizational effectiveness
    c. society benefits
    d. to help attract quality employees
    e. all of the above

5. A retrenchment strategy implies a management decision to:
    a. slow down
    b. cut back
    c. seek performance improvement
    d. all of the above
    e. none of the above

6. The official objectives of organizations help:
    a. clarify purpose
    b. integrate objectives of the organization with those of the individual employees
    c. adapt to change
    d. revitalize the organization
    e. all of the above

7. The common operating objective which is most difficult to control is usually:
    a. productivity
    b. profitability
    c. innovation
    d. social responsibility

8. The purpose of strategic planning is to help clarify for the organization members:
    a. the goods and services that the organization intends to provide
    b. the methods it will use to produce them
    c. performance targets
    d. all of the above

9. Which sequence of the "elements" of strategic planning is correctly quoted:
   a. mission set, threats/opportunities analyzed, managerial values stated, and internal strengths and weaknesses identified
   b. threats/opportunities analyzed, managerial values stated, mission set, and internal strengths and weaknesses identified
   c. strengths and weaknesses identified, mission set, managerial values stated, threats/opportunities analyzed
   d. managerial values stated, internal strengths and weaknesses identified, mission set, threats/opportunities analyzed
   e. none of the above

10. Major components of the external environment are:
    a. economic
    b. political
    c. social
    d. technological
    e. all of the above

Matching Self Test

Directions: Write the letter of the description that best fits each numbered item in the blank provided.

_____ 1. Operating objectives

_____ 2. Strategy

_____ 3. Superordinate goal

_____ 4. Contingency strategies

_____ 5. Programmed strategies

_____ 6. Operating management

_____ 7. Failure of process

_____ 8. Strategic planning principle one

_____ 9. Strategic planning principle two

_____ 10. Strategic planning principle three

a. The means through which these ends are pursued.

b. The specific ends toward which organizational resources are allocated.

c. Poor handling of the activities through which the elements were addressed.

d. Represents the overall purpose of the organization to its members.

e. Strategy and objectives must direct effort toward accomplishment of the organization's basic mission.

f. Strategy and objectives should target effort on specific results.

g. Strategy and objectives should build upon strengths and minimize weaknesses.

h. Uses resources to do the things necessary to implement strategy.

i. Strategies used when dealing with uncertain environments.

j. This strategy is used when dealing with stable environments.

LEARNING ACTIVITIES — PART 2

Number 1 — Supplemental Reading and Discussion

Directions: Read the following reprinted business journal article and write short responses to the questions that follow.

Lead Question: How sick is the Penguin?

MUNSINGWEAR AIMS AT INCREASED SALES

Munsingwear promoted a former marine drill instructor to be its president two months ago, and the new man is putting the ailing apparel-maker through a close-order drill.

Staff cuts, reduced inventories, and stiff production controls allowed Munsingwear to nearly triple its first-quarter profit this year ($1.1 million) compared with last year, even though sales fell by more than $6.1 million.

But Munsingwear traditionally turns a first-quarter profit on strong spring sportswear sales. It still managed to lose money for the last three years—in growing amounts—and it hasn't shown two consecutive years of profit growth in 20 years.

Observers say that George Hansen, the no-nonsense operations expert, will have to maintain his first-quarter performance through three more quarters before skeptical investors and retailers are convinced and the Penguin can smile again.

"The operations of the company have been corrected," Hansen told stockholders at Munsingwear's annual meeting Friday, "and now our biggest task is to increase our sales." He predicted that Munsingwear will break even this year.

Hansen is moving cautiously on the sales front.

"I'm of the school of thought that if it ain't broke, don't fix it," he said in an interview last week. In the opinion of Munsingwear executives, the familiar Penguin shirts and Vassarette women's underwear are just fine with quality-conscious consumers.

On the cost side, however, Hansen has dug in.

Even the annual meeting, held at L'hotel Sofitel, reflected the new austerity. Gone were last year's croissants and sportswear giveaways. And the annual report lacked the traditional color photography of models in tennis shirts and nightgowns. This year's stockholders had to settle for a cup of coffee and a chance to complain about poor management.

But there was a new table of executives to field the complaints—the result of an executive housecleaning that started last fall, when it became clear that the company would lose money for the third straight year.

Gone was Raymond Good, hired away from Pillsbury Co. in 1979 to become president. Gone were David Ehlen and William Walker, senior vice-presidents whom Good hired from Pillsbury. And gone was Donald P. Brown, the chief financial officer who served briefly as president between Good and Hansen.

Observers said Good was hired for his marketing expertise—and Munsingwear's sales grew substantially in 1979 and 1980. But operating costs grew even faster, and the company lost $3.8 million in 1980, $6.3 million in 1981, and $14.8 million in 1982. It was not uncommon for Munsingwear to miss retailers' crucial seasonal deadlines, then have to dump huge quantities of sportswear at close-out prices.

Hansen, 53, who has 20 years of experience in manufacturing and operations with two other major apparel firms, was hired for just that expertise, said Harry Piper, Jr., a Munsingwear director.

"It's no secret that this company had trouble meeting its orders on time—or at all," Piper commented before Friday's meeting.

The company already has improved deliveries, said J. Raymond Donnelly, president of the men's apparel division. He said so far this year, Munsingwear has filled a better percentage of orders than in the last five years.

On the expenses side, Hansen is proud of his cost-cutting measures.

"First, operating expenses." Pointing to a first-quarter financial sheet that showed a $1.75-million saving, he said, "staff—that's what we're talking about."

"The message so often in reduction of staff is: Go out and fire the janitor. We didn't do it that way."

Will the managerial staff cuts hurt the company? "No. They were overloaded with staff."

Second, Hansen cited inventories that he called "just incredibly high." He said he has cut inventories by $20 million—from $52 million to $32 million. Reflecting on the lack of coordination between sales and inventory levels, Hansen commented, "Well, you don't think that was all good inventory, do you?"

"Third, they were not doing a good job with their receivables collections." Hansen said he has tightened up collections procedures.

But industry experts said Munsingwear will have to make progress on the sales front as well.

"They've got a challenge ahead of them to regain the shelf space with the retailers who got skeptical," said Richard Pyle, an analyst who used to follow Munsingwear for Piper, Jaffray and Hopwood, Inc.

Hansen, though, is staying with the no-nonsense approach.

"In my opinion, sales are off because of the way the company's operated in the past few years. First, they haven't been profitable, so retailers become reluctant to deal with you. Second, the company did not deliver well. We're not perfect, but we're getting better every day. Third, there was a lot of direction-changing during these past three years." That refers to efforts to spiff up products by, for example, changing waistband colors on underwear and pushing specialty golf and tennis wear.

Donnelly said Munsingwear may change its direction back toward general leisure wear. "We concentrated on smaller sectors of the market, such as golf and tennis wear. That's an important market for us, but it's not the whole picture."

But Hansen said that, for the time being, the company plans "nothing dramatic" in the way of new products or merchandising techniques.

"You do have to be aware of the trends. Colors, for example—whether they're muted one year or bright the next.

"But there's nothing new under the sun. What people wear today you've probably seen before."

Munsingwear Sales and Profits

	Net sales	Net earnings
1973	$ 91,928,000	$ 3,231,000
1974	97,675,000	326,000*
1975	98,391,000	2,474,000
1976	104,984,000	1,835,000
1977	115,702,000	4,013,000
1978	117,988,000	2,913,000
1979	121,998,000	1,482,000
1980	133,530,000	− 3,848,000
1981	131,168,000	− 6,251,000
1982	103,069,000	− 14,817,000

*A change in inventory accounting methods reduced this figure by $1,512,000.

Source: *Minneapolis Star and Tribune*, Sunday, May 1, 1983.

Questions for Discussion

1. What are some of the problems or factors cited in the article that seem to have contributed to the huge losses at Munsingwear?

2. How would you explain an apparent contradiction that Munsingwear failed to meet retailer deadlines, yet there is a problem of incredibly high inventories?

3. Based upon the nearly 15 million dollar loss in 1982, how do you react to Mr. Hansen's optimism when he says Penguin shirts and Vassarette underwear are "just fine," and he expects to break even in 1983?

4. What strategies can you suggest in product development, marketing, or management that might help Munsingwear in the long run?

Number 2 — Exercise: Projecting the Future

Planning is the focus of Part 2 of the text, and the author skillfully explains a variety of strategies and tactics managers can use to do their planning. Managers and most other people doing serious planning tend to base plans upon current variables. It might be more exciting to base planning, in part, on what is called premising—making different assumptions about the future.

Directions: Complete the following projecting exercise, and for each item, briefly respond to what the implications for business or society might be!

Answer	*Projecting*
_____	1. In what year will a woman be elected president of the U.S.? a. If this were to occur, how would this affect the business/planning environment? b. How would it affect you?
_____	2. What will be the major means of transportation in the year 2000? a. If it is to be substantially different from now, how will it affect business/planning? b. What impact will the different means have on you?
_____	3. What will be the trend in housing in the year 2005? a. If it is to be substantially different from the present, how will it affect business/planning? b. What impact will the different transportation methods have on you?
_____	4. What will be the mainstay of the majority of people's diets in 2010? a. If it is to be substantially different, how will it affect business/planning? b. What impact will the different diet patterns have on you?
_____	5. What will constitute "family" in 2005? a. If it is to be substantially different, how will it affect business/planning? b. What impact will the "family" have on you?

6. What will be the major social/societal problem in 2000?
   a.   If it is to be substantially different, how will it affect business/ planning?

   b.   What impact will this problem have on you?

7. What will be the major health problem in 2008?
   a.   If it is to be substantially different, how will it affect business/ planning?

   b.   What impact will this have on you?

8. In what year will a male give birth to a baby?
   a.   If it is to actually happen, how will it affect business/planning?

   b.   What impact will this have on you?

9. In what era will do-it-yourself medical physiological treatment become commonplace?
   a.   If it is to be substantially different, how will it affect business/ planning?

   b.   What impact will this have on you?

10. In what year will there be complete weather control?
    a.   If it will be controllable, how will it affect business/planning?

    b.   What impact will this have on you?

11. In what year will the Cubs win a pennant and World Series?
    a.   If this were to occur, how would it affect business/planning?

    b.   What impact would this have on you?

_____   12. How will you be earning a living in 1998?
                              a.   If it is to be substantially different, how will it affect business/
                                   planning?

                              b.   What impact will this have on you?

Summary: Please answer or discuss with classmates the significance of premising, the assumptions managers make about the future, and how new sets of assumptions can drastically affect their planning. For example, use any one of the premises you stated above to show impact on planning.

Number 3 — Exercise: Personal Strategic Planning Through MBO

Brief reference is made in Chapter 5 to MBO, Management by Objectives, a popular device currently being used by many organizations to get individual employees personally involved in organizational planning. MBO is usually done in the short term, a time frame of 6 to 18 months.

Directions: Write your own MBO, but call it PBO, Planning by Objectives. Use the following framework:

Framework for Personal Planning Example

Area in which personal planning is to be done	*Identify specific goals that are both qualitative and quantitative*	*List activities necessary to reach goal*
EXAMPLE	EXAMPLE	EXAMPLE
A. Recreation: Trip to Disney World	A-1 By March 15, 1985 Will take family on a prepaid flight to a prepaid vacation to Disney World in Florida; purpose to achieve complete relaxation for two weeks within a $3,000 budget for family of five, including all expenses.	A-1 By January 1, 1984 Will set up a monthly savings account of $200 per month.

A-2 By February 15, 1984 Will prepare a vacation itinerary to Florida, while in Florida and back to Minneapolis. |

Student Starts Here:

Framework for Personal Planning for Student

Area in which personal planning is to be done	*Identify specific goals that are both qualitiative and quantitative*	*List activities necessary to reach goal*
A.	A-1	A-1
	A-2	A-2
	A-3	A-3
	A-4	A-4
	A-5	A-5

Number 4 — Matching Wits with the Experts

Throughout the text the question of productivity recurs. Managers are held responsible for productivity of the units or organizations in which they lead. Productivity is also a broad economic issue in the United States, and in recent years there have been cited a number of reasons that the U.S. rate of growth has been slowing.

Directions: The following are some of the reasons cited by business/economic experts in business publications regarding the lackluster growth of productivity in the U.S. Circle the number representing the extent that you agree with the statement, and write a one-line clarification of your response. Response choices are arranged from 1 to 5: 1=strongly agree, 2=agree, 3=not sure, 4=disagree, 5=strongly disagree. Be prepared to discuss your ideas with peer members and with your professor.

Answer choices	*Expert opinion explaining reasons for productivity slowdown*
1 2 3 4 5	1. Poor employee attitude. Comment:
1 2 3 4 5	2. Labor unions or collective bargaining units set low standards. Comment:
1 2 3 4 5	3. Managers do not know how to "motivate" employees. Comment:
1 2 3 4 5	4. Wages and salaries are too low to inspire hard work. Comment:
1 2 3 4 5	5. Major industries in the U.S. such as steel are becoming obsolete in technology. Comment:
1 2 3 4 5	6. Research and development capital is inadequate. Comment:
1 2 3 4 5	7. The percent of organization profits set aside for reinvestment is too small. Comment:
1 2 3 4 5	8. There are too many protective tariffs and similar protection for U.S. business, and this discourages competitiveness and innovation. Comment:
1 2 3 4 5	9. There are too many laws and regulations imposed on business. Comment:
1 2 3 4 5	10. Not enough entrepreneurship and starting of new small businesses. Comment:

Summary

Regarding items 1-10 above, which ones do you feel are the major ones that need to be addressed now in order to help U.S. productivity improve? What other factors would you add that can help improve productivity? Discuss.

Number 5 — Experiential Learning

Organizations are finding that inequity of treatment between men and women, minority and nonminority employees is not only unjust, it is usually in violation of equal employment laws. Therefore, the following experiential exercise is offered to provide you with a first-hand managerial experience in trying to rectify inequity in pay between two employees. It requires that you directly apply fundamental planning to maintain equity.

Directions: Read the following short case, "A Question of Equitable Salary Program," and then set up a MBO, Management by Objectives, system to insure that future wage decisions will be based on something specific and less arbitrary than is the case presently. Use the following format, and do at least four major functions, writing at least one specific quantitative and/or qualitative goal for each of the four job functions.

A Question of Equitable Salary Program

You have just been confronted in the hall by two of your employees, Mary and Bill, who are arguing and seem most highly incensed with you. Normally you would expect them to be happy because they have just received what seem to you to be "fat" salary increases.

Mary exclaims, "I'm very upset! I have compared notes with Bill who has been doing the same kind of work for the same period of time as I have, but you gave him $20 more per month in his raise! Why? I'm not complaining about the amount that you gave me, but I'm just not clear, and Bill isn't either, about the criteria you used to determine these raises. How did you decide?"

Mary continues, "We both feel that we worked dutifully on our functional areas shown below. However, when you went over our work, your general reactions didn't help us much. We both feel that you could help us do a better job if you were more specific about how our functions are tied to salary. Also, we would like a clearer picture of how salaries are established in the first place."

You are caught without a good answer to any of Mary's questions, and you have no immediate criteria. However, you promise Mary, as you slither away, to meet with all the sales people soon to discuss this whole compensation subject. Hopefully, Mary won't file a discrimination suit.

Your department is shoes, and there are five full-time sales people who rotate on the two eight-hour shifts that you have. They earn a straight salary which you consider pretty good for this business.

Directions: Set up an alternate compensation and benefit system which is more progressive in the sense that it can be tied to employees' efforts, especially as such efforts increase sales and profits. The job functions are shown below:

Functions

Sales people will:

1. Display merchandise effectively and maintain attractive displays.

2. Sell shoes achieving highest volume of most expensive shoes, but sell other lines where customer shows interest:

    Lines

    • Exclusive, high-priced, all-leather: 30% of inventory generating, hopefully, 50% of dollar volume and 50% of profits.

    • Medium-priced, but popular styles for young people: 50% of total shoes inventory, 30% of the dollar volume and profit.

    • Lower-priced, low margin, high-rate-of-return shoes: 20% of shoes inventory and sales, but only 10% of gross profit.

    • Accessory items such as socks, shoe trees, polish—the remainder of sales and profits.

3. Maintain accurate records of items sold, dollar amounts, inventory, and reorder requests.

4. Customer relations: Keep customers happy by being courteous and patient. Present return business estimated at 20% of total; could be better.

5. Cooperate with other employees in all department duties. Sharing of duties, especially clean-up and hang-ups, has not worked out well.

6. Keep theft and sales returns to a minimum. Returns are running 3%; theft 1% of gross sales.

7. Miscellaneous housekeeping chores.

MBO for Retail Shoe Sales People

Major function	Goal statement	Activity
EXAMPLE	EXAMPLE	EXAMPLE
A. Selling	A-1 Each sales person will sell — — —	A-1 Each sales person will use the following steps in selling the high-priced line to customers: — — —
1. Exclusive line of shoes		
2.		
3.		
4.		

Summary

Discuss in what ways MBO planning can help avoid inequitable treatment of employees. What problems might still occur?

LOOKING BACK; LOOKING AHEAD

Part 2 of the text and this learning guide dealt with planning, the first management function which must precede other functions such as organizing and controlling. Unless management makes strategic and tactical plans, the organizational activities are likely to be haphazard and unfocused. As individuals, you are encouraged to develop the planning habit now.

In Part 3, the author continues the quest for increased productivity on the part of management via improved organizational design and formalizing of individual roles in business.

Both formal organizations, designed by management, and informal organizing by employees occur in organizations. You should think about your own networks or groups which you have joined and why! What advantages are inherent in group formation? What benefits do individuals get from membership in organizations, either formal or informal? What potential is there for increased productivity when a loose collection of people becomes a cohesive group?

PART III
ORGANIZING FOR PRODUCTIVITY

INTRODUCTION — PART 3

(Chapters 6 — 9)

Highlights

Part 3, Chapters 6—9 of the text, focuses on another key functional area of management called organizing. In Chapter 6 the formal process of organizing is explained in terms of structure—putting employees into particular jobs, coordinating their efforts, and getting them to focus on common goals. Both organization principles and related management principles are introduced. Certain questions that managers often have are answered. How many people, for example, can any one manager effectively supervise? Why, for example, do problems develop when employees have to report to more than one boss? In what ways does the organization process facilitate delegation?

Chapter 7 continues the topic of organization by focusing on variations in design. "Bureaucracy," for example, is a traditional design that has been given bad connotation by virtue of the use of the term "bureaucracy" as something impossible to deal with. Actually, many of the characteristics of a bureaucracy were meant to help organize and simplify employee existence, not to make it more difficult for them to function. Throughout Chapter 7, the author traces the evolvement of organizational design from bureaucratic to mechanistic and organic to more recent designs such as participatory and contingency types.

In Chapter 8, the author adds meaning to organization design by focusing on jobs and the design of jobs as the building blocks of organizations. The point he makes is that organizations are really made up of people who operate in the structures previously discussed. They help make up organizations, but they also derive satisfaction or dissatisfaction from the organizations in which they work and from the jobs that are designed for them.

Chapter 9 brings to life the dynamic organizational activities of staffing. Organizations do not simply appear from space. They must be staffed and constantly renewed with new people. An organization has a life cycle, and so do the personnel working within it. As people mature in their jobs and terminate or retire, new ones are needed. In this chapter, the author adroitly explains the staffing process, the role of the human resource department, how human resource planning is done, and how recruiting and selecting employees is carried out. Gone are the days of "good old folks" network hiring in which organizations would simply bring in a friend or relative without concern for other people's civil or human rights. The advent of EEO laws requires that hiring and promotion practices be done in valid and reliable ways.

Chapter Titles for Part 3

Chapter 6 — Fundamentals of Organizing
Chapter 7 — Organizational Design
Chapter 8 — Designing Jobs for Individuals and Groups
Chapter 9 — Staffing the Human Resources

CAREER PERSPECTIVE — PART 3

Getting Yourself Organized for the Job Interview

In Part 1 you were directed to write a resume which by definition is a very brief summary of a person's qualifications for employment in a formal organizational setting. This section of the text focuses on organizing and organizational design in which human resources are placed in relation to each other. Job design and staffing these designed jobs are topics included in this section, and staffing in particular ought to be of great personal interest to you as a prospective job seeker. Probably one reason that you are taking this course and pursuing a formal education is to improve your prospects for employment and advancement in the organizational world.

Does a degree guarantee employment in the field of your choice? Does a formal education single you out as a prospect when job hunting? The answer is usually "no" for both questions. The reason for the negative response is that competition for jobs is becoming keener even among college graduates. For each opening that is advertised, firms are reporting that response rates of qualified candidates often run into the hundreds. Therefore, your chances for employment, even when you may be highly qualified, may be slim. The issue, therefore, is how to distinguish yourself. How can this be done? The answer in part is to get organized for employment interviewing.

The employment interview is the downfall of many excellent prospects. Right or wrong, fair or unfair, many very qualified job prospects fail to get their ideal job because they do not interview well. The following exercise, therefore, is meant to help you get your "stuff" together in terms of interviewing well.

Directions

The following statements reflect personnel department reasons as reported in journal articles for rejecting job applicants in the interview phase of employment selection process. Read each statement and then answer questions that relate to how you would avoid the potential dilemmas posed here. That is, get yourself organized for the employment interview by doing this exercise.

Interview Related Factor and Appropriate Response

A. Appointment pitfalls
    1. Arriving late or at the wrong place

Discussion:
    What specific preparation would you recommend for yourself to avoid this problem? List ideas.

B. Poor personal appearance (one of the most common rejection factors)
    1. Inappropriate dress

Discussion:
    What is the current accepted attire for you in your field when going for the interview? List specific wardrobe items, colors, styles, etc.

2. Poor grooming, hygiene

Discussion:

   What particular grooming might be considered by you? For men, for example, is facial hair okay? Shoulder-length hair? Pierced ears and earrings?

   For women, what type of coiffure is appropriate? Does hair styling make a difference? Does the "perm" look, for example, convey a different image than does straight hair styling?

C. Poor etiquette
   1. Inappropriate greeting or salutation
   2. Inappropriate topics raised by the applicant in the interview
   3. Inappropriate departing comments when the interview is over

Discussion:

   What is the appropriate greeting and salutation when meeting a male or female company representative? What titling should be used? Besides sexual titling, does the applicant use rank, position or degree titling, for example, when addressing company representatives. Is first name basis okay in a formal interview setting? Give your written responses to these questions.

   What things should not be asked by the applicant in the initial interview?

   What should be the closing comments and departure by the applicant?

D. Poor personal expression; poor self-direction (often listed as the number one reason interviewees are downgraded in interview ratings)
   1. Unclear response to questions by interviewer on the part of the interviewee regarding **why** he/she is interested in a particular career, job, or firm.

Discussion:

   Select your ideal job or career and explain why it is.

2. Unclear response to self-assessment. That is, the applicant does not cite clearly his/her perception of strengths and weaknesses.

Discussion:
    List what you feel are your own strengths and weaknesses in the context of employment.

3. The applicant does not respond clearly to longer term interests—where he or she would like to be in three to five years.

Discussion:
    List what type of work and position you would like or prefer in, say, five years and ten years.

4. Unclear response to rationale for major taken in college and favorite or unfavorite subject.

Discussion:
    List and briefly explain your rationale for your choice of major and favorite subjects.

5. Negative demeanor displayed toward authority figures in the academic setting. In other words, expressions of dislike or disrespect for professors comes across badly.

Discussion:
    Explain how you would express likes and dislikes of faculty with whom you have been associated?

E.   Negative body language
    1.   Poor posture, closed appearance

    2.   Facial expressions

    3.   Nervous antics

    4.   Over-gesturing

Discussion:
    What, if anything, can you do to avoid problems under body language or nonverbal behaviors?

F.   Follow-up
    1.   Applicant does not know what should be done in terms of post interview follow-up

Discussion:
    What things should the interviewee do in terms of follow-up?

6 Fundamentals of Organizing

STUDENT LEARNING OBJECTIVES

After completing the chapter material you should be able to:

1. Explain the concept of organization.
2. List how the organization is important in terms of facilitating other management work.
3. Draw a simple organization chart to illustrate the concept of structure and its sub-parts.
4. Contrast the formal structure with the informal.
5. Elicit the structure concept from a manager's perspective.
6. Compare ways that both internal and external determinants can affect structural design.
7. Explain the value of departmentation in designing structures, and give examples of different types of structural designs.
8. Define vertical coordination, and explain four fundamental elements involved.
9. Define horizontal coordination and related concepts of functional and line and staff authority.

CHAPTER HIGHLIGHTS

Organizing as a management function
Organization structure
Structure from a manager's perspective
Departmentation
Vertical coordination
Horizontal coordination

PROGRAMMED LEARNING

The following statements are drawn from actual textbook content in abbreviated form. The blanks within the statements are numbered to correspond with the answer blanks at the left.

Organization defined

1. _____

According to Peter Drucker, the first job of the manager is to make the organization _____(1).

2. _____
3. _____
4. _____
5. _____

An organization is defined as a collection of _____(2) in a division of _____(3) working _____(4) to achieve a common _____(5).

Organizing as a management function

6. _____

The process of dividing work into manageable components and coordinating results to serve the organization's purpose is called _____(6).

7. _____

Organizing arranges or mobilizes organizational _____(7) for action.

8. _____
9. _____
10. _____
11. _____
12. _____
13. _____
14. _____

The benefits of good organizing efforts by managers include: clarifying the _____(8) of work, providing _____(9) for individual performance, aiding _____(10) and _____(11), establishing channels for _____(12) and _____-_____(13), and focusing_____(14).

Organizing as a decision process

15. _____
16. _____

In the vocabulary of the management, this decision process addresses two fundamental questions: how should work efforts and workers be _____(15), and how should work efforts and workers be _____(16) in return or integrated to insure a common result?

Organization structure

17. _____

The formal system of working relationships that both divide up and coordinate the task activities of multiple people and groups to serve a common purpose is called organization _____(17).

18. _____
19. _____

In the organization performance equation, performance depends upon both _____(18) and _____(19) being appropriate to the task at hand.

Organization charts and the formal structure

20. _____

A diagram that describes the basic alignment of work positions within an organization is called an organization _____(20).

21. _____
22. _____
23. _____
24. _____
25. _____

From an organization chart, one can typically determine: the division of _____(21), superviser-subordinate _____(22), type of _____(23) performed, _____(24), and the levels of _____(25).

The informal structure

26. _____ The set of unofficial but very critical working relationships is called the _____(26) structure.

27. _____ Informal structures can benefit the organization by helping its members
28. _____ to accomplish their _____(27), overcome _____(28) in the
29. _____ formal structure, and _____(29) with one another.

30. _____ The potential costs of informal structures include: resistance to
31. _____ _____(30), diversion of _____(31) attention from other issues,
32. _____ diversion of _____(32) from organizational objectives, and suscep-
               tibility to rumor.

Structure from a manager's perspective

33. _____ Structure represents two things to a manager, something within which a manager must work, but also something managers _____(33).

External and internal determinants of structure

34. _____ There are five major external determinants of structure: _____(34),
35. _____ _____(35), _____(36), _____(37), and _____(38).
36. _____
37. _____
38. _____

39. _____ One management configuration task is the process through which multiple work tasks are arranged in a division of labor called _____(39).

40. _____ Specialization can be done by job _____(40) and _____(41).
41. _____

42. _____ Once specialization has been accomplished, steps must be taken to in-
               tegrate the resulting division of labor by a process called _____(42).

43. _____ Two types of coordination are _____(43) and _____(44).
44. _____

Departmentation

45. _____ The process of grouping people and activities together under the super-
               vision of a common manager is called _____(45).

46. _____ When departmentation is done well, it contributes to organizational
47. _____ success by: clarifying _____(46), facilitating _____(47) and
48. _____ _____(48), and increasing quality of _____(49).
49. _____

50. _____ Forming departments by grouping people together in common organiza-
               tional units performing similar or closely related activities is called depart-
               mentation by _____(50).

51. _____ Departmentation by functions relies on specialization of _____(51).

52. _____ Functional structures are best suited for _____(52) environments.

53. _____ Departmentation based on product, client, territory, time or project
               differences are called divisions, and are quick in responding to rapidly
               changing _____(53) and opportunities.

54. _____ The organization type that combines functional and divisional forms of
               departmentation to take best advantage of each is called _____(54).

55. _____ The matrix form of departmentation provides a mechanism for handling _____(55) products or services in a balanced manner.

56. _____ The matrix form of organization is designed to force _____-_____(56) down to the lowest possible level.

57. _____ It does this by creating permanent _____-functional(57) teams for decision-making.

58. _____ The matrix is suited for organizations pursuing _____(58) strategies
59. _____ in _____(59) and complex environments.

60. _____ Some things to watch for and guard against when establishing or working
61. _____ within a matrix structure include: _____(60) struggles, _____(61),
62. _____ "_____itis"(62), and excessive _____(63).

Vertical coordination

64. _____ Besides organizing people and resources, management must also _____(64) results.

65. _____ The central element in this coordination process is _____(65).

66. _____ The process of using the hierarchy of authority to help integrate the separate components of an organization is called _____(66) coordination.

67. _____ Through vertical coordination management forms an unbroken line of authority that links all persons in an organization with higher levels of authority, and this is called chain of _____(67).

68. _____ The chain of command principle that states that there should be a clear and unbroken chain of command linking different levels of people in the organization is called _____(68) principle.

69. _____ A related principle that states each person in an organization should report to one and only one boss is called _____(69) of command.

70. _____ Another "chain" principle that states there is a limit to the number of persons one manager can effectively supervise is called _____(70) of control.

71. _____ Organizations with generally larger spans of control tend to be _____(71).

72. _____ Organizations with generally small spans of control tend to be _____(72).

73. _____ The vertical coordination process of entrusting work to other persons is called _____(73).

74. _____ Three steps in delegation are assigning _____(74), granting
75. _____ _____(75), and creating employee _____(76).
76. _____

77. _____ The foundation elements in the delegation process include: _____(77),
78. _____ _____(78), and _____(79).
79. _____

80. _____ Classical advice is that authority should equal _____(80).

81. _____ When authority is dispersed through extensive delegation throughout all levels of management it is called _____(81).

Horizontal coordination

82. _____   The process through which activities are integrated across rather than up and down levels in the chain of command is called _____(82) coordination.

83. _____   Authority to act in relation to the activities of other persons or units lying outside of the formal chain of command is called _____(83).

84. _____   A good example of functional authority in most organizations is found with the _____(84) department.

85. _____   Another means for achieving horizontal coordination is through a clear designation of line and _____(85) units.

86. _____
87. _____   The authority of staff in relationship to line personnel varies along a continuum, from purely _____(86) to _____(87) authority.

88. _____
89. _____   In summary, managers must _____(88) work and _____(89) the results to accomplish organizational objectives.

TESTING YOUR KNOWLEDGE

True and False Self Test

Directions: Circle the letter (T or F) of the correct response for each of the following statements.

T F   1. Authority is the arrangement of work positions in order of increasing authority at management levels.

T F   2. Organizing is the basis for defining task activities.

T F   3. Structure, chain of command, centralization, decentralization, departmentalization, staff, levels of management and job functions, represent the basic organizing concepts for organizations of all types.

T F   4. The key element in what we can now call the organizational performance equation is called planning.

T F   5. An example of an informal structure component might be a consulting engineer.

T F   6. Middle or lower-level managers are responsible for helping top level managers create a structure.

T F   7. There are two major determinants of structure: technology and people.

T F   8. A manager's major concern with specialization is departmentation.

T F   9. Specialization by departmentation is creation of work units or groups by arranging several jobs under the authority of a common manager.

T F 10. The two dimensions of coordination are veritcal and horizontal.

Multiple Choice Self Test

Directions: Circle the letter of the response that best completes each of the following statements.

1. An organization by definition includes:
   a. a collection of people
   b. a division of labor
   c. coordination of people
   d. common purpose
   e. all of the above

2. Good organizing normally results in:
   a. clarification of work flow
   b. guidelines for individual performance
   c. clarification of planning
   d. improved communication
   e. all of the above

3. From an organization chart one can typically determine:
   a. "power" and "politics" in informal management networks
   b. a division of work
   c. superior-subordinate relationships
   d. levels of management
   e. all but a above

4. Informal structures can benefit organizations by helping:
   a. fill employee needs
   b. employees communicate
   c. overcome gaps in the formal structure
   d. accomplish formal organization tasks
   e. all of the above

5. Informal structures may lead to:
   a. resistance to change
   b. diversion of managerial attention
   c. spreading of rumors
   d. all of the above
   e. none of the above

6. External determinants of structure include the need for:
   a. specialization of labor
   b. coordination of employee work
   c. clarification of authority/responsibility
   d. none of the above are external

7. A hybrid form of organization used to force decision-making down the hierarchy is called:
   a. functional
   b. exceptional
   c. divisional
   d. matrix

8. Divisional departmentation is based on:
   a. products
   b. clients
   c. territories
   d. projects
   e. all of the above are possible divisional departments

9. The principle that states that each person in an organization should report to one and only one boss is called:
   a. scalar
   b. unity of command
   c. span of control
   d. delegation

10. According to your text, the authority of staff in relationship to line personnel ranges from:
   a. advisory to functional
   b. soft line to hard nosed
   c. no authority to absolute
   d. mini-min. to maxi-max.

Matching Self Test

Directions: Write the letter of the description that best fits each numbered item in the blank provided.

_____ 1. Unity of command principle

_____ 2. Matrix organization

_____ 3. Chain of command

_____ 4. Span of control

_____ 5. Functional authority

_____ 6. Horizontal coordination

_____ 7. Scalar principle

_____ 8. Specialized staff

_____ 9. Organizational chart

_____ 10. Hierarchy of authority

a. Each person in an organization should have only one boss.

b. Unbroken line of authority that links all persons in an organization with higher levels of authority.

c. Combines functional and divisional forms of departmentation.

d. Total number of employees reporting to one manager.

e. Process through which activities are integrated across the organization.

f. Personnel department is an example of.

g. Performs a technical service as a source of special problem-solving expertise.

h. Arrangement of work positions from low to high levels of management.

i. Represents the formal structure of an organization.

j. Providing service in a range from advisory to functional.

k. Buck stops at the top!

7 Organizational Design

STUDENT LEARNING OBJECTIVES

After completing the chapter material you should be able to:

1. Define organizational design and list the variables that affect design.
2. List the bureaucratic features or characteristics of a bureaucracy.
3. Explain what modern industrialized developments exist that will likely bring about the death of the bureaucratic form of organization.
4. Contrast differences in mechanistic and organic structures.
5. Define the contingency approach to organizational design and explain its strategic components.
6. List examples of both environmental and contextual factors that affect organizational design.
7. Define such concepts as differentiation and integration as issues of major significance in the design of subsystems.

CHAPTER HIGHLIGHTS

Bureaucracy as a type of organization
Mechanistic and organic structures
Strategic factors in organizational design
Environmental factors in organizational design
Organizational context's impact on design
Subsystems in organizations

PROGRAMMED LEARNING

The following statements are drawn from actual textbook content in abbreviated form. The blanks within the statements are numbered to correspond with the answer blanks at the left.

Nature of organizations

1. _____

The process of choosing and implementing an appropriate structural configuration is called organizational _____(1).

2. _____
3. _____
4. _____
5. _____
6. _____

Good organizational design is based on the examination of relationships between _____(2) and _____(3), _____(4), _____(5), _____(6), and people.

Bureaucracy

7. _____

An organization carefully structured with clear-cut division of labor, hierarchy of authority and a system of rules is called _____(7).

8. _____
9. _____
10. _____
11. _____

The characteristics of an ideal bureaucracy include: a clear-cut _____(8) of labor, positions arranged in a _____(9) of authority, positions staffed on the basis of _____(10) competence, and a system of impersonal rules and _____(11).

12. _____

However, there are times when very _____(12) organizations seem nothing more than sources of endless lines, red tape, insensitivity to unique problems, and resistance to change.

13. _____
14. _____
15. _____
16. _____

Four relevant threats to bureaucracy in today's business setting are: rapid and unexpected _____(13), growth in _____(14), _____(15) of modern business and technology, and a psychological threat springing from a change in managerial _____(16).

17. _____
18. _____
19. _____

The classical bureaucratic model of organization is prone to the following limitations in actual practice: too _____(17), too _____(18), and too specialized reducing employee _____(19).

Mechanistic and organic organizations

20. _____
21. _____

The organization is an open _____(20) that transforms resource _____(21) into product or service outputs.

22. _____

For an organization to survive and be successful over time it must continuously adapt to its environment by developing a structure which exploits the opportunities and solves the problems at hand. This is called the _____(22) approach.

23. _____

Mechanistic organizations are very _____(23) in form.

24. _____

Structures that have decentralized authority, few rules and procedures, less strict division of labor, wider spans of control, and informal and personal means of coordination are called _____(24).

25. _____
26. _____

Mechanistic structures are usually adopted under _____(25) conditions, whereas _____(26) structures are developed for changing conditions.

Strategic factors in organizational design

27. _____

28. _____

Environmental and contextual forces are considered _____(27) factors in organizational design because they influence situational _____(28).

29. _____

30. _____

Strategic design consideration leads to the following organization view: structure must fit _____(29) and _____(30).

Environment

31. _____

32. _____

Organizational design guideline number 1 states that when environmental complexity is high a more _____(31) structure is best; when environmental complexity is low a more _____(32) structure is best.

33. _____

34. _____

Environmental uncertainty is the _____(33) and _____(34) associated with environmental elements.

35. _____

The _____(35) environment is composed of the cultural values, economic, legal-political, and educational conditions in the region within which an organization conducts most of its business.

36. _____

The _____(36) environment consists of all external organizations and persons with whom an organization must interact in order to grow and survive.

Organizational context

37. _____

In addition to the external environment, a manager must be prepared to analyze the _____(37) context for action.

38. _____

39. _____

40. _____

41. _____

This includes its _____(38), _____(39), _____(40), and the _____(41).

42. _____

Each of these contextual elements is an additional _____(42) factor to consider in organization design.

43. _____

The combination of equipment, knowledge, and work methods that allows the organization to transform resource inputs into product or service outputs is called _____(43).

44. _____

The availability of proper technology is a major element in efforts to increase _____(44).

45. _____

In the _____(45) technology there is uncertainty as to how to produce desired outcomes.

46. _____

A _____(46) technology links together parties seeking a mutually beneficial exchange.

47. _____

A mass production process relying upon highly specialized jobs performed in a closely controlled sequence to create a final product is called _____-_____(47) technology.

48. _____

Organizational design guideline number 2 states that when technological complexity is high, such as in small batch, continuous process and intensive technologies, a more _____(48) structure is best.

49. _____

When technological complexity is low, as in long-linked and mass production technologies, a more _____(49) structure is best.

50. _____

Organizational design guideline number 3 states that organizations tend to adopt more _____(50) structures as they increase in size. However, the author goes on to say this may not always be best.

51. _____   Organizational design guideline number 4 states that stability strategies
52. _____   will be more successful when supported by _____(51) structures;
                       growth strategies will be more successful when supported by _____(52)
                       structures.

53. _____   Organizational design guideline number 5 states that people with greater
54. _____   technical skills and expertise will prefer working in more _____(53)
                       structures; people with less technical skills and expertise will prefer work-
                       ing in more _____(54) structures.

55. _____   Because mechanistic structures are stable and well-defined, they appeal to
56. _____   people wanting _____(55) direction and more _____(56) in their
                       work.

57. _____   Because organic structures are flexible and less-defined, they appeal to
58. _____   people wanting task _____(57) and more _____(58) in their
                       work.

Subsystem relationships

59. _____   A single department or work unit headed by a manager and which repre-
                       sents a smaller part of a larger organization is called a _____(59).

60. _____   Subsystems in a given firm face _____(60) whose characteristics may
                       differ from one another.

61. _____   The overall structures of successful firms in each industry matched their
                       respective _____(61) challenges.

62. _____   As the text said, organizational structure must match _____(62)
                       factors in environment and context.

63. _____   Within an organization, differences among _____(63) will emerge
                       as each subunit tries to position itself to best meet the special demands of
                       its subenvironment.

64. _____   This point highlights both differentiation and _____(64) as issues of
                       major significance in the design of subsystems and in the maintenance of
                       good working relationships among them.

65. _____   A term used to represent the degrees of difference that exist among sub-
                       units is called _____(65).

66. _____   Lawrence and Lorsch identify four dimensions of differentiation that
67. _____   become important for managers seeking to understand and manage
68. _____   differences among organizational subunits: (1) _____(66) orientation,
69. _____   (2) _____(67) orientation, (3) _____(68) orientation, (4) dif-
                       ferences in _____(69).

70. _____   Organizational design guideline number 6 states that organizations facing
                       more uncertain external environments will require greater internal
                       _____(70) among subsystems than will organizations facing more
                       certainty.

71. _____   Increased differentiation creates a need for increased _____(71).

72. _____   Coordination becomes more difficult as _____(72) increases.

73. _____   Organizational design guideline number 7 states that the greater the need
74. _____   for and difficulty of achieving integration among highly differentiated
75. _____   subsystems, the more an organization's mechanism for creating lateral
                       relations must shift toward task _____(73), _____(74), and the
                       _____(75), and away from rules, procedures, and hierarchical referral.

76. _____   The process of subsystem design requires fulfillment of two basic manage-
77. _____   ment responsibilities: _____(76) and _____(77).

TESTING YOUR KNOWLEDGE

True and False Self Test

Directions: Circle the letter (T or F) of the correct response for each of the following statements.

T F 1. The ideal bureaucracy is based on logic, order, and legitimate authority.

T F 2. Burns and Stalker suggest that two different organizational structures could be successful depending upon the nature of environmental conditions.

T F 3. Changing environmental conditions call for mechanistic structures.

T F 4. The specific environment consists of people and other organizations of immediate consequence.

T F 5. A mediating technology links together parties seeking a mutually beneficial exchange.

T F 6. Coordination in an organization becomes more difficult as differentiation increases.

T F 7. The ultimate goal in organizational design is to provide structures which help organizations achieve high levels of productivity.

T F 8. Technology is the combination of equipment, knowledge, and work methods that allows organizations to transform resource inputs into product or service outputs.

T F 9. Tailoring to meet customer specifications would be an example of small batch production.

T F 10. Growth strategies are most likely to be successful when supported by mechanistic structures.

Multiple Choice Self Test

Directions: Circle the letter of the response that best completes each of the following statements.

1. The process of choosing and implementing an appropriate structure is called organizational:
    a. decisions
    b. design
    c. planning
    d. strategy

2. Good organizational design is based upon the examination of the relationships between structure and which of the following variables?
    a. environment
    b. technology
    c. size
    d. strategy
    e. all of the above

3. The founder of bureaucracy as an organizational concept was:
    a. Weber
    b. Von Strutz
    c. Heiden
    d. Burns

4. Bureaucracies are particularly helpful in meeting:
    a. rapid change
    b. growth
    c. advances in technology
    d. changes in managerial behavior
    e. none of the above

5. Classical bureaucratic models of organization tend to be too:
   a. rigid
   b. tall
   c. specialized
   d. flexible
   e. all but **d** above

6. Structures that have decentralized authority, few rules, less strict divisions of labor, and wider spans of control are called:
   a. generic
   b. biological
   c. organic
   d. none of the above

7. Mechanistic organizations work best under what conditions:
   a. stable
   b. uncertain
   c. rapidly changing
   d. out of control

8. Under strategic design considerations the organization structure must fit:
   a. environment
   b. context
   c. bureaucratic parameter
   d. both **a** and **b** above
   e. none of the above

9. The general environment in which organizations operate is composed of:
   a. culture
   b. economic/political factors
   c. educational conditions
   d. all of the above

10. The organizational context refers to:
    a. technology
    b. size
    c. strategy
    d. people
    e. all of the above

Matching Self Test

Directions: Write the letter of the description that best fits each numbered item in the blank provided.

_____ 1. Cultural values

_____ 2. Organizational design

_____ 3. Organic

_____ 4. General environment

_____ 5. Long-linked technology

_____ 6. Chemical plants and refineries

_____ 7. Environmental complexity

_____ 8. Integration

_____ 9. Subsystem

_____ 10. Technology, size, people

a. An organization with few rules and procedures.

b. Cultural values, economic and legal conditions.

c. A single department or work unit.

d. Contextual elements that influence an organizational structure.

e. Measure of rate of change and degree of uncertainty associated with environment.

f. Level of coordination achieved among subsystems.

g. Process of choosing and implementing an appropriate structure.

h. Indicates what actions are important and desireable from a societal perspective.

i. Automobile assembly line.

j. Continuous process technology.

8 Designing Jobs for Individuals and Groups

STUDENT LEARNING OBJECTIVES

After completing this chapter material you should be able to:

1. Explain the meaning of work to individual employees.
2. Define psychological contract in terms of an employee's productivity in the organization.
3. Describe how work can contribute to quality of life.
4. Explain job satisfaction and its relationship to performance.
5. Relate the terms job content and context to the process of job design.
6. Compare and contrast the concepts of job simplification, job enlargement, and job enrichment.
7. Give examples of some of the author's creative work group designs and alternative work schedules.

CHAPTER HIGHLIGHTS

The meaning of work
Satisfaction and performance
Job design in concept and practice
A diagnostic approach to job enrichment
Creative work group designs
Alternative work schedules

PROGRAMMED LEARNING

The following statements are drawn from actual textbook content in abbreviated form. The blanks within the statements are numbered to correspond with the answer blanks at the left.

Job design

1. _____ A fundamental part of the organizing process in any work setting is designing _____(1) for individuals and groups.

2. _____ Jobs combine into _____(2) or work units which together create
3. _____ _____(3).

4. _____ A collection of tasks performed in support of an organization's purpose is called a _____(4).

The meaning of work

5. _____ Work is an activity that produces _____(5) for other people.

6. _____ The shared set of expectations held by the individual and the organization, specifying what each expects to give to and receive from the other in the course of their working relationship, is called a _____(6) contract.

7. _____ A _____(7) contract represents the exchange of _____(8) result-
8. _____ ing from an individual's decision to work for the organization and the organization's decision to employ the individual in return.

9. _____ An individual offers _____(9) or work activities of value to the organization.

10. _____ The things of value that the organization gives to the individual in return for his/her contributions are called _____(10).

11. _____ When the exchange of values between the individual and the organization is fair, a state of inducements-contributions _____(11) exists and a positive or healthy psychological contract results.

12. _____ A high quality _____ _____(12) for the individual and
13. _____ _____(13) for the organization should be the ideal results.

Satisfaction and performance

14. _____ The degree to which an individual feels positively or negatively about various aspects of the job tasks, the work setting, and relationships with co-workers is called job _____(14).

15. _____ According to the Hygiene theory, items causing feelings of job dissatisfaction were most often associated with job _____(15).

16. _____ Sources of job dissatisfaction are called _____(16) factors and include
17. _____ such things as working _____(17), _____(18) relations, organi-
18. _____ zational _____(19) and administration, _____(20), and
19. _____ _____(21).
20. _____
21. _____

22. _____ The hygiene factors in Herzberg's theory only affect job _____(22).

23. _____ Hygiene factors exist in job _____(23) and affect job dissatisfaction.

24. _____ To improve job satisfaction, Herzberg argues that a manager's attention
25. _____ must shift away from _____(24) and toward _____(25) factors,
26. _____ which are identified as job _____(26).

27. _____   Satisfier factors exist in job _____(27) and affect job satisfaction.

28. _____   Job satisfaction alone is probably not a good predictor of individual work _____(28).

29. _____   However, there is an important relationship between job satisfaction and employee _____(29).

30. _____   Job satisfaction is also of recognized _____(30) importance to the individual.

31. _____   If performance leads to greater job satisfaction, then management might concentrate on rewarding high _____(31).

32. _____
33. _____   If management is interested in creating both high job satisfaction as well as high performance, then it should allocate _____(32) contingent upon _____(33).

Job design in concept and practice

34. _____
35. _____   When a job is properly defined, both task _____(34) and job _____(35) should be facilitated.

36. _____   The process through which specific work tasks are allocated to individuals and groups is called _____(36).

37. _____
38. _____   A manager's efforts in job design will be directed toward both job _____(37) and job _____(38).

39. _____
40. _____   Job content refers to _____(39) employees do, and job context refers to the _____(40) in which they work.

41. _____
42. _____   The design of task attributes involves determining appropriate job _____(41), that is the number and combination of _____(42) an individual or group is asked to perform.

43. _____   In designing the scope of the task, the manager might standardize work procedures and employ people in clearly defined and very specialized tasks. This is called job _____(43).

Job enlargement, job rotation, and job enrichment

44. _____
45. _____   Job _____(44) and job _____(45) are strategies of job design that increase the number and variety of tasks performed by a worker.

46. _____
47. _____   According to Herzberg's two-factor theory, it is illogical to expect high levels of _____(46) and _____(47) among employees whose jobs are designed according to the rules of simplification, enlargement, or rotation.

48. _____
49. _____   What is needed is job _____(48), the expansion of job _____(49) rather than job scope.

50. _____
51. _____   Job depth is expanded by adding to a job some of the _____(50) and _____(51) duties normally performed by the supervisor.

A diagnostic approach to job enrichment

52. _____   Modern management theory, however, recognizes that job _____(52) is not for everyone.

53. _____
54. _____
55. _____
56. _____   Instead, managers need to use a diagnostic approach to job enrichment including determination of: skill _____(53), task _____(54), task _____(55), individual _____(56), and _____(57) from the job.

57. _____

58. _____   These five job diagnostic characteristics, if present, provide critical
59. _____   psychological states that promote job satisfaction and performance
60. _____   for the worker: meaningfulness in the _____(58), experience
                        _____(59) for outcomes of work, and see actual _____(60).

61. _____   The key variable in the diagnostic approach is _____(61) need strength
                        of the individual.

62. _____   That is, the individual's desire to achieve a sense of _____(62) growth
                        in his or her work.

63. _____   A person high in growth need strength seeks _____-_____(63)
                        need satisfaction.

64. _____   In many cases it is the nature of the work flow _____(64) that makes
                        job enrichment costly.

65. _____   The employee satisfactions of performing _____(65) tasks often will
                        be adequate compensation.

Creative work group designs

66. _____   A method of job enrichment in which there are self-managed work teams
                        responsible for accomplishing defined production goals, deciding how tasks
                        will be distributed among individuals, and determining at what pace work
                        will progress in order to meet these goals is called _____(66) work
                        groups.

Alternative work schedules

67. _____   There are at least three alternatives to the traditional eight-hour per day,
68. _____   five days per week work schedule as a way of trying to improve job
69. _____   satisfaction: the _____(67) work week, _____(68) working hours,
                        and _____(69) sharing.

70. _____   Some organizational benefits attributed to "flextime" include: reduced
71. _____   _____(70), reduced _____(71), reduced _____(72), and
72. _____   higher individual work _____(73).
73. _____

TESTING YOUR KNOWLEDGE

True and False Self Test

Directions: Circle the letter (T or F) of the correct response for each of the following statements.

T F 1. Sources of job dissatisfaction are called hygiene factors and include such things as working conditions.

T F 2. The hygiene factors in Herzberg's theory affect all aspects of the job for the employee.

T F 3. Herzberg argues that if employees are being paid a truly competitive wage or salary, then the satisfactions of performing enriched tasks will be adequate compensation.

T F 4. Job sharing is a work schedule in which one full-time job is split between two people.

T F 5. A satisfied worker will be the cause of high performance.

T F 6. Compressed work weeks, flexible working hours and job sharing are ways of arranging work schedules to accomodate individual preferences.

T F   7. If a manager is interested in creating high job satisfaction, s/he should allocate rewards to employees in proportion to performance.

T F   8. Work is an activity that produces value for other people.

T F   9. Contributions are forms of compensation that an organization gives to an individual in return for his or her services.

T F   10. The two-factor theory argues that improvements in job content, i.e., adding satisfier factors to a job, can increase satisfaction.

T F   11. Improvements in hygiene factors will improve job satisfaction.

Multiple Choice Self Test

Directions: Circle the letter of the response that best completes each of the following statements.

1. The fundamental building block of formal organization structure is:
    a. people
    b. jobs
    c. machinery
    d. informal relationships

2. A job is a collection of:
    a. responsibilities
    b. outcomes
    c. tasks
    d. goals

3. The psychological contract sums up the mutual exchange between employees and employers of:
    a. input-outputs
    b. communication
    c. values
    d. factors of economic importance

4. According to Herzberg's research, items causing job satisfaction would be:
    a. working conditions
    b. interpersonal relations
    c. organizational policies
    d. supervision
    e. none of the above

5. Improving hygiene factors will lead to:
    a. greater employee motivation
    b. greater employee productivity
    c. lower dissatisfaction
    d. greater satisfaction
    e. both c and d

6. Job satisfaction can be improved through:
    a. enriched jobs
    b. challenging work
    c. added responsibility
    d. opportunity to achieve
    e. all of the above

7. Job satisfaction alone will **not** predict individual:
    a. turnover
    b. psychological reactions of employees
    c. performance
    d. any of the above

8. Job design includes context which means:
   a. tasks to be done
   b. jobs to be done
   c. setting
   d. responsibilities

9. The process of standardizing work procedures and specializing tasks is called:
   a. job simplification
   b. job enlargement
   c. job enrichment
   d. employee motivation

10. Highly enriched jobs would have:
   a. skill variety
   b. task identity
   c. task significance
   d. autonomy
   e. all of the above

Matching Self Test

Directions: Write the letter of the description that best fits each numbered item in the blank provided.

_____ 1. Job design

_____ 2. Work

_____ 3. Hygiene factors

_____ 4. Inducements

_____ 5. Job rotation

_____ 6. Psychological contract

_____ 7. Modern management theory

_____ 8. Autonomous work grouping

_____ 9. Strategies for job design

_____ 10. Job enlargement

a. Simplification, enlargement/rotation, and enrichment.

b. Emphasizes satisfaction and performance as key results for people at work.

c. Interpersonal relations, working conditions, salary, and policies.

d. Things of value an organization gives to the employee in return for such contributions.

e. Process of defining a job as a collection of specific tasks to be performed by individuals or groups.

f. Building one job from two or more tasks which were previously assigned to separate workers.

g. A shared set of expectations held by the individual and the organization.

h. Increases task variety by periodically shifting workers among jobs involving different tasks.

i. An activity that produces value for other people.

j. Technique for enriching job content at the group level.

9 Staffing the Human Resources

STUDENT LEARNING OBJECTIVES

After completing the chapter material you should be able to:

1. Define the staffing process and explain the performance equation.
2. List and explain the elements in the staffing process.
3. Define human resource planning and explain its central importance in staffing.
4. Delineate job analysis procedures and how the analysis helps to shape the job description.
5. Describe the human resource forecasting factors, both need and supply.
6. Explain the intent and value of EEO laws.
7. Relate human resource planning to recruiting, and explain the recruitment process.
8. Compare relative merits of external and internal recruiting.
9. Distinguish between recruiting and selecting, and describe selection tools and processes.
10. Explain the value of the new-hire orientation programs.
11. Restate what the text says constitutes good training, and give samples of training types.
12. Explain the processes used in replacement.

CHAPTER HIGHLIGHTS

The staffing process
Human resource planning
Recruitment
Selection
Orientation
Training and development
Replacement

PROGRAMMED LEARNING

The following statements are drawn from actual textbook content in abbreviated form. The blanks within the statements are numbered to correspond with the answer blanks at the left.

The staffing process

1. _____ The managerial process of filling jobs with appropriate persons is called _____(1).

2. _____
3. _____ Management tries to acquire employees with ability, but in order to get performance, ability must be multiplied by _____(2) and _____(3).

4. _____
5. _____ Support is achieved, in large measure, through proper design of organization _____(4) and _____(5).

6. _____ Effort is influenced via _____(6).

7. _____ _____(7) is a staffing issue.

8. _____
9. _____ The basic objective in the staffing process is to match _____(8) and _____(9) in a manner that facilitates _____(10).
10. _____

11. _____
12. _____ The managerial elements in the staffing include: human resource _____(11), _____(12), _____(13), _____(14), _____(15), and replacement.
13. _____
14. _____
15. _____

Human resource planning

16. _____ The identification of staffing needs of the organization, forecasting staff supplies, and the determination of what additions and/or replacements are required to maintain a staff of the desired size and quality is called _____ _____(16) planning.

17. _____ Personnel or human resource planning involves establishing _____(17)
18. _____ needs and forecasting human resource _____(18).

19. _____ The beginning point in any systematic effort to identify staffing needs is called _____ (19) analysis.

20. _____ From a job analysis one can create the job _____(20) and job
21. _____ _____(21).

22. _____ Job _____(22) usually include education, experience and ability requirements for the job.

23. _____
24. _____ Forecasting supply of human resources involves projecting future staffing _____(23) and _____(24).

25. _____
26. _____ When forecasting the need for human resources, consider such things as:
27. _____ organization _____(25), _____(26) trends, _____(27) of
28. _____ employees, and introduction of new _____(28).

29. _____ Determining the availability of required talent in external labor markets and outside competition are part of forecasting the _____(29) of human resources.

30. _____ A method of identifying promotable employees within the organization is called the human resource _____(30).

31. _____   The right of people to employment and advancement without regard to race, sex, religion, color, or natural origin is called _____(31) employment opportunity.

32. _____   Programs that are designed to increase employment opportunities for women and other minorities including veterans, the aged, and the handicapped are called _____(32) Action Programs.

Recruitment

33. _____   A set of activities designed to attract a qualified pool of job applicants to an organization is called _____(33).

34. _____   Human resource planning leads to recruiting which sets the stage for _____(34).

35. _____   The three steps in the recruitment process itself are: _____(35) of
36. _____   a job vacancy, preliminary _____(36) with potential job candidates,
37. _____   and initial _____(37) to create a pool of qualified applicants.

38. _____   Making current employees aware of job vacancies through job posting and personal recommendations is called _____(38) recruitment.

39. _____   Instead of overselling the organization, the _____(39) recruitment process tries to provide the job candidate with all pertinent information and without destortion.

Selection

40. _____   The process of choosing from a pool of applicants the person or persons best meeting job specifications is called _____(40).

41. _____   Events in a typical selection process are: completion of a formal
42. _____   _____(41) form, further _____(42), _____(43), _____(44)
43. _____   checks, _____(45) examination, and final analysis and decision to
44. _____   _____(46) or reject.
45. _____
46. _____

47. _____   The written summary of the applicant's personal history and job qualifications that usually becomes a permanent part of the personnel file is the _____(47) form.

48. _____   The interview is an extremely important part of the selection process because of the two-way _____(48) exchange.

49. _____   A selection tool used to screen applicants on the basis of intelligence, aptitudes, skills and personality is called a _____(49).

50. _____   The goal of any employment test is to gather information which will help predict the eventual _____(50) success on the job.

51. _____   To predict success on a job, a test must be both _____(51) and
52. _____   _____(52).

53. _____   A valid test measures exactly what it intends to relative to the job _____(53).

54. _____   A reliable test yields approximately the same results over _____(54) if taken by the same person.

55. _____   A thorough process of involving job candidates in a series of experiential activities over a one or two day period is an _____(55) center.

Orientation

56. _____ The process of systematically changing the expectations, behavior and attitudes of a new employee in a manner considered desirable by the organization is part of _____(56).

57. _____ An initial set of activities designed to familiarize new employees with their jobs and co-workers, as well as with the policies, rules, objectives and services of the organization as a whole is also called _____(57).

58. _____ The anticipated results of orientation are higher _____(58) and
59. _____ _____(59) and increased employee _____(60).
60. _____

Training and development

61. _____ A set of activities that provide learning opportunities through which people can acquire and improve job-related skills is called _____(61).

62. _____ Good training is implemented by: assessing _____(62), setting
63. _____ _____(63), selecting _____(64), implementing a _____(65),
64. _____ and _____(66) the program.
65. _____
66. _____

67. _____ Good training can only occur when trainees want to _____(67) and
68. _____ trainees are _____(68) for learning.

69. _____ A training method discussed as a job design strategy is called _____(69) rotation.

70. _____ The communication of specific technical advice to an individual is referred to as _____(70).

71. _____ An assignment of an employee to serve as understudy or assistant to a person already having the desired job skills is called _____(71).

72. _____ A process of demonstrating through personal behavior that which is expected of others is called _____(72).

73. _____ Lectures, discussions, demonstrations, case studies, simulations, and role-plays are examples of _____-_____-_____(73) training.

74. _____ The act of sharing experiences and insights between a seasoned executive and junior manager is a management development technique called _____(74).

Replacement

75. _____ When a selection error occurs or a person outgrows a job or gets demoted, the step called _____(75) occurs.

76. _____ Replacement relates to the management of _____(76), _____(77),
77. _____ _____(78), layoffs, and _____(79).
78. _____
79. _____

80. _____ A service to help terminated employees that ranges from personal counseling to direct assistance in seeking alternative employment is called _____(80).

81. _____ The most extreme form of termination is _____(81).

TESTING YOUR KNOWLEDGE

True and False Self Test

Directions: Circle the letter (T or F) of the correct response for each of the following statements.

T F 1. It is a matter of economic necessity to improve human resource planning.

T F 2. Organized labor is a major external influence on human resource planning.

T F 3. Good staffing begins with human resource planning.

T F 4. Affirmative action requirements only apply to a few certain organizations doing business with the federal government.

T F 5. Traditional recruitment often seeks to "sell" the organization to outsiders.

T F 6. The reliability of a test refers to its measuring exactly what it intends to relative to the job specification.

T F 7. In order to gather information which will help predict performance success on the job, a test must be both valid and reliable.

T F 8. The assessment center is a special technique often used in selecting people for management jobs.

T F 9. The orientation process reduces start-up costs and time, reduces anxiety, and reduces turnover.

T F 10. Orientation is often considered a managerial responsibility.

Multiple Choice Self Test

Directions: Circle the letter of the response that best completes each of the following statements.

1. Ability x (times) support x effort results:
   a. performance
   b. motivation
   c. satisfaction
   d. success

2. The "core staffing issue" when seeking employees who will perform is:
   a. age
   b. ability
   c. education
   d. experience

3. The basic objective in the staffing process is to match:
   a. supply with demand
   b. employee and organization interests
   c. people and jobs
   d. wits with dishonest applicants

4. Staffing activity is described as:
   a. planning
   b. recruitment
   c. selection
   d. orientation and training
   e. all of the above

5. The identification of staffing needs, forecasting, and determination of what additions or replacements are needed is called human resource:
   a. planning
   b. recruiting
   c. selection
   d. orientation

6. The first step in determining staffing needs is to:
   a. forecast needs
   b. do job analysis
   c. determine future turnover
   d. hire an EEO officer

7. Precise identification of qualifications needed of a person to do a job is called:
   a. job summary
   b. job description
   c. job specifications
   d. job title

8. When forecasting human resource needs, the factor to consider is:
   a. organization growth
   b. budget trends
   c. employee turnover
   d. technological development
   e. all of the above

9. Title VII of the 1967 Civil Rights Act makes it illegal to discriminate under all the factors below except:
   a. age
   b. race
   c. sex
   d. religion
   e. color or national origin

10. Interviewing, testing, and job application blank are all used in which staffing step?
    a. planning
    b. forecasting
    c. recruiting
    d. selecting

Matching Self Test

Directions: Write the letter of the description that best fits each numbered item in the blank provided.

_____ 1. Staffing

_____ 2. Recruitment process

_____ 3. Mentoring

_____ 4. Affirmative action program

_____ 5. Replacement

_____ 6. Instructional methods

_____ 7. External recruitment

_____ 8. Human resource planning

_____ 9. Orientation

_____ 10. Events in a selection process

a. Identifying staffing needs of the organization.

b. Increasing employment opportunities for women and minorities.

c. Final stage of the staffing process.

d. Process of filling jobs with appropriate personnel.

e. Rotation, coaching, modeling, and apprenticeship.

f. A process of searching for new employees.

g. Sharing experiences and insights between a seasoned executive and a junior manager.

h. Activities designed to familiarize new employees with work and the work environment.

i. Completing an application, interviewing, testing, and reference check.

j. Newspapers, employment agencies, colleges, personal contacts, referrals, etc.

LEARNING ACTIVITIES — PART 3

Number 1 — Supplemental Reading and Discussion

Directions: Read the following report from a consulting engagement investigated by Professor Kroll, your learning guide writer, and respond to the questions that follow.

THE INNOVATIVE ORGANIZATION
(Small New England City)

Francis Miller, founder and owner of a small toy manufacturing firm has nearly 70 employees, four of whom are supervisors, five are sales people, fifty are production employees, one personnel administrator, two accountants, and five office/secretarial people. Recently, Professor Kroll was called in to help her with what she called "management" problems. (Names have been changed to protect anonymity.)

When Francis began the company five years ago, she was the only manager, and she had ten assemblers of her cootie-type toys that are made of wood and entertain children because they can be assembled into a variety of funny animals.

The original informal chart is shown by the circle below, with Francis in the center of a tidy little "family" of employees all relating to Francis, the hub of the wheel design. The circle or wheel design worked well and the close-knit feeling made for a happy, productive group.

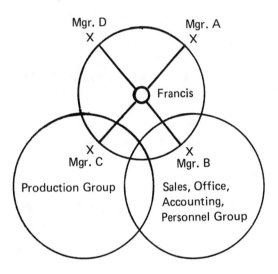

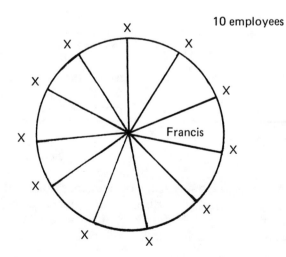

With the very rapid growth of the firm, the original circle has now become what Francis calls three interacting circles: there is her management circle; a large production circle; and the circle of accounting, office, and sales employees.

The above configuration was contrived by Francis to stress the relationships and feelings of equality among all employers and employees among management. This is an offshoot of Francis' original single circle that worked well and led to the present company. By all counts, a successful company, but lately problems have developed.

In the management circle each manager and Francis have served as a team dealing with each functional issue—production, selling, personnel, and finance. Every two weeks the management circle meets with the other two circles and participation in company matters is encouraged. With the growth of the company, a lot more time goes into this participatory approach to things. Delays are developing in decision making. Irrelevant issues often get aired, and employees' personal gripes enter into more substantive questions or issues.

Accountability is also becoming an issue. Sales people, for example, not having a particular supervisor (rather 4 or 5) to report to are delaying sales and marketing reports. Furthermore, when a sales person calls from the field for expert advice, he/she often gets mixed and sometimes conflicting advice when two or more managers respond.

The smallest circle of mixed accountants, office, and personnel employees seems confused about their roles within the circle. On the production scene, the 50 interacting employees circle is becoming cumbersome. The "family" seems to be breaking up, but Francis was not sure how to regroup. Thus, she called in consultant, Mr. Kroll.

Questions Regarding the Innovative Organization

1. What merits or potential merits does the present organization structure offer?

2. Why did the current design or wheel structure work well with the original ten employees, but is faltering now?

3. What are some of the traditional organization/management principles that seem to be violated or not practiced in the current structure?

4. What structural changes would you recommend at this time?

Number 2 — Exercise: Organization Redesign

John Ford Custom Cleaners
Metropolitan USA

```
                    ┌──────────────────┐
                    │   John Ford      │
                    │  Owner/Manager   │
                    └──────────────────┘
```

5 office workers	10 sales personnel who also inspect jobs done by janitors and deliver cleaning products	1 accountant	34 cleaning personnel including 20 full-time and 14 half-time janitorial workers

In the past five years John Ford Custom Cleaners has grown from a one-man janitor service to the business organization illustrated above.

John, the original employee and founder, is "enjoying" growing pains as his business has doubled each year for the past several years resulting in 18-hour days for John. He is director and supervisor of everything including janitorial services and cleaning product sales which is the pleasant surprise. Cleaning products such as detergents, waxer, and utensils, now constitute 40% of dollar volume and 60% of total profits.

Especially difficult for John to keep in order is his janitorial staff many of whom are part-time, thus irregular, not always available, and not particularly loyal to the company.

Geographically, John and his sales people are getting spread out since 30% of new customers have come from East Metropolitan, and John's main office is in West Metropolitan, twenty-five miles away and across a major river which serves as a natural divider of the two areas.

John has an executive secretary and four other office helpers.

Directions:
1. Reorganize the above organization and draw a new chart to illustrate your improvements. Correct the various problems it has, and try to improve its use of personnel as well as its service to its customers.

2. List the various organization principles that seem to be violated or neglected.

Management/Organization Principles Needing Improvement

		Explanation
a)	Span of control	Corrected in the janitorial service department.
b)		
c)		
d)		
e)		
f)		

Number 3 — Training Exercise

Your author describes a variety of training methods used to help develop managerial knowledge and skills. One way corporations help trainees build these skills is through simulation, particularly via "in-basket" exercises. In-basket exercises refer to the nitty-gritty type of day-to-day nuisance issues that come along and need some attention, but also should be dispensed with quickly and put in the "out basket".

Directions: Make decisions for each of the following in-basket memos addressed to you in a variety of settings. Give yourself three minutes each to state what to do and give one- or two-sentence rationale for each decision.

Memo No. 1

To: Personnel Administrator
From: Security
Subject: Obscene phone calls

Ginny Babs and Tom Trouble, two accounting clerks, were caught yesterday during their break making obscene phone calls to Melody Proper, the receptionist. While Melody wasn't too upset with the phone calls, she feels the calls might possibly be overheard by anyone (outsiders) waiting in the reception area.

Your recommended action:

Your rationale:

Memo No. 2

To: Sales Manager
From: Your Secretary
Subject: Additional expense money

As field sales manager you have just received a phone call, according to your secretary, from one of your better sales people requesting an additional expense allowance of $100 above and beyond normal per diem and/or allowance for entertaining clients. The sales person claims he/she needs to do a "first-class" wine and dine for client and spouse to restore regular business which has been slipping to competitors in recent months. To your knowledge your product quality and customer service have not been lacking; prices are competitive.

Your recommended action:

Your rationale:

Memo No. 3

To: Sales Manager
From: Yourself
Subject: Missed deadlines

Bill Hanratly, one of your top sales people, has missed (handed in 4 days late) his third sales report deadline in as many weeks. These reports are crucial for you and others in the firm for internal reporting and planning. Bill knows their importance, but offers no good excuse, except "too busy" concerning the late reports. What do you suggest?

Your recommended action:

Your rationale:

Memo No. 4

To: Head of Women's Wear Department
From: Sue Swift, employee
Subject: "Punch out" early

One of your sales people, Sue Swift, in a 12-person clothing specialty shop wants to punch out two hours early on Friday to beat the traffic on her way up North for the holiday weekend. Her leaving early should not affect sales any, although customers in these highly stylish shops do seek out "their" sales person when buying.

Swift has been doing a very good job and is a willing worker both in sales and in shop maintenance.

Your recommended action:

Your rationale:

Summary

After completing this exercise on your own, compare notes with classmates.

Number 4 — Matching Wits with the Experts

The Worth of Employment Interviewing as a Selection Device

In the selection process your author identifies the employment interview as a commonly (predominantly) used device to help employers determine qualifications of job applicants.

Directions: You are to circle **yes** or **no** as answers to the following statements regarding the worth of the employment interview as a selection device. Each statement is a generalization which is based on research reports in personnel journals. One of the most current comprehensive studies from which some of the generalizations were made is footnoted below.

Yes No   1. The employment interview has been proven time after time to be a highly valid selection device.

Yes No   2. The employment interview has similarly been proven time after time to be a highly reliable selection device.

Yes No   3. The employment interview is susceptible to bias and distortion on the part of the interviewer.

Yes No   4. Certain interpersonal dimensions of behavior such as verbal skill can be validly assessed.

Yes No   5. Similarly, assessments of applicant's motivation to perform have been done consistently and with validity.

Yes No   6. The employment interview has been shown to be a valuable device to communicate job information to the applicant.

Yes No   7. Regarding interviewers' decisions regarding favorable or unfavorable impressions of the interviewee, the decision is formed very early (i.e., within the first several minutes) in the interview.

Yes No   8. Interviewers tend to have stereotypes of idealized successful applicants against which real applicants are judged.

Yes No   9. Females are generally given lower evaluations than males even though they possess similar or identical qualifications.

Yes No   10. Using a group or panel of people to interview or rate interviewees results in higher validity and reliability of ratings.

Responses of experts based upon research data:

1. No	3. Yes	5. No	7. Yes	9. Yes
2. No	4. Yes	6. Yes	8. Yes	10. Yes

Number 5 — Experiential Learning Exercise

Challenge of Informal Leadership

You are a recently-transferred supervisor whose responsibility is to supervise five employees. Their jobs are primarily service-oriented, direct one-to-one contact with the public. These five employees are equal in rank, but not equal in seniority, experience, or pay. They are briefly described as follows:

Margaret Mode: Two years with your company; young, eager to do well. She has asked, several times, about future opportunities in the company. When you arrived six months ago, she often volunteered for extra assignments. Lately, she has seemed subdued and hasn't volunteered. Mike Smith has

---

Source: Arvey, Richard O. and Campion, James E. "The Employment Interview: A Summary and Review of Recent Research." *Personnel Psychology*, Volume 35, 1982.

been subtly "putting down" her ideas and also her enthusiasm. Her getting "put down" surprises you since Margaret seems like such an independent self-starter. Lately, customer complaints in her area have increased sharply.

Mike Smith: Eight years with the company in his present position. He is well-polished as a public servant when he wishes to be. He has great flair with an impressive line of words that please even the most hard-to-please customers. However, he has another "face" in his public work. Rarely, but increasingly, he resorts to his recording-like message filled with sarcastic "We're here to please" jargon when a customer has a complaint. Even the less perceptive individual sees through his line. Mike is very influential over Robert Johnson, the "rookie" in this group.

Robert Johnson: Is the newest employee who arrived shortly before you did. When Robert came to work, there was only a temporary supervisor filling the interim between regulars, and this temporary person took little interest in Robert. Mike Smith took Robert under his "wing," taught him the job, and helped Robert gain confidence. Now, even though you can see clearly that Robert would like to become more independent in his thinking and actions on the job, he still feels loyal to Mike who plays on this loyalty. In a recent group meeting, for example, you heard Robert responding enthusiastically to your "Customer Courtesy" idea, but he quickly turned against it with Mike's negative facial expressions. Robert's customer contact had been improving as he was learning, but lately his progress has come to a halt.

Sylvia Latts: Has been with the firm two years, returning to work after raising her children to school age. She plays a neutral role in any group matter, especially if it is controversial. Doesn't say much unless asked. She sits on the "fence." Very nice person; excellent customer record. Seems to be content, for now, in her present assignment.

Jane Adams: Is the oldest of the group, and she has been with your company for six years. She disdains Mike, and Mike can't stand her. However, in most verbal confrontations between Jane and Mike, Mike wins through superior articulation. Jane's work is steady with predictable error rates; seems unable to get them down. Jane is loyal to you to a "pain." Often, she stops in to report on even the most minor incident involving Mike. She feels Mike is subverting the work group. You do not, although you know Mike is still mildly upset over not getting this supervisory job which you are eminently qualified to fill.

Ms./Mr. Hyatt: (You) are the new supervisor of this group. You were transferred from another district office of the same company where you supervised a similar operation. Although you were treated as an outsider, initially, this work group seems to respect you and follows your orders quite well.

After six months as supervisor you are finding the day-to-day work going fairly well. Employees have shown increasing responsiveness to you, except for Mike, who is cool, but not openly antagonistic. One major problem is handling Mike in situations where you or some other employee has a new idea to try. Mike tends to curtail new ideas or enthusiasms in his role as informal leader. The formal organization lines and informal lines appear below:

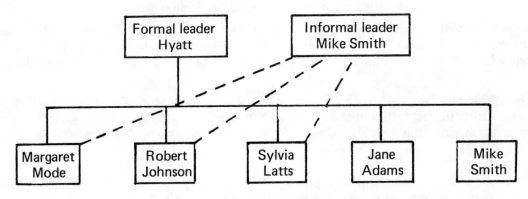

A specific example of Mike's influence came up two days ago when you asked employee reactions to a "Customer Check Card" method for analyzing how customers react to the five individuals providing service. Each employee would hand a customer a card requiring only 10 seconds of check-off answers concerning the business transacted, impact of company procedures, and effectiveness of the employee administering the service.

Each employee would personally get the card back and would not have to share specific service complaints with the supervisor or the other employees. This method had reduced customer complaints to management by 50% in a three-month period in your previous district assignment before you were transferred here.

Unfortunately, after you gave a brief introduction, Mike did his thing, whatever it is, to influence a shutdown. Margaret reacted excitedly, but quickly shut up. Robert thrust his hand up for additional thoughts, but let it wilt when Mike gave him the "eye." Sylvia said she didn't care one way or the other, but would go along with the group. Mike was clever, verbally giving support, but not really. And Jane Adams emoted too strongly against Mike and really didn't help your situation.

Directions:

1. First, you should try to role play this scenario since brief personality sketches of each individual are available. The key role players, Hyatt and Smith, need to play conflicting roles of power and leadership.

    The other employees can play the roles as described in the respective character descriptions. Each role might be elaborated such as Jane Adams being argumentative with Mike.

    Have fun with it, but also see if your group can develop some problem-solving techniques in spite of leadership conflicts and personality clashes between Smith and Hyatt.

2. Discussion questions appropriate for either role play or for using the situation above as a case problem:

    a. What organizational principles can be brought to focus here in interpreting both formal organization and informal organization structure?

    b. What elements of group dynamics can you identify? Why, for example, is Mike successful in gaining a following?

    c. From a problem-solving perspective, what is/are the problems here? What solution(s) can you suggest?

    d. Of course, an easy out for Hyatt would be the termination or transfer of Smith. How would you react to such a move? Would it solve all the problems cited in the case? Explain.

LOOKING BACK; LOOKING AHEAD

In Part 3 you directed your effort toward learning about the formal organization structure and how managers organize human resources for greater productivity. It is interesting to note that the ways organizations were designed historically reflect in part how people were viewed in terms of productive resources. Under scientific management approaches, for example, people were merely extensions of the machinery. They were organized, therefore, for efficiency. In more current enlightened organizations, people are viewed as thinking, creative individuals, and they are organized for achievement as well as productivity.

In Part 4, Chapters 10—13, the emphasis is on the leadership role of managers in trying to achieve high rates of employee productivity. Is there a difference between "leadership" and "management"? This question should be of interest to you since you probably have experienced the influence of both. Your author contends that there is significant difference between the two terms and the way managers with and without leadership ability operate. Under which type of manager would you prefer to work—one with leadership ability or without? Why? How do they differ in terms of handling subordinates?

Part 4 should be of special interest to you since it focuses on the "flesh and blood" of the organization—people leading, following, and cooperating to achieve greater productivity.

PART IV
LEADING FOR PRODUCTIVITY

INTRODUCTION – PART 4

(Chapters 10 – 13)

Highlights

In the previous part of the text, the author focused on management organization as an avenue through which to pursue greater productivity. Productivity continues to be the underlying theme in Part 4 of the text, but there is a shift from organization skills to leadership skills. There should be a sense of the "real" and "life-like" for you in this part of the text as you learn about the dynamic nature of interpersonal relationships that comprise leader/follower pairings.

In Chapter 10 fundamentals of leadership are introduced by your author and placed in context through lively examples such as union members talking bitterly about their bosses. Throughout Chapter 10, the author portrays a variety of situations in which the need for both formal and informal leadership arises.

Are you a leader? Do you have leadership potential? How do you know? These questions and your responses can help you personalize the text material so that it will have additional meaning for you. You probably have been involved in the leader/follower dyad. That is, you have played either the leader or follower role, or both in different settings. Under what circumstances have you been led? Led others? What dynamics were involved? The author helps explain the dynamics of leadership including such things as power, individual traits, and contingent situations which generate leader/follower roles.

Throughout the leadership material, the author links leadership to management and distinguishes between the two. That is, some managers lack leader skills, while some nonmanagement personnel develop considerable leadership talent. Styles of leadership are also explained and linked to situations as well as to personalities of individuals playing leader roles.

In Chapter 11 leadership is directed toward communication. In today's rapidly changing business environment the potential for individuals, particularly managers, to lead depends upon their ability to communicate. In Chapter 11 you will learn more about this management skill area, an area that you, of course, experience daily. While we all practice communication skills on a daily basis, achieving clear communication is one of the biggest challenges for management. There is considerable communication breakdown in most organizations, and the author offers excellent ideas for overcoming these barriers to effective communication.

In Chapter 12 leadership is directed toward improving employees' motivation to work and to improve their productivity. Can management "motivate" employees? The answer is no, but do you know why? Chapter 12 reveals the answer plus considerably more about motivation. The role of the manager and leader in the quest for employee behavior directed toward productivity in the formal organization is often referred to as the motivational role. And, the chapter on leading through motivation explains in theory and application how leaders influence motivated behavior of employees.

Chapter 13 continues the exploration of employee behavior, but the focus is turned to group dynamics, the interpersonal relationships that form in work environments that may contribute to or detract from organizational productivity. In Chapter 13, you will be able to readily identify with group material since you have experienced membership in a number of the group types and group scenarios depicted by the author.

The manager's task of achieving productivity through individual employees becomes more complicated when individuals become group members and submit to group membership rules, roles, and purposes. Do subgroups that form within a business help or hinder the manager's task? This chapter on group dynamics reveals a variety of answers to that question.

Chapter Titles for Part 4

Chapter 10 – Fundamentals of Leadership
Chapter 11 – Leading Through Communication
Chapter 12 – Leading Through Motivation
Chapter 13 – Leading Through Group Dynamics

CAREER PERSPECTIVE — PART 4

Assessing Your Leadership Talents

Part 4 of the text focuses on leadership. Each chapter is developed with the undergirding of leadership as an important management skill. Hopefully you will sense the "flesh" and "blood" of managing in these chapters since leadership potential exists in the one-to-one interpersonal relationships between managers and subordinates as well as between peers in the organization. In other words leadership may emerge within employee ranks without any formal designation. This section should have the "flesh" and "blood" referred to above since you already have personally experienced followership roles in your life, if not leadership roles as well.

How would you describe your leadership potential? Perhaps you feel little interest in the question. However, even if you care little about leading in the formal organization setting, you will be joining, by virtue of taking a job, the leadership/followership scenario. Therefore, when you are confronted by an employment representative in an employment interview, don't be surprised by queries regarding your propensity to lead and follow. There is usually a sequence of questions raised by interviewers regarding prospective employee interest in and talent for leading. In other words, employment representatives will ask about both formal and informal leadership roles in which you were involved while in college.

The following career-related exercise is offered to help you assess your leadership/followership interests, experiences, and apparent skills.

Directions

Answer the following questions regarding leadership as it relates to you.

1. What degree of interest do you have in the topic of leadership? High? Low? Explain your level of interest.

2. In what volunteer, extra curricular, and informal activities such as recreation have you taken part? Describe what role(s) you played.

3. In what formally-structured organizations have you been a member? What position(s) did you hold?

4. In what type of organized sporting events or team activities have you participated? What role(s) or position(s) did you hold?

5. What elected positions have you held?

Summary for items 1—5: Is there a pattern regarding the type of role you have played in the above situations in which you have participated? That is, do you seem to have the propensity to play leader roles? Do others around you tend to put you in leader positions? Please write about your leadership experiences under the following comments section.

Comments:

Interpersonal Situations Where Leader/Follower Roles Develop

6. How frequently do you initiate small group, social activities? Often? Seldom? Explain.

7. In a conversation with a group of acquaintances what is your ratio of listening to talking? Mostly listening? Half and half? Mostly talking and being listened to? Explain.

8. In a heated disagreement in a small group of acquaintances trying to do a particular task, what role do you tend to play? Peacemaker? Soother of hurt feelings? Director of activities toward achieving the task? Explain.

9. What personal traits do you have that seem particularly influential over others? Example, size? Discuss.

10. Forced to make a choice, which do you prefer? Power over others? Opportunity to achieve? Close friendships? Discuss.

Summary for items 6—10: Is there a pattern regarding the type of role you have played or the traits you have displayed in items 6—10? For example, do you tend to be highly goal or task oriented? Or, do you tend to be more concerned in group settings with avoiding hurt feelings of individual members? Or, are you constantly striving for team building?

10 Fundamentals of Leading

STUDENT LEARNING OBJECTIVES

After completing the chapter material you should be able to:

1. Define leadership and list the knowledge and skills associated with it.
2. Distinguish between leadership and management.
3. Explain power as a leadership resource, and sources and types of power.
4. Define the three major approaches to studying leadership and distinguish respective differences among the three: traits, behavioral, and contingency.
5. Give trait examples that could have some potential for identifying leader potential, but also explain why traits are least reliable in identifying leader potential.
6. Explain leader behaviors and orientations such as concern for task versus concern for people.
7. Identify leadership contingencies and how they come to bear on leader situations and styles.
8. Distinguish between directive, supportive, and participative leadership behaviors and under what situations and behaviors relate to each.
9. Define contingency approach to leadership.

CHAPTER HIGHLIGHTS

Leadership concepts
Power: a leadership resource
Approaches to studying leadership
Fiedler's Contingency Theory
House's Path-Goal Theory
The Vroom-Yetton leader participation
Leadership in managerial perspective

PROGRAMMED LEARNING

The following statements are drawn from actual textbook content in abbreviated form. The blanks within the statements are numbered to correspond with the answer blanks at the left.

Leadership defined

1. _____ — The process of directing human resource efforts toward organizational objectives is called _____(1).

2. _____ — Leading requires knowledge and skills in: _____(2), _____(3)
3. _____ relations, _____(4), and _____(5) dynamics.
4. _____
5. _____

6. _____ — The manager's use of power to influence the behavior of other persons in the work setting is called _____(6).

7. _____ — The ability to get someone else to do something you want done is called _____(7).

Leadership concepts

8. _____ — Leading is not synonymous with being a _____(8).

9. _____ — When a manager leads through the exercise of the authority of his or her official position in the organization it is called _____(9) leadership.

10. _____ — When a person without formal authority proves influential in directing the behavior of other persons it is called _____(10) leadership.

11. _____ — Informal leadership exists outside of the _____(11) of command.

Power: A leadership resource

12. _____ — A force or capability which, when successfully activated, makes things happen is called _____(12).

13. _____ — In a positive sense, a manager's need for power is defined **not** as a need to _____(13).

14. _____ — Three bases of power that relate to a manager's official position in a
15. _____ hierarchy of authority are: _____(14), _____(15), and
16. _____ _____(16) power.

17. _____ — The capability to offer something of value, a positive outcome, as a means of controlling other people is called _____(17) power.

18. _____ — The capability to punish or withhold positive outcomes as a means of controlling other people is called _____(18) power.

19. _____ — The right to command and to act in the position of managerial responsibility is called _____(19) power.

20. _____ — The two bases of personal power are _____(20) and _____(21).
21. _____

22. _____ — The capability to control other people because of specialized knowledge is called _____(22) power.

23. _____ — The capability to control other people because of their desires to personally and positively identify with the power source is called _____(23) power.

24. _____ — Managerial power = position power + _____(24) power.

25. _____ Power is the potential to control the _____(25) of other people.

26. _____ The limits to power are established in terms of _____(26) by employees.

27. _____
28. _____
29. _____
30. _____
A manager's orders are most likely to be accepted when, and only when, the subordinate: understands the _____(27), feels _____(28) of carrying out the directive, that it is in the best interests of the _____(29), and it is consistent with his/her _____(30) values.

31. _____ Power in organizations is also limited to that range of directives and requests that people consider appropriate to their basic employment or _____(31) contracts with the organization.

32. _____ This range is called a zone of _____(32).

33. _____ Managerial directives falling within the zone tend to be _____(33) automatically.

Managerial guidelines for acquiring and using power

34. _____ Managers need _____(34) to succeed in both their formal and informal leadership roles.

35. _____
36. _____
Leadership depends on an ability to acquire and use power from both _____(35) and _____(36) sources.

37. _____
38. _____
39. _____
40. _____
41. _____
In exercising managerial leadership, the following guidelines are suggested: don't deny your _____(37) authority; don't be afraid to create a sense of _____(38); create feelings of _____(39); build and believe in _____(40); allow others the opportunity to _____(41) with you as a person.

Approaches to the study of leadership

42. _____
43. _____
44. _____
Management theory includes the three major approaches to the study of leadership: _____(42), _____(43), and _____(44) approaches.

45. _____ The goal of trait research was to find a set of _____(45) characteristics which separates effective and ineffective leaders.

46. _____ However, researchers have been unable to isolate a definitive profile of leadership _____(46).

47. _____
48. _____
49. _____
50. _____
51. _____
Recent studies concluded that, if traits could be identified that affect leadership, they would include a person's: _____(47) ability, need for occupational _____(48), _____(49), _____(50), and _____-_____(51).

Understanding leader behaviors

52. _____ The inability of researchers to isolate a set of personal traits uniquely characteristic of successful leaders led to a subsequent focus on actual leader _____(52).

53. _____ A recurring pattern of behaviors exhibited by a leader is called leadership _____(53).

54. _____
55. _____
Two basic orientations a leader may display in his or her behavior vis-a-vis followers are (1) concern for the _____(54) to be accomplished, and (2) concern for the _____(55) doing the work.

56. _____
57. _____

Directive or autocratic leadership means showing a high concern for the _____(56) and low concern for _____(57).

58. _____
59. _____

A manager with this style would make most _____(58) for the work unit, and issue work _____(59).

60. _____
61. _____

Supportive or human relations leadership means showing a high concern for _____(60) and low concern for _____(61).

62. _____
63. _____

A leader showing a high concern for both people and task would be labeled _____(62) or _____(63).

64. _____

A leader showing a low concern for both people and task is called a _____-_____(64) leader.

65. _____
66. _____

Most leadership theorists now recognize that the critical question is no longer "which is the **best** leadership _____(65)?" but really becomes "when and under what _____(66) is a given style preferable to the others?"

67. _____

This is referred to as a _____(67) approach to leadership.

Contingency theory in leader behavior

68. _____
69. _____
70. _____
71. _____

Under the Fiedler's contingency model, the manager or aspiring leader's challenge is threefold: to understand one's predominant _____(68) style, to diagnose _____(69) in terms of the amount of control offered the leader, and to achieve a good match between _____(70) and _____(71).

72. _____
73. _____
74. _____

Three situational variables are important in determining the amount of control a situation allows the leader: _____-_____(72) relations, _____(73) structure, and _____(74) power.

75. _____

House's contingency theory argues that effective leadership clarifies the paths through which subordinates can achieve both work-related and personal goals, assists them to progress along these paths, and removes any barriers on the paths which may inhibit goal accomplishment is called _____-_____(75) model.

76. _____
77. _____
78. _____
79. _____

According to House's research on the path-goal theory: supportive leadership complements _____(76) tasks; directive leadership complements _____(77) tasks; achievement leadership complements _____-_____(78) workers; participative leadership complements highly _____(79) workers.

The Vroom-Yetton Leader-Participation Theory

80. _____
81. _____

According to the Vroom-Yetton contingency theory, various problems present different _____(80) that require different _____(81) methods.

82. _____

The type of decision making in which all group members participate and finally agree is called _____(82).

83. _____
84. _____
85. _____

Acording to Vroom and Yetton, a good decision is one that is of high _____(83), _____(84) by the people who have to implement it, and time _____(85).

Leadership in a managerial perspective

86. _____
87. _____
88. _____
89. _____

A good manager uses _____(86) and contingently applies a variety of _____(87) behaviors to facilitate _____(88) and _____(89).

90. _____
91. _____
92. _____
93. _____

Substitutes for leadership basically reduce the manager's need to exercise direct leadership in a situation. Substitutes include: having subordinates with high levels of task _____(90); having an organization structure that is _____(91); having tasks that are _____(92); and having tasks controlled by highly automated _____(93).

94. _____

You must understand your leadership _____(94).

95. _____

You must be able to properly diagnose leadership _____(95).

TESTING YOUR KNOWLEDGE

True and False Self Test

Directions: Circle the letter (T or F) of the correct response for each of the following statements.

T   F   1. Formal leadership occurs when a manager leads through the exercise of the authority of his/her official position in the organization.

T   F   2. Managers use power to achieve interpersonal influence through which leadership is ultimately exercised.

T   F   3. Coercive power is the capability to control other people by virtue of the rights of office.

T   F   4. A leader's personal characteristics always determine leadership success.

T   F   5. Democratic leadership shows a high concern for both people and task.

T   F   6. According to Blake and Mouton, a "9 - 9" leader is a person whose behavior is that of a team manager, one who is able to integrate task and people concerns to the benefit of the organization and its members.

T   F   7. Task oriented leadership style is predicted successful in high and low control situations all the time.

T   F   8. A successful manager is one who is able to direct activities of others in order to achieve high performance.

T   F   9. Managers report that House's path-goal theory is the most successful method of leading people.

T   F   10. Researchers conclude that leader behaviors vary from supportive to participative to directive extremes.

Multiple Choice Self Test

Directions: Circle the letter of the response that best completes each of the following statements.

1. The ability to get someone else to do something you want them to do is called:
   a. influence
   b. manipulation
   c. power
   d. leadership

2. Leading and managing are:
   a. synonymous terms
   b. inseparable, one cannot manage without being a leader
   c. not the same
   d. equal in importance

3. Formal leadership occurs when a manager leads through the exercise of:
   a. creativity
   b. spontaneity
   c. authority
   d. Karate

4. Managers can be more effective if they also exercise power which can be derived from a base called:
   a. reward power
   b. coercive power
   c. legitimate power
   d. all of the above

5. According to the text, the one thing that definitely puts a limit on a person's power is:
   a. his/her physical strength
   b. acceptance of it by those susceptible to it
   c. economic reality
   d. education level

6. Guideline(s) for acquiring and using power include:
   a. using your formal position well
   b. creating a sense of obligation
   c. creating feelings of dependence
   d. building your expertise
   e. all of the above

7. According to your author, the most unreliable way to try to identify an individual's leadership potential is through determination of:
   a. personal traits
   b. past behavior patterns
   c. analysis of the situation
   d. none of the above was talked about by the author

8. A person showing a high concern for the task to be done and a low concern for people doing it is called:
   a. participative
   b. supportive or human relations oriented
   c. directive
   d. laissez-faire

9. Based upon Fiedler's research, the type of leadership most likely to work in both high and low control situations is:
   a. task-oriented
   b. relationship-oriented
   c. individually-oriented
   d. externally-oriented

10. Substitutes for leadership include:
    a. employee task expertise
    b. mechanistic organizational structure
    c. routine and repetitive tasks
    d. all of the above

Matching Self Test

Directions: Write the letter of the description that best fits each numbered item in the blank provided.

_____ 1. Reward powers

_____ 2. Zone of indifference

_____ 3. Trait, behavioral, and contingency approaches

_____ 4. Autocratic

_____ 5. Laissez-faire

_____ 6. Contingency assumption

_____ 7. Fiedler's contingency theory

_____ 8. Power

_____ 9. Informal leadership

_____ 10. Vroom-Yetton Model

a. The major approaches to the study of leadership.

b. A person showing low concern for both people and task.

c. The capability to offer something of value, a positive outcome, as a means of controlling other people.

d. Power which is limited to a range of managerial requests that are acceptable on the part of employees who must carry out the requests.

e. Effective leadership results when the decision method used to resolve a problem matches the problem characteristic.

f. The match of leadership style and situation determines leadership success.

g. Potential to control the behavior of others.

h. When a person without authority is influential in directing behavior of others.

i. Successful leadership depends on a good match between the style of the leader and the demands of the situation.

j. A person showing a high concern for the task and a low concern for people.

11 Leading Through Communication

STUDENT LEARNING OBJECTIVES

After completing the chapter material you should be able to:

1. Define communication in the organizational context and explain how management functions and roles are facilitated via communication.
2. Identify via Figure 11.4 the key elements in the communication process and distinguish between effective and efficient communication.
3. List and explain barriers to communication.
4. Define perception and how it affects communication.
5. List and explain the author's four perceptual distortions.
6. Distinguish between interpersonal and organizational communication.
7. Compare and contrast formal and informal communication channels.
8. Explain the communication of role expectations.
9. List and explain the author's guidelines for effective communication such as active listening.

CHAPTER HIGHLIGHTS

Communication and the managerial role
Communication as an interpersonal process
Barriers to effective communication
Perception and communication
Organizational communication
Guidelines for effective communication

PROGRAMMED LEARNING

The following statements are drawn from actual textbook content in abbreviated form. The blanks within the statements are numbered to correspond with the answer blanks at the left.

Communications and the manager

1. _____

The interpersonal process of sending and receiving symbols with meanings attached to them is called _____(1).

2. _____

Any manager's job builds around the need to _____(2).

3. _____

It is through communication that vital information for _____-_____(3) is gained and the results of those decisions are conveyed to others.

4. _____
5. _____
6. _____

Communication makes other people aware of a manager's _____(4) and _____(5), and thereby sets the foundation for _____(6) to take place.

7. _____

Research indicates that up to 80% of a manager's time is spent in _____(7).

8. _____
9. _____
10. _____
11. _____

Communication is essential to each of the four basic management functions: _____(8), _____(9), _____(10), and _____(11).

Communication as an interpersonal process

12. _____
13. _____
14. _____
15. _____
16. _____
17. _____

In the communication process, the _____(12) is responsible for _____(13) an intended meaning into a _____(14) and sending it through a _____(15) to a receiver, who then _____(16) the message into a perceived _____(17).

18. _____
19. _____

Effective communication occurs when the _____(18) meaning of the sender and _____(19) meaning of the receiver are one and the same.

20. _____

Efficient communication occurs at minimum _____(20) in terms of resources expended.

Barriers to effective communication

21. _____

Anything that interferes with the effectiveness of the communications process is called _____(21).

22. _____
23. _____
24. _____
25. _____
26. _____
27. _____

Six major sources of noise that can threaten communication in work settings are: _____(22) problems, the absence of _____(23), improper choice or use of _____(24), _____(25) distractions, _____(26) differences, and _____(27) effects.

28. _____

The advantage of two-way communication over one-way is that it allows for _____(28).

29. _____

One-way communication, by contrast, is usually more _____(29) efficient.

30. _____
31. _____
32. _____

When done well, the written message compared to oral can be very advantageous in providing _____(30) records reaching a large number of people _____(31) and appearing formal and _____(32).

33. _____

Communication that takes place through body language, voice intonations, and physical appearance is called _____(33).

34. _____

A _____(34) message occurs when a person's words communicate one message while actions, body language, or appearance communicate something else.

35. _____

Cross-cultural communication problems are often _____(35) based.

36. _____
37. _____

Given the authority and status of their positions, managers may be inclined to do a lot of "_____"(36), but not much "_____"(37).

Perception and communication

38. _____

The process through which people receive and interpret information is called _____(38).

39. _____
40. _____

Perception acts as a _____(39) or _____(40) through which information must pass.

41. _____
42. _____

Depending upon individual values, needs, cultural background, and other circumstances of the moment, information will pass through this screen with varying _____(41) and degrees of _____(42).

43. _____
44. _____
45. _____
46. _____

Four common perceptual distortions that can have a significant impact on the quality of a manager's decisions and actions are: _____(43), _____(44) effects, selective _____(45), and _____(46).

47. _____

When an individual or event is assigned to a group or category, and then the attributes associated with the group are associated with the individual or event in question, this is called _____(47).

48. _____

When one attribute is used to develop an overall impression of a person or situation, this is called _____(48) effecting.

49. _____

Halo effects cause the same problem for managers as do stereotypes— _____(49) differences become obscured.

50. _____

The tendency to single out for attention those aspects of a situation or attributes of a person which reinforce or appear consistent with one's existing beliefs, values, or needs is called _____(50) perception.

51. _____

A classic projection error is the manager who assumes that subordinates want or desire the same from their _____(51) as the manager does from his/her own job.

52. _____
53. _____
54. _____
55. _____
56. _____

A manager who is skilled in the perception process will: have a high level of _____-_____(52); seek information from various sources to confirm or disconfirm personal impressions of a _____(53) situation; be _____(54); influence the _____(55) of other people; and avoid the common perceptual _____(56) that bias our views of people and situations.

Organizational communication

57. _____ The specific process through which managers systematically give and receive information in interactions with other persons inside the organization is called _____(57) communication.

58. _____ Communication that follows the chain of command established by an organization's hierarchy of authority is called _____(58) in channeling.

59. _____
60. _____ Communication channeling not sanctioned as official or authoritative by the organization is called _____(59) or _____(60).

61. _____ The primary disadvantage of grapevines occurs when they transmit _____(61) or untimely information.

62. _____ Managers are responsible for communicating job instructions, standards, and other work expectations via _____(62) communication.

63. _____
64. _____
65. _____
66. _____ A taskforce at the Johnson and Johnson company concluded that upward communication should keep a higher level manager informed about: what _____(63) are doing, unsolved work _____(64), suggestions for _____(65), and how _____(66) think and feel about their jobs, their associates, and the organization.

67. _____ _____(67) communication occurs among persons working at the same level.

68. _____ One of the most important of a manager's communications is the sending and receiving of _____(68) expectations.

69. _____
70. _____ Difficulties in the communication of roles can result in role _____(69) and/or _____(70).

71. _____ Role ambiguity occurs when the person in a role is uncertain about the _____(71) held by others and relating to his or her behavior.

72. _____ Role conflict occurs when the person in a role is unable to respond to the _____(72) held by one or more others.

73. _____
74. _____ Role dynamics in the form of ambiguities and conflicts can create tensions that have adverse effects on work _____(73) and _____(74).

Guidelines for effective communication

75. _____
76. _____ Active listening refers to managers attempting to listen for both message _____(75) and _____(76) of the source.

77. _____ Feedback is the process of telling how you _____(77) about something they did or said.

78. _____
79. _____
80. _____
81. _____
82. _____
83. _____
84. _____
85. _____
86. _____
87. _____ The ten commandments of good communication, according to the American Management Association, are: clarify your _____(78) before communicating; examine the true _____(79) of each communication; consider the total physical and _____(80) setting; _____(81) with others in planning communications; be mindful of the overtones as well as the basic content of your _____(82); take every opportunity to communicate something of _____(83) or value to the receiver; follow up your _____(84); communicate for _____(85) as well as today; be sure your actions support your _____(86); and be a good _____(87).

TESTING YOUR KNOWLEDGE

True and False Self Test

Directions: Circle the letter (T or F) of the correct response for each of the following statements.

T   F   1. A "mixed" message occurs when a person's words communicate both good news and bad news.

T   F   2. Physical distractions, hierarchy of authority, and differences in cultural backgrounds are a few areas that can cause communication breakdowns.

T   F   3. Projection is the assignment of personal attributes to other individuals.

T   F   4. Role conflict occurs when the person in the role has certain expectations of others that are not being filled.

T   F   5. Stereotypes, halo effects, selective perceptions, and projections are various personality types often seen in a typical work setting.

T   F   6. Feedback is the process of telling someone else how you feel about something they did or said, or about the situation in general.

T   F   7. Role ambiguity is achieved when a person bites into a doughnut and discovers it is a bagel.

T   F   8. Lateral communication takes place when managers talk negatively about someone in the back room.

T   F   9. Upward communication involves messages flowing from higher levels to lower levels in an organization's hierarchy of authority.

T   F   10. An example of an "informal" communication channel might be the boss giving the summer picnic welcome in a leisure suit.

Multiple Choice Self Test

Directions: Circle the letter of the response that best completes each of the following statements.

1. Research indicates that managers who responded to how much time they spent on oral communication report that it is up to:
   a. 20% of their time spent
   b. 40%
   c. 60%
   d. 80%

2. "Efficient" communications occur:
   a. when you have the bosses' attention
   b. when you can reverse charge long distance calls
   c. at a minimum cost to your organization
   d. the intended meaning of the message gets through

3. A barrier to communication could be:
   a. unclear encoding
   b. improper choice of channel
   c. noise
   d. poor decoding
   e. all of the above

4. Comparing oral and written styles of communication, which application below would be in-effective if delivered via written format?
   a. Settle an on-the-floor verbal dispute
   b. Reprimand a poorly performing employee
   c. To communicate something urgent
   d. All of the above

5. An example of a common perceptual distortion is:
   a. stereotyping
   b. halo effect
   c. selective perception
   d. all of the above

6. The perception problem in which there is the tendency to single out for attention those aspects of a situation which reinforce our own beliefs is:
   a. stereotyping
   b. halo effect
   c. selective perception
   d. projections

7. What should be communicated upwards?
   a. What subordinates are doing
   b. Unsolved work problems
   c. Suggestions for improvement
   d. How subordinates think and feel about their jobs
   e. All of the above

8. One of the most important of the manager's communications is sending and receiving role:
   a. conflict
   b. verbal
   c. expectations
   d. perception

9. Active listening refers to a manger's:
   a. listening while doing calisthenics
   b. listening for both content and feelings of a message
   c. responding with feelings
   d. noting all cues, verbal and nonverbal
   e. all but a above

10. Under the "Ten Commandments" of communication, it is recommended that you:
    a. clarify your ideas before communicating
    b. examine the true purpose of each communication
    c. follow-up
    d. communicate for tomorrow as well as for today
    e. all of the above

Matching Self Test

Directions: Write the letter of the description that best fits each numbered item in the blank provided.

_____ 1. Stereotype

_____ 2. Disseminator role

_____ 3. Chain of command

_____ 4. "Grapevine"

_____ 5. Downward, upward, and lateral

_____ 6. Monitor role

_____ 7. Communication

_____ 8. Semantic barrier

_____ 9. Halo effect

_____ 10. Projection

a. Gathering appropriate information from sources—internal and external.

b. When one attribute is used to develop an overall impression of a person.

c. Types of organizational communication.

d. Informal communication channel.

e. Distributing information within the work unit.

f. When an individual is assigned to a group or category, and then the attributes associated with the group are associated with the individual.

g. When a manager assumes that subordinates want the same from their work as does the manager.

h. Encoding and decoding errors and received as mixed messages.

i. Interpersonal process of sending and receiving symbols with meaning.

j. Formal channel of communication.

12 Leading Through Motivation

STUDENT LEARNING OBJECTIVES

After completing the chapter material you should be able to:

1. Define motivation in terms of the forces within individuals that affect their levels, directions, and persistence of effort in the work force.
2. Explain rewards and their value in enhancing employee motivation.
3. Define and distinguish between content, process, and reinforcement theories of motivation.
4. Give examples of content (need) theories and ways managers can apply need theory both in interpreting employee behavior and influencing it.
5. Give examples of process theories and ways managers can apply them both in interpreting employee behavior and influencing it.
6. Reemphasize from objective three above how reinforcement theory is unique in that it is environmental, not cognitive.
7. List and explain concepts associated with reinforcement theory such as operant conditioning and how organization behavior can be modified.
8. Explain the text's integrated approach components to motivation.

CHAPTER HIGHLIGHTS

The concept of motivation
Motivation and rewards
Understanding individual needs
Equity Theory
Expectancy Theory
Reinforcement Theory
An integrated approach to motivation

PROGRAMMED LEARNING

The following statements are drawn from actual textbook content in abbreviated form. The blanks within the statements are numbered to correspond with the answer blanks at the left.

The concept of motivation

1. _____ In order to achieve high performance, even people with ability and support must _____(1) to perform.

2. _____ Willingness to exert effort, in turn, reflects a _____(2) to work.

3. _____ Motivation is a term used in management theory to describe forces within
4. _____ the individual that account for the _____(3), _____(4), and
5. _____ _____(5) of effort expended at work.

6. _____ In order to enhance other people's motivation to work, managers must be able to establish a work _____(6) that makes such motivation possible.

7. _____ This work environment will be one that makes the right kinds of _____(7) available to persons who work to perform high output levels.

Rewards and motivation

8. _____ A _____(8) is a work outcome of positive value to the individual.

9. _____ Rewards are a means of paying _____(9) to people and their work.

10. _____ Any reward, if used _____(10), can assist the manager in establishing a motivational climate for individual employees.

Types of motivation theories

11. _____ There are three types of motivational theories: _____(11),
12. _____ _____(12), and _____(13).
13. _____

14. _____ Content theories of motivation use individual _____(14) to explain the behavior and attitudes of people at work.

15. _____ Needs cause _____(15) which influence attitudes and behavior.

16. _____ In Maslow's need hierarchy, lower order needs include: _____(16),
17. _____ _____(17), and _____(18).
18. _____

19. _____ Higher order needs include esteem and _____-_____(19).

20. _____ Under A. H. Maslow's need hierarchy, the _____(20) principle holds that a satisfied need is not a motivator of behavior.

21. _____ The progression principle holds that the five needs exist in a strict _____(21) of prepotency such that a need at one level doesn't become activated until the next lower-level need is already satisfied.

22. _____ Only when the level of self-actualization is reached does Maslow see the
23. _____ _____(22) and _____(23) principles ceasing to operate.

24. _____ Alderfer's model of needs includes just three: existence, relatedness, and _____(24).

25. _____ McClelland also has a three-part need theory including achievement,
26. _____ _____(25), and _____(26).

27. _____ A person high in need for achievement is most likely to prefer explicit and challenging _____(27).

28. _____ A high need for _____(28) usually should appear in the profiles of successful executives.

Equity theory

29. _____ Equity theory is a _____(29) theory of motivation.

30. _____ The essence of equity theory is that felt _____(30) is a motivating state.

31. _____ Inequities occur whenever people feel the _____(31) received for
32. _____ their work inputs are _____(32) to the rewards other persons appear to have received for their work inputs.

33. _____ When perceived inequity exists, the individual is predicted to engage in
34. _____ one or more of the following ways in order to restore a sense of equity
35. _____ to the situation: change work _____(33), change _____(34)
36. _____ received, _____(35) the situation, change the comparison
37. _____ _____(36), and psychologically _____(37) the comparisons to a more favorable perspective.

Expectancy theory

38. _____ Expectancy theory argues that work motivation is determined by in-
39. _____ dividual beliefs regarding _____-_____(38) relationships and the desirabilities of _____(39) associated with various performance levels.

40. _____ Three employee perceptions must be in place if the manager is to under-
41. _____ stand expectancy theory: the person's belief that working hard will
42. _____ enable various levels of task performance to be achieved is called _____(40); the person's belief that various work-related outcomes will occur as a result of task performance is called _____(41); the value the individual assigns to these work outcomes or rewards is called _____(42).

43. _____ For a reward to have a high and positive motivational impact, expectancy,
44. _____ instrumentality, and valence must all be _____(43) and _____(44).

Reinforcement theory

45. _____ Reinforcement theory views human behavior as determined by its _____(45) consequences.

46. _____ Reinforcement theory avoids looking within the individual and examining _____(46) processes.

47. _____ It focuses on the _____(47) environment and the _____(48) it
48. _____ holds for the individual.

49. _____ Reinforcement theory is based on the law of effect which states that behavior that results in a pleasing outcome will be likely to be _____(49); behavior that results in an unpleasant outcome is not likely to be repeated.

50. _____ There are four OB Mod or law of effect strategies: _____(50) re-
51. _____ inforcement, _____(51) reinforcement, _____(52), and
52. _____ _____(53).
53. _____

54. _____ A means for decreasing the frequency of or eliminating an undesirable behavior by making it an unpleasant consequence contingent with the occurrence of the behavior is called _____(54).

55. _____ In order for a reward to have maximum reinforcing value, it must be delivered only if the desired behavior is exhibited which is called _____(55) reinforcement.

56. _____ The sooner the delivery of a reward after the occurrence of a desirable behavior, the greater the reinforcing effect on behavior which is called _____(56) reinforcement.

57. _____ To shape new behavior, reinforcement should be given on a _____(57) basis until the desired behavior is achieved.

58. _____ Then an _____(58) reinforcement schedule should be used to maintain the behavior at the new level.

59. _____ A means for eliminating undesirable behavior by administering an unpleasant consequence immediately and contingently upon the occurrence of that behavior is called _____(59).

60. _____ Critics and supporters of behavior modification agree that it involves the control of _____(60).

61. _____ It's inevitable that managers influence the _____(61) of other people.

62. _____
63. _____ An integrated approach to management points out that performance is determined by individual _____(62), work _____(63), and organizational _____(64).
64. _____

TESTING YOUR KNOWLEDGE

True and False Self Test

Directions: Circle the letter (T or F) of the correct response for each of the following statements.

T F 1. Pay is the best reward in the work place.

T F 2. The higher order needs of Maslow's theory include physiological, safety, and social concerns.

T F 3. Both ERG theory and Maslow's theory agree on the progression principle.

T F 4. According to the Equity theory, equity will occur when people feel the rewards received for their work inputs are equal to the rewards other people appear to have received for their work inputs.

T F 5. The key to motivation lies in an ability to allocate rewards in a manner that positively responds to individual needs and goals.

T F 6. Willingness to exert effort reflects a motivation to work.

T F 7. Shaping is the creation of new behavior by the positive reinforcement of successive approximations to the desired behavior.

T F 8. Intermittent reinforcement rewards behavior only periodically.

T F 9. A major aspect of any work environment is the set of rewards which are made available to the worker.

T F 10. Reinforcement theory introduces the important dynamic of social comparison.

Multiple Choice Self Test

Directions: Circle the letter of the response that best completes each of the following statements.

1. The motivation theory type that explains worker behaviors in terms of their needs is labeled a _____theory.
   a. content
   b. context
   c. process
   d. reinforcement

2. The correct order of Maslow's need hierarchy form low to high is:
   a. social, physiological, safety, ego, self-fulfillment
   b. safety, social, physiological, ego, self-fulfillment
   c. physiological, safety, social, ego, self-fulfillment
   d. physiological, ego, safety, social, self-fulfillment

3. Alderfer's need theory differs from Maslow's in what way?
   a. Alderfer's theory reduces the five needs in Maslow's hierarchy to only three.
   b. Alderfer's theory does not assume that lower-level needs must be satisfied before higher-level needs become activated.
   c. Alderfer's theory has a regression component.
   d. All of the above.
   e. None of the above.

4. Based upon McClelland's need theory and application, it appears people with a high need for _____would make the best managers.
   a. affiliation
   b. achievement
   c. power
   d. recognition

5. When an individual employee perceives that an inequity exists, it is predicted that he will restore a sense of balance by:
   a. changing work inputs
   b. trying to change rewards received
   c. leaving the situation
   d. psychologically distorting comparisons to a more favorable perspective
   e. all of the above might be done

6. Under Expectancy theory people will be motivated to perform if they have positive perception about:
   a. valence
   b. instrumentality
   c. expectancy
   d. all of the above must be perceived positively

7. The person's belief that his extra effort will lead to greater rewards is labeled:
   a. valence
   b. instrumentality
   c. expectancy
   d. equity

8. Reinforcement theory views human behavior as determined by:
   a. signs of the Zodiac
   b. electrical force fields
   c. environment factors
   d. none of the above

9. An OB Mod strategy that is done by making the results of an employee's behavior an unpleasant consequence is called:
   a. positive reinforcement
   b. negative reinforcement
   c. punishment
   d. extinction

10. To use operant conditioning properly, a manager should:
   a. clearly identify the desired behaviors
   b. maintain an inventory of rewards
   c. recognize individual differences
   d. let subordinates know how to achieve rewards, and administer them contingently and immediately
   e. all of the above

Matching Self Test

Directions: Write the letter of the description that best fits each numbered item in the blank provided.

_____ 1. Content theory

_____ 2. The "Law of Effect"

_____ 3. Expectancy theory

_____ 4. Reward

_____ 5. Operant conditioning

_____ 6. Progression principle

_____ 7. Victor Vroom

_____ 8. Reinforcement theory

_____ 9. ERG theory

_____ 10. J. Stacy Adams

a. Work outcomes of positive value to the individual.

b. Maslow's need hierarchy is an example of this theory.

c. A need at one level doesn't become activated until the lower-level one is satisfied.

d. Introduced the Equity theory.

e. Examines how people learn patterns of behavior based upon the environment.

f. Controlling behavior by manipulating its consequences.

g. Work motivation based upon individual beliefs regarding effort-performance relationships and the attractiveness of work outcome.

h. Behavior that results in a pleasing outcome will be likely repeated.

i. Collapses Maslow's hierarchy into three needs.

j. Introduced Expectancy theory.

13 Leading Through Group Dynamics

STUDENT LEARNING OBJECTIVES

After completing the chapter material you should be able to:

1. Define the concept of group, the formal group, and its characteristic components.
2. Distinguish differences in formal and informal groups.
3. Explain the synergy potential of a group, and when and how groups might be organized to achieve synergy.
4. Explain the contributions groups can give to individual members, but also what individuals must sacrifice to become members of groups.
5. Explain the input/output relationship that affects group effectiveness.
6. List and explain stages of group development.
7. Define group dynamics and list some of the characteristics from Table 13.2 that contribute to an effective group.
8. Explain Homans' Model of group dynamics and the managerial implications.
9. Compare and contrast the influence of inter-group and intra-group dynamics on task and and maintenance activities of groups.
10. Define "team" as a group concept and how teamwork can contribute to group productivity.

CHAPTER HIGHLIGHTS

Types of groups in organizations
Understanding groups in terms of organization productivity
Group dynamics
Group norms and cohesiveness
Group task and maintenance activities
Team building: managing group effectiveness
Inter-group dynamics

PROGRAMMED LEARNING

The following statements are drawn from actual textbook content in abbreviated form. The blanks within the statements are numbered to correspond with the answer blanks at the left.

Types of groups in organizations

1. _____   A collection of people who regularly interact with one another over time and in respect to the pursuit of one or more common goals is called a _____(1).

2. _____   A work group or formal group is created by formal _____(2) within
3. _____   an organization to transform _____(3) inputs into product or service
4. _____   _____(4).

5. _____   It is appropriate to view organizations as interlocking _____(5) of work groups.

6. _____   Because each manager acts as a superior in one group and as a subordinate in another, all work groups become _____(6) in the hierarchy and across the hierarchy of authority.

7. _____   This interconnection helps _____(7) the many separate components in an organization.

8. _____   A temporary and interdependent group that can solve the problem and make appropriate recommendations to management is called a _____(8) force.

9. _____   Basic guidelines for setting up and leading a task force include: selecting
10. _____   appropriate task force _____(9), clearly defining the purpose and
11. _____   _____(10), carefully selecting the person who will serve as task force
12. _____   _____(11), and periodically reviewing _____(12).

13. _____   Spontaneous subgroups or cliques which develop within formal work groups are called _____(13) groups.

14. _____   Informal groups help individuals satisfy _____(14) that are thwarted or left unmet by their formal work group affiliations.

15. _____   Among the things which informal groups provide their members are:
16. _____   _____(15) satisfaction, _____(16), and _____(17).
17. _____

18. _____   In groups where members are truly aware of one another's needs and potential resource contributions it is called a _____(18) group.

Understanding groups in organizations

19. _____   In work groups managers can be either the formally appointed
20. _____   _____(19) or regular _____(20).

21. _____   The creation of a whole, via group formation, that is greater than the sum of its parts is called _____(21).

22. _____   When synergy occurs in groups, groups accomplish more than the total of their members' _____(22) capabilities.

23. _____   Research shows that synergism is likely when the presence of an "_____"(23) is uncertain; then groups make better judgments than would the average individual.

24. _____ Problem solving can be handled by a division of _____(24) and the sharing of information; then groups are typically more successful than individuals.

25. _____ When risk taking is involved in decisions, groups can be more _____(25) and innovative than individuals in their task accomplishments.

26. _____ Both formal and informal groups provide for social _____(26) and
27. _____ interpersonal _____(27).

28. _____ In the group context, satisfaction relates to the broader concept of
29. _____ human resource _____(28), an ability of the group to maintain its _____(29) fabric as a working entity over time.

30. _____ An effective work group achieves and maintains high levels of **both**
31. _____ task _____(30) and human resource _____(31) over time.

32. _____ A group's ability to be effective depends, in part, upon how well it trans-
33. _____ forms resource _____(32) into group _____(33).

34. _____ We refer to this transformation stage as the group _____(34).

35. _____ Another important influence on group effectiveness is the nature of the _____(35) themselves.

36. _____ Even the most positive group process will fail to yield effective results
37. _____ when _____(36) or _____(37) inputs are the only ones available.

38. _____ Among the basic inputs having the potential to impact group effective-
39. _____ ness are the _____(38) setting, nature of the _____(39), and
40. _____ _____(40) characteristics.

Stages of group development

41. _____ A synthesis of the research on small groups suggests that there are four
42. _____ distinct phases of group development: _____(41), _____(42),
43. _____ initial _____(43), and _____(44) integration.
44. _____

45. _____ In the forming stage, people are concerned to discover what is considered
46. _____ acceptable _____(45) and what the real _____(46) of the group is.

47. _____ Whereas, the storming phase is characterized by _____(47) among group members.

48. _____ The initial integration stage stresses _____(48).

49. _____ Here, the group begins to become coordinated as a _____(49) unit.

50. _____ A mature, organized, and well-functioning group characterizes total _____(50).

Group dynamics

51. _____ Forces operating in groups which affect task performance and member-ship satisfaction are called group _____(51).

52. _____ Group dynamics enact the transformation process through which resource
53. _____ _____(52) are turned into task _____(53) and human resource
54. _____ _____(54) as group outputs.

55. _____ Those behaviors the organization requests from group members by way of job performance and in return for the right of continued membership and support are called _____(55).

56. _____   Required behaviors fall in the "contributions" side of the _____(56) contract.

57. _____   Three basic elements of group dynamics which have both required and
58. _____   emergent forms are labeled by Homans as _____(57), _____(58),
59. _____   and _____(59).

60. _____   To the extent that a group's required and emergent behaviors
61. _____   _____(60) rather than contradict one another, and to the extent the
62. _____   activities, interactions, and sentiments of group members _____(61)
63. _____   organizational goals, the group process is likely to be more _____(62),
                        and higher group _____(63) is likely to result.

Group norms and cohesiveness

64. _____   Behavior expected of group members is called _____(64), often
                        referred to as rules.

65. _____   Norms serve the group by allowing members to predict one another's
                        _____(65) and to select appropriate behaviors for themselves.

66. _____   One of the most important norms in any group relates to the level of
67. _____   work _____(66) and _____(67) which members are expected to
                        contribute to the group task.

68. _____   The degree to which members are attracted to and motivated to remain
                        part of the group is called group _____(68).

69. _____   Persons in a highly cohesive group value their _____(69) and strive
70. _____   to maintain positive _____(70) with other group members.

71. _____   Members of highly cohesive groups are concerned about their group's
72. _____   _____(71) and _____(72).

73. _____   Cohesive groups generally have stable _____(73) and foster feelings
74. _____   of _____(74), _____(75), and high _____-_____(76)
75. _____   among their members.
76. _____

77. _____   Group norms can breed _____(77) of members which can cause
                        negative results.

78. _____   The worst situation for a manager is a highly cohesive work group with
                        negative performance _____(78).

79. _____   The norms and cohesiveness of any group, formal or informal,
                        _____(79) with one another to affect the behavior of group members.

80. _____   Group cohesion results in a loss of willingness and ability among group
                        members to critically evaluate one another's ideas and suggestions, and
                        is called _____(80).

Group task and maintenance activities

81. _____   Research on the social psychology of groups identifies two types of
82. _____   activities that are essential if group members are to work well together
                        over time—_____(81) and _____(82) activities.

83. _____   Activities that contribute directly to the group's performance purpose
84. _____   are called _____(83), and activities that support the emotional life of
                        the group as an ongoing social system are called _____(84).

85. _____   Both _____(85) and _____(86) activities are required for groups
86. _____   to be effective over the long run.

87. _____   Task and maintenance activities are _____(87) skills.

Inter-group dynamics

88. _____   Organizations require good coordination among the activities of many groups in order to achieve their production or service goals, and this is called _____-_____(88) dynamics.

89. _____   A common reason for breakdowns in inter-group coordination is inter-group _____(89).

90. _____
91. _____   There is a tendency for groups to develop rivalries and even antagonisms with one another that detract from the goals of inter-group _____(90) and _____(91).

92. _____
93. _____
94. _____
95. _____   Strategies for minimizing the negative consequences resulting from groups in competition include: identifying a common _____(92), appealing to a common _____(93), bringing representatives of the groups into direct _____(94), and training members of the competing groups in group process and interpersonal _____(95).

96. _____   A sequence of planned activities to gather and analyze data on the functioning of a group and implement constructive changes to increase its operating effectiveness is called _____(96) building.

TESTING YOUR KNOWLEDGE

True and False Self Test

Directions: Circle the letter (T or F) of the correct response for each of the following statements.

T   F   1. Committees and task forces are examples of temporary groups.

T   F   2. George Homans identifies activities, interactions, and sentiments as three basic elements of group dynamics.

T   F   3. Sanctions are often referred to as "rules" or "standards" of behavior that apply to group members.

T   F   4. Task and maintenance activities contribute to the group's performance, purpose, and support the emotional life of the group as an ongoing social system.

T   F   5. The informal group process helps transform resource inputs into product or service outputs.

T   F   6. Effective, well-trained managers will not try to influence group norms or cohesion.

T   F   7. Emergent behaviors arise by the requests of the organization.

T   F   8. In order to increase cohesion a manager can increase membership heterogeneity.

T   F   9. In order to decrease cohesion a manager can increase group size.

T   F   10. An example of inter-group dynamics is in colleges and universities where numerous separate departments are responsible for teaching specialized subjects.

Multiple Choice Self Test

Directions: Circle the letter of the response that best completes each of the following statements.

1. A "group" doesn't exist unless there is:
   a. a collection of people
   b. regular interaction of these people
   c. interaction for a prolonged period of time
   d. common goals
   e. all of the above must occur

2. Basic guideline(s) for setting up and leading a task force include:
   a. selecting appropriate task force members
   b. clearly defining its purpose and goals
   c. carefully selecting a task force leader
   d. periodically reviewing progress
   e. all of the above

3. Informal groups emerge because they help satisfy which need of individual members?
   a. social
   b. security
   c. identification
   d. could be all three of above

4. Synergy occurs in groups:
   a. when the presence of an "expert" is missing.
   b. when problem solving can be handled by a division of labor.
   c. because groups tend to be better risk takers and more creative.
   d. all of the above.

5. Key ingredient(s) for an effective group include:
   a. organizational setting
   b. nature of task
   c. membership characteristics
   d. all of the above
   e. none of the above

6. According to Homans, three basic elements of group dynamics come into play when groups form. The one in which group members direct behaviors toward other members is:
   a. activity
   b. interaction
   c. sentiments
   d. problem-solving

7. If a member of a group fails to comply with certain rules of the group, s/he may be punished with:
   a. sanctions
   b. norms
   c. rules
   d. cohesiveness

8. Cohesion of groups tends to be high in groups whose members share similar:
   a. needs
   b. attitudes
   c. socio-economic background
   d. all of the above

9. A highly cohesive group compared to a less cohesive group tends to:
   a. be more energetic
   b. be absent less
   c. feel happy about performance
   d. feel loyal towards one another
   e. all of the above

10. Competition may be good for members within each separate unit, but between competing groups:
    a. each group tends to view the other as enemy
    b. each group develops a very positive self-image but negative image of the competition
    c. each group tends to overestimate its strengths
    d. all of the above

Matching Self Test

Directions: Write the letter of the description that best fits each numbered item in the blank provided.

_____ 1. Quality circle

_____ 2. Cohesive group

_____ 3. Norms

_____ 4. Group development phases

_____ 5. Groupthink

_____ 6. Informal groups

_____ 7. Performance norms

_____ 8. Synergy

_____ 9. Group dynamics

_____ 10. Team building

a. Forming, storming, initial integration, total integration.

b. Forces operating in groups which affect task performance and membership.

c. A sequence of planned activities to gather and analyze data on the functioning of a group, and implement positive changes.

d. A special form of a group to facilitate quality control.

e. Rules or standards of behavior.

f. An energetic, success motivated group.

g. A tendency for a highly cohesive group to lose its evaluative critical capabilities.

h. Satisfy the individual needs of members.

i. Key characteristics of work groups.

j. Creation of a whole that is greater than the sum of its parts.

LEARNING ACTIVITIES — PART 4

Number 1 — Supplemental Reading and Discussion

Directions: Read the following journal report from *The Royal Bank Letter* of Canada on teamwork in business, and answer the discussion questions that follow:

TEAMWORK IN BUSINESS

As recently as the early part of this century, the word "team" was associated primarily with beasts of burden. Only as an afterthought would people then have taken it to mean an aggregation of athletes pooling their energies and abilities in a common pursuit. They certainly would never have visualized a team as a group of people working together within an organization. The concept of teamwork on the job had not yet been hatched.

In fact, many workers in those days were driven in much the same way as draught animals. The head of an organization could run it more or less single-handedly through the medium of overseers who kept employees in an invisible harness enforced by the fear of losing their jobs. The overseers used their authority as a whip to press the pace of activity. There could be no deviation from the course they steered.

This horse and buggy style of management lingers on in some quarters even now, and it is likely to bring horse and buggy productivity. The age of one-owner, one-product, one-market companies in which it flourished has long since passed. In a new age of diverse and complex organizations, egalitarian attitudes and occupational mobility, teamwork in business is modelled on teamwork in modern sports, not old-fashioned agriculture. Workers today cannot be driven to optimum performance. They must be led.

Study after study has shown that the best business results are obtained when people work together with a sense of commitment to one another as well as to the organization. Researchers have found that "unity of purpose" is the chief distinguishing feature of an outstanding managerial group. To do a really exceptional job, then, a work unit should have the same characteristics as a competitive sports team. Among these are:

— A team is organic. It is made up of components in the persons of its players, but these come together to form a cohesive whole which is greater than the sum of its parts.

— A team is interdependent. Each player supports the others. If the team succeeds, they all succeed; if it fails, they all fail.

— A team is stimulating. The actions and attitudes of the players spur their teammates on to greater efforts and achievements—achievements which they might have thought beyond their own personal abilities.

— A team is enjoyable. People get a thrill from being on one. They like the camaraderie, the sense of belonging, the sheer fun of being with a group.

Above all, perhaps, a team is civilized. Though they may have their personality clashes and differences of opinion, the players have learned to interact and to share. They submerge their individual aspirations in a greater objective. And yet when the common goal is reached, they find that their individual goals are satisfied too.

Speaking of the game he played for years with the New York Knicks, Bill Bradley once said: "Basketball can serve as a metaphor for ultimate co-operation. It is a sport where success, as symbolized by the championship, requires that the dictates of the community prevail over selfish personal impulses."

Bradley was a star, but he realized that he could not have shone so brightly without the back-up he received from players of lesser ability. Team sports do not demand equal skill or strength or attainment, but they do demand equal effort. Each player is expected to perform to the limit of what ability he has.

It is not inexcusable on a team to have an off day or to make mistakes; it *is* inexcusable to let the side down by not trying hard enough. A chronic shirker may be ostracized by his colleagues, because by not pulling his weight, he has hurt everyone concerned.

Recognition may be lacking when people work in groups

Teams demand a certain conformity. A player must attend to his position and must follow the game plan and the rules of the sport. This does not, however, lead to uniformity. Individuals are expected to take their own initiative within the pre-determined limits, but when an individual makes a brilliant play to score, it is on behalf of the team as an entity. Every member of it can take pride in what that one player has achieved.

In most respects, a team is like a well-ordered family. It is in the give and take and mutual support of the family circle that most of us learn how to con-

The independence of action in team sports—the hockey player on a break-away, the football player running back a punt for a touchdown—is what makes the game worthwhile.

Confronted with the desirability of giving their subordinates a freer rein, some managers may protest that this means abandoning their authority. Not necessarily: the head of a work unit occupies much the same position as a coach in sports, and coaches have a good deal of disciplinary power. They can reprimand players, "bench" them, suspend them, fine them, demote them, banish them or fire them. A winning coach, however, uses sanctions only as a last resort.

In his book *Team Building: Issues and Alternatives*, William G. Dyer introduces a fictional character named Jim Thomas, an industrial plant manager who's an avid supporter of the Dallas Cowboys of the National Football League. If Jim could only talk to the Cowboys' coach, he could tell him exactly where the team was going wrong. "What raises Jim's boiling point higher than anything," Dyer writes, "is to watch his team fail to play together. He can spot in an instant when somebody misses a block, loafs on the job, fails to pass on obvious information to the quarterback, or tries to 'shine' at the expense of the team."

It never occurs to Jim to draw a parallel between his own job and coaching the Cowboys. As Dyer says, "A football team practises over and over again how it will execute its plays. The team has 'skull' practice—they talk over plans and strategies. They review films of past games, identify mistakes, set up goals for next week. Unfortunately, Jim Thomas's management group does not engage in any similar type of activities."

A professor of organizational behaviour at Brigham Young University, Dyer is an advocate of "team building," a practice which concentrates on training an entire group and not just its leader in "management" methods. Team building calls for employee participation in decision-making, working arrangements, setting targets, and quality control. It emphasizes task specialization to make the most of the unique personal traits and skills of members of a team.

More and more work will be done in a team environment

Team building takes into account a growing phenomenon in organizational affairs, namely what Alvin Toffler in his *Future Shock* called "adhocracy." Toffler noted that an ever-increasing proportion of work is being done by task forces and other *ad hoc* groups that are peeled off from the conventional organizational structure. A number of organizations lately have lent "adhocracy" a kind of permanence

by adopting the matrix system of management. Under this, special task managers are appointed outside of functional departments to head up teams devoted to particular projects or product lines.

Matrix management is designed to stimulate innovation and the development of new and better products. As its application spreads, more and more people will be working in a team environment. "The typical operational unit is coming to be the small group—several people working together on some large problem," says organizational expert Harold J. Leavitt. "Work, these days, is moving much more toward working with rather than for others, more toward co-operation than toward competition."

In view of this, it only makes sense to teach people to work together, and to develop managers who are more interested in coaching a team than in climbing to individual stardom. The team building concept strives to do this by training work groups, with the help of an outside consultant more often than not. Teams can also be developed less formally through sensitive management and steps to bolster an employee's sense of participation and personal worth.

In recent years western businessmen have been casting an envious eye on Japan, whose highly productive work force and flair for innovation have made it such a powerful trading nation. So imbued are Japanese workers with corporate team spirit that they start their shifts by singing the company song. Family and other groups play a central role in Japanese culture, so they may be more amenable to working in groups than individualistic westerners. But while they appear regimented, Japanese workers do much more original thinking on the job than their western counterparts. One survey showed that employees of large Japanese concerns make an average of 22 suggestions per employee per year.

Management Japanese-style : Teamwork from bottom to top

The Japanese style of management puts a premium on policy consultation at every level of the corporation. Many Japanese enterprises deploy small "business teams" in plants and offices which are responsible for their own output, quality control, objectives and rewards.

When Nissan Motor Manufacturing Co. U.S.A. recently opened a truck plant in Tennessee, its president, Marvin T. Runyon, remarked that management practices in Japan are mainly responsible for that country's industrial prowess. An executive of Ford Motor Co. before becoming associated with the Japanese firm, Runyon said: "Perhaps some of these practices cannot be transferred successfully to the American operation,

duct ourserves as members of a team. People in western nations take up team play at an early age, whether in organized children's leagues or in their neighbourhoods. This continues into adult life in school, college, and sports clubs. Team play is an extension of the familial and social instincts that are part of a normal, well-adjusted personality.

From this we might jump to the conclusion that teamwork in business comes naturally. It would seem like a simple transfer to a different milieu of a mode of behaviour which we have practised all along. There are, however, strong built-in obstacles to it. For while teamwork in sports and business have much in common, there are crucial differences between the two which make the ideal of organizational teamwork harder to realize than it would appear.

One of these concerns identity. With their uniforms, their supporters, a league to compete in and a championship at stake, athletes can idenfity whole-heartedly with their team because they know what they represent and where they stand. Things are seldom so clear-cut for a work unit. Its opposition is out of sight and its ultimate objectives are often vague. Members may not know how well or poorly they are doing because it is difficult to measure accurately how a work unit in one organization compares with its counter-part in another.

To muddy the waters further, managers and supervisors may be members of two or more teams —teams of their peers concerned with planning, admin-istration or project development, and a team of sub-ordinates. The interests of these groups may clash when, for instance, one wants to save money and the other to spend it to improve working conditions. Unionized workers may also be caught between conflicting forces in cases where unions and management see each other as adversaries. They are subject to pressure to choose between "them and us."

The identity problem is compounded by a lack of recognition. Athletes have their fans to cheer them, but members of a work team rarely have a chance to taste the glory that is such a powerful incentive for competing in sports. Unless corporate policy makes a deliberate point of giving the credit that is due to employees, most of them labour in obscurity. When credit *is* forthcoming, it all too often goes to an individu-al (mainly the boss) rather than to the whole group.

The traditional system of career development does little to encourage teamwork. By concentrating on personal advancement, it has more in common with training people to compete in solo sports such as box-ing or tennis than with training them to play on a team. Their competitive instincts are channelled into domi-nating rivals, including rivals among their own colleagues.

As Douglas McGregor observed in his classic work, *The Human Side of Enterprise*: "Most so-called man-agerial teams are not teams at all, but collections of individual relationships with the boss in which each individual is vying with every other for power, prestige, recognition and personal autonomy ... Many executives who talk about their 'teams' of subordinates would be appalled to discover how low is the actual level of collaboration among them, and how high is the mutual suspicion and antagonism."

Co-ordination minus co-operation will take any team only so far

The assumption that people are working together as a team when they are in fact doing the very opposite is not uncommon. It prevails even among the worst offenders. D.L. Landen, an organizational director with General Motors Corp., recently wrote: "People engage in tugs-of-war, have territorial disputes, play one-upmanship, sabotage one another's programs, cut one another's throats, while all the time proclaiming what a great team they are."

The rhetoric of management is studded with references to teamwork which take its existence for granted. This is somewhat understandable, since it is so easy to mistake the illusion of teamwork for the real thing. A group may function like clockwork and yet be nothing like a team. "One can rather readily manage people so that the work proceeds in a co-ordinated way, as for example in a concentration camp," writes New York management professor James J. Cribben. "It is a far cry from this to managing them so that they are stimulated to co-operate willingly with each other, to offer mutual help spontaneously when needed, and to have pride in their work force—to think of themselves as damned good."

Co-ordination without co-operation can take any team only so far. In business this is almost always the result of managers trying to control every aspect of the operation. When people are ordered about without consultation, they are unlikely to volunteer their efforts or ideas. And they are unlikely to take on any more responsibility than the minimum expected of them, because by making all the decisions, the boss has taken all the responsibility upon himself.

At a time when workers are more individualistic and better-educated than ever before, it is counter-productive not to afford them a reasonable measure of independence. In a situation where the boss insists on running a one-man (or one-woman) show, the contributions their subordinates are capable of making go to waste. It might be thought that independence de-tracts from teamwork, but as consulting psychologist Bruce Sanders argues, " it's an important part of it."

but my staff and I are determined that we're going to apply the Japanese principle that underlies all of them—teamwork and interaction from bottom to top."

"From bottom to top"—that is an illuminating way of putting it. Teamwork will remain confined to management pep-talks as long as anyone from the shop floor up is made to feel like a cog in an inhuman machine. The spirit and practice of teamwork must be manifest throughout an organization if the stubborn institutional barriers to it are to be eliminated. Only then can it become more than just a word.

Source: *The Royal Bank Letter*, Vol. 63, No. 1, Jan./Feb. 1982.

Questions for Discussion

1.   In what ways does the concept of teamwork in the reading above relate to the Part IV theme on leatership? Explain.

2.   Restate from the article what appear to be common ingredients of teamwork. Then add your own ideas about teamwork to the list.

3.   The author of the article says that team players submerge their individual aspirations. If this is true, isn't the team spirit detrimental to the potential for emerging leaders? Agree or disagree and explain.

4.   List some of the difficulties that the article cites in business for achieving teamwork. Then answer how a leader/manager might overcome such problems as individual feelings of loss of identity or lack of recognition.

Number 2 — Exercise: Identifying Your Personal Power Sources

In Chapter 10 the author identifies sources of power such as personal and position. Under personal power he adds "expert" and "referent" sources of power. Several current popular paperbacks in the "trade" section of bookstores also delineate a variety of power sources and uses for would-be managers and/or manipulators. For example, charismatic power, one's magnetism, seems to be in each book's table of contents.

Directions: List what you believe are your personal, if not charismatic, power sources that might have potential for influencing other people with whom you develop interpersonal contact. Then put a check mark in one of the columns to indicate the power value of the characteristics identified.

Personal power source	Adds greater power	Lessens power	Neutral or not sure
1. Physical stature			
a. Height			
b. Weight			
c. Conditioning/Build			
d. Posture			
e. Attractiveness/Looks			
f. Skin, coloring, appearance			
g. Sex			

Personal power source	Adds greater power	Lessens power	Neutral or not sure

2. Dress/Hygiene

    a.   Appearance/Health/ Grooming

    b.   Clothing Style/Fit

    c.   Clothing colors

    d.   Clothing: Extent of Formality/Informality

3. Personality/Attitude/ Quirks

    a.   Demeanor overall

    b.   List your own:

        1)   Extent of intro-version, or

        2)   Extroversion

        3)   Bubbly, or

        4)   Laid back

        5)   Funny, or

        6)   Serious

        7)   Openness to others, or

        8)   Closed

    c.   Other? List. (i.e. voice)

4. Socio/Economic Background

    a.   Heritage/Background

    b.   Education

    c.   Wealth

    d.   Cultural traditions

    e.   Memberships and reference groups

Summary

1. Based on the factors above, plus others you have sensed in relating to others, what are your primary power attributes? How useful to you is knowing how you and others view you? Discuss the value of power as a concept in organizational settings.

2. In what ways can you add to or extend your own power base?

3. In what positive and negative ways do people use power?

Number 3 — Exercise: Self Analysis of Group Skills

Directions: This group skills assessment form is to be done in two steps. First circle the number on the scale for each item describing your present behavior. Next place an X mark over the number representing your ideal ranking.

1. Clarity in expressing my thoughts.

   0   1   2   3   4   5   6   7   8   9

   Quite vague   Exceptionally clear

2. Ability to listen in an alert and understanding way.

   0   1   2   3   4   5   6   7   8   9

   Low   Very high

3. Ability to present ideas forcefully and positively.

   0   1   2   3   4   5   6   7   8   9

   Low   Very high

4. Ability to "stay with" the topic discussed.

   0   1   2   3   4   5   6   7   8   9

   Very poor   Excellent

5. Tendency to trust others

   0   1   2   3   4   5   6   7   8   9

   Quite suspicious   Very trusting

6. Willingness to tell others what I feel (express emotions).

   0   1   2   3   4   5   6   7   8   9

   Conceal all   Reveal all

7. Readiness to accept direction from others.

   0   1   2   3   4   5   6   7   8   9

   Very reluctant   Very accepting

8. Tendency to "take charge" of group.

   0   1   2   3   4   5   6   7   8   9

   Don't try   Try very much

9. Usual behavior toward others.

   0   1   2   3   4   5   6   7   8   9

   Cool   Very warm

10. Reactions to comments about or evaluation of my behavior.

   0   1   2   3   4   5   6   7   8   9

   Ignore   Take them seriously
                                            & emotionally

11. Sensitivity to other's group member needs.

    0   1   2   3   4   5   6   7   8   9
    Low   High

12. Understanding why I do what I do (insight).

    0   1   2   3   4   5   6   7   8   9
    Don't know   Really understand

13. Tolerance for conflict and antagonism in the group.

    0   1   2   3   4   5   6   7   8   9
    Can't stand it   Like very much

14. Tolerance for expressions of affection and warmth.

    0   1   2   3   4   5   6   7   8   9
    Can't stand them   Like them very much

15. Thinking creatively in groups.

    0   1   2   3   4   5   6   7   8   9
    Seldom contribute ideas   High idea production

16. Tolerance of opposing opinions.

    0   1   2   3   4   5   6   7   8   9
    Low   High

17. Interest in team building.

    0   1   2   3   4   5   6   7   8   9
    Low   High

18. Ability to focus on the task.

    0   1   2   3   4   5   6   7   8   9
    Low   High

Discussion:

1. List the items above in which there is a large difference (such as 5 points) between current ranking and ideal score.

2. Regarding items where there is a major point difference between current ranking and ideal ranking, list steps that you could take to improve upon the ranking.

Number 4 — Matching Wits with the Experts

"20 Top Status Items for the Office"

Power sources go beyond individual traits. In the formal organizational environment there are "status" symbols which serve to both reflect power and position of managers and at the same time contribute added symbolic power.

Directions: What do you believe are the physical, decorative trappings in the business office setting that are considered "the" status symbols? List what you believe them to be. Example, executive coffee pot. List your top 20. Then, turn the page and compare your list with the list from an anonymous large corporation.

Number or rank

1.
2.
3.
4.
5.
6.
7.
8.
9.
10.
11.
12.
13.
14.
15.
16.
17.
18.
19.
20.

"20 Top Status Items for the Office"

1. How big? A large corner office still rates tops on the prestige scale, especially in the era of Open Office when any private office is considered a coup.

2. Windows—how many and what can you see? A lot of glass and a spectacular view can't be beat. The executive desk should be placed in front of windows so that the terrible glare is inflicted only on visiting subordinates.

3. Proximity of an office to that of the chief executive officer. Even an interior office without windows close to the CEO's might be more prestigious than one with windows several floors below.

4. A sofa. It will fit only in the larger offices, many of which are designed to include a work area (desk), a conference area (table), and an informal area (sofa).

5. A fireplace. Not found in most offices.

6. Sauna and/or kitchenette and bar.

7. Choice of how to achieve "the power look". It includes choice of wall coverings or rosewood paneling if you are a prime mover in a prime company, and a choice of wall hangings, preferably a few tasteful original prints, certainly not university diplomas even if from Ivy League schools. A long narrow office with the big desk at the far end shows sufficient power to make an employee "crawl" before he reaches you.

8. A lamp. Or as it is now called "task lighting," not to be confused with ambient or overhead lighting.

9. A metal desk or a wooden desk? Wooden, of course, carries more status and the bigger the better, especially if it has few drawers and visitors can see your legs.

10. A private restroom.

11. Plants paid for by the company.

12. A more expensive grade of carpet (important in some firms).

13. Walnut ashtrays and wastepaper baskets. They are much more prestigious than metal or plastic.

14. A touchtone phone (or a phone that is a link in a complex communications network).

15. A gatekeeper. Also known as a secretary, this person is prized at middle management levels for preventing visitors from sticking their heads into an office unannounced.

16. Which elevator you take. The top executives use the elevator marked to serve the uppermost floors.

17. A conference table.

18. A stereo sound system or a TV with video cassette recording capability. (Particularly important for public relations vice presidents.)

19. A coat closet in the office.

20. A door. This sounds like a simple item but some companies keep close track of which employees are entitled to doors to their offices. Doors also may affect life in the upper echelons. One executive had a button installed on his desk to automatically close the door to his office. Unfortunately for him, it went on the fritz one day and he was locked in his office for 2½ hours.

*Source unknown

Number 5 — Experiential Learning Exercise

Communicating: Good News and Bad News

This experiential scenario is a continuation of the case described in Part 3 on organization membership in which the informal organization interfered with formal organization in pursuit of formal organization goals. The organization chart is recreated below. You will benefit by reviewing the original employee descriptions.

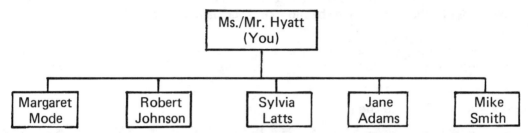

You, Hyatt, are the manager supervising five employees as was previously described.

Official communication in the organization is handled in a variety of ways as illustrated below:

1. Delegation is done directly through the formal chain usually in writing.
2. Division meetings are conducted six times per year in the large cafeteria by the division manager to whom you report in the chart.
3. Question/suggestion boxes are placed conveniently to solicit employee input.
4. Twice per month communications meetings are conducted by Hyatt with subordinates.
5. The personnel department uses the official posting areas to describe job openings at certain levels, promote educational opportunities, post EEO laws, etc.
6. The corporate president sends out a monthly newsletter to all employees at their home address.
7. A social events bulletin board is open to all to use.

Good News: You will be promoted to a mid-management position leaving your supervisor position open to some division employee to be recommended for promotion. Besides your own group of five employees who will be informed of the opening there are two other similar groups of five employees doing similar bank teller work.

Bad news: Jane Adams, who was previously described as a marginal performer, is getting even more errant in her work; and she must be terminated. Of course, this will be against her will. Although she is conscious of her error rates, she will still be surprised and hurt by termination notice.

Questions

In pursuit of good leadership examples as well as effective communication, please answer the following questions:

1. Who should announce the good news? Examples . . . Have it posted on the bulletin board as the original source? Have the personnel department do it? Have your own (Hyatt's) manager announce it? Explain your choice of sender of meaasges.

2. Who should communicate the bad news? How? Refer to possible senders of the bad news alluded to in question one.

LOOKING BACK; LOOKING AHEAD

Part 4 was devoted to the management function labeled leadership. Leadership is important in the quest for increased productivity on the part of employees. Yet few managers have the natural ability to lead. Therefore, the material offered was very meaningful since it offered the content through which managers and potential managers could learn about leadership and begin to develop leadership skills—communicating, influencing motivation, and affecting group dynamics.

In Part 5 yet another management function, controlling, is taught through the author's text material. Chapter 14, "Fundamentals of Controlling," sets the tone of the topic controlling by defining its purpose in terms of monitoring performance to make sure that actual performance is consistent with plans. Plans! What plans? The answer lies with your ability to recall at this point the earlier chapters on planning in which goals and objectives were explained as part of the planning process. Inherent in goals are performance targets, and once you have performance targets you have the foundation for carrying on effective control functions.

Part 1 includes three chapters which will stretch your comprehension of controlling via a variety of management techniques—performance appraisal systems, pay and reward systems, discipline, management by objectives, budgets, and management information systems.

PART V

CONTROLLING FOR PRODUCTIVITY

INTRODUCTION — PART 5

(Chapters 14 — 16)

Highlights

Part 5 introduces you to yet another key managerial function—controlling for productivity. Controlling is a logical continuation of the managerial functional responsibilities including planning, organizing, and leading, which your text covered in previous parts. Your author is diligent in linking the control function to the previously covered functions. For example, in Figure 14.7 of the text he illustrates how skillful planning, organizing, leading and controlling take us from where we have been toward the direction we want to go. This illustration is very meaningful since it emphasizes that productivity, or whatever other success measures in business we choose to pursue, does not just happen. That is, all the managerial functions need to be carried out regularly and thoroughly.

Perhaps controlling is the least understood of the managerial functions. For example, when we identify something as being out of control, we often attribute such a state as the result, perhaps, of chance or fate or accident. This logic gets carried into the business setting so that something out of control seems to continue indefinitely, as if there were nothing management could do about it. This inaction is true particularly in dealing with the human resource element of the business. Employees' work behaviors seem to perpetuate even though their behaviors are less than fully productive. The author emphasizes in Chapter 14, in particular, that good managerial control can satisfy the needs and goals of both the organization and the individuals employed by the organization.

You may gain more from Chapter 14 by thinking of yourself as a system susceptible to varying degrees of being in or out of control. How would you improve your own control? Try adopting the control material directly to yourself. For example, take the author's four basic elements in the control process, and improve your own control. That is, set a goal for yourself this week. Then set up a monitoring procedure. Next, as each day goes by compare your own progress with the goals you have set. If you fall behind, what can you do? Take corrective action as the last step in the control process.

Chapter 15 continues the controlling theme via budget and management information systems topics. Budgeting is an excellent management controlling activity and is also very helpful as a self-controlling activity. Do you budget regularly? Are you financially in control or out of control? What are the symptoms of being financially out of control? Through budgeting and utilizing management information systems, the author adeptly expands the content of management control.

In the last chapter of Part 5, you will learn about management production/operation activities. Perhaps the most difficult chapter in any management text to make meaningful to readers, production and operations is brought to light with lively vignettes such as Peter Smith's meteoric rise in General Signal Company. Does anyone with a degree really want to work in production? Yes, and apparently there is excitement and good growth potential in manufacturing.

In Chapter 16 you will learn how managers generate a product or service by coordinating the inputs of raw material, equipment, and people.

Chapter Titles for Part 5

Chapter 14 — Fundamentals of Controlling
Chapter 15 — Control Via Budgets and Information Systems
Chapter 16 — Production and Operations Control

CAREER PERSPECTIVE — PART 5

Career Occupations of Control

Introduction

To what extent are you interested in or have an aptitude for exercising control or being controlled in your job or career field? In what particular occupations do you feel there are opportunities to exercise control? For example, police officer compared to counselor. These questions are important in your determining the likelihood that you will be satisfied or dissatisfied with your employment.

Directions

A.   Use the table format below to do the following:
1.   In the first column list occupations in which you have some interest. Try to do at least three.
2.   In the second column list occupational descriptors from, for example, the *Dictionary of Occupational Titles*. Look for controlling words such as authority, independence, and relationships of control over others.
3.   In the last column you should make your own evaluative comments regarding your feelings (likes/dislikes) about the descriptive information you found. In short, is each job that you listed still of interest to you after the career perspective exercise?

List of occupations/ positions in which you have an interest	*Brief description of characteristics of each occupation**	*Your comments about controlling aspects of the occupation*
1.		
2.		
3.		
4.		
5.		

B.   To further explore the likelihood that you would be satisfied in a particular occupation, you should make an appointment with a counselor who very likely has information about your measured vocational needs. Ask the counselor to help you go one step further. That is, ask the counselor to do an occupational reinforcement profile. There are instruments available, and your counseling staff should have one of these. Occupational reinforcers are factors such as independence, ability utilization, opportunity for achievement and authority that through a questionnaire are determined on your behalf. Once your profile (how you react to job reinforcers) is known, it can be matched with your occupational needs. That is, a need—ORP (occupational reinforcement profile)—comparison can be made, and your own interpretation can be done about the degree that you want controlling factors in your work.

*See *Dictionary of Occupational Titles*, for example, for information. Your counseling office or the library should have this book.

14 Fundamentals of Controlling

STUDENT LEARNING OBJECTIVES

After completing the chapter material you should be able to:

1. Define controlling as a management function and express its importance in relationship to other management functions, particularly planning.
2. Explain the text's forces that also lend importance to the controlling function.
3. List and explain the three purposes the controls fulfill.
4. Identify the manager's controlling responsibilities.
5. List and explain the text's four basic elements in the control process.
6. Delineate the various types of controls explained by your author.
7. Compare and contrast internal and external controls.
8. Define performance appraisal as a system and how it is used to impact on control, and list the benefits that accrue for organizations.
9. List and explain the text examples of performance appraisal methods.
10. Explain pay and reward systems in terms of the several purposes they serve, particularly in the area of controlling.
11. Define MBO, the procedures used, and explain its contributions as a control mechanism.
12. Explain author's suggestions for making controls effective.

CHAPTER HIGHLIGHTS

Controlling as a management function
Organizational control systems
Performance appraisal systems
Pay and reward systems
Employee discipline systems
Management by objectives
Making controls effective

PROGRAMMED LEARNING

The following statements are drawn from actual textbook content in abbreviated form. The blanks within the statements are numbered to correspond with the answer blanks at the left.

Controlling concepts and the importance of controlling

1. _____

A process of monitoring performance and taking corrective action to insure desired results is called _____(1).

2. _____

Its purpose is to make sure that actual performance is consistent with _____(2).

3. _____
4. _____

Control is a means for making sure actual _____(3) is consistent with intentions and that organizational _____(4) are thereby achieved.

5. _____
6. _____
7. _____

Controls help managers to make sure that people in organizations do _____(5) is necessary, _____(6) it is necessary, and in the _____(7) it is required.

8. _____
9. _____
10. _____
11. _____

There are four forces that lend importance to the controlling function: an _____(8), _____(9), human _____(10), _____(11) and decentralization.

12. _____
13. _____

Control fulfills certain basic purposes in the organization: provides a means of _____(12) performance, and helps ensure that action _____(13) and performance accomplishments are consistent with one another.

14. _____
15. _____
16. _____

The emphasis of control is on action designed to _____(14) problems, _____(15) problems and exploit _____(16).

Elements in the control process

17. _____
18. _____

The text example of thermostatic control represents an ideal or _____(17) control system, i.e., one that is entirely _____-_____(18) in its monitoring and correction capabilities.

19. _____
20. _____
21. _____
22. _____

The four basic elements in the control process are: establishing performance _____(19) and standards, monitoring actual _____(20), comparing actual performance with _____(21) and standards, and taking _____(22) action.

23. _____

Objectives and standards set performance targets and means for evaluating _____(23).

24. _____

In the measurement stage of the control process, measurement must be done well enough to spot _____(24) or variances between what actually occurs and what is desired.

25. _____
26. _____

Management by exception in controlling allows managers to conserve valuable time and energy by focusing attention on areas of _____(25) and _____(26).

27. _____
28. _____

There are two ways in which the control process influences behavior in organizations: _____(27) control or self control and _____(28) control.

Types of control

29. _____
30. _____
31. _____

Four basic types of external controls are: _____(29), _____(30), _____/_____(31) controls and postaction controls.

32. _____

_____(32) controls act in anticipation of problems.

33. _____

Control that takes place after an action is completed is labeled _____(33).

Organizational control systems

34. _____

Regardless of the type of control, the goal of exercising control in organizations is to increase or insure the predictability of _____(34).

35. _____
36. _____

Control via performance objectives occurs when work _____(35) are appropriately directed toward the right end _____(36).

37. _____
38. _____

Control via _____(37) and _____(38) occurs by setting guidelines for behavior and including specified rules for solving problems.

39. _____

Control via staff _____(39) and training involves the maintenance of a qualified work force.

40. _____
41. _____

Control can also be achieved via structural _____(40) design, _____(41) relations, and via positive norms.

42. _____

Leadership is the use of _____(42) to influence other people to act in ways that serve organizational objectives.

43. _____

The type of control that allocates resources to specific activities is called an _____(43).

Performance appraisal systems

44. _____

The process of formally evaluating performance and providing feedback upon which performance adjustments can be made is called _____(44) appraisal.

45. _____

Managers use performance appraisal to help control individual _____(45).

46. _____
47. _____

The purposes served by good performance appraisal systems are _____(46) and _____(47).

48. _____
49. _____

Both _____(48) and _____(49) roles by managers are essential to the performance appraisal process.

50. _____
51. _____
52. _____

Regardless of the approach used, the evaluation of employees must be _____(50), _____(51), _____(52), and practical.

53. _____
54. _____

One of the most common performance appraisal methods is the graphic _____(53) _____(54).

55. _____

The _____(55) incident technique of performance appraisal involves the preparation of a running log or inventory of examples of very effective and ineffective job behaviors.

56. _____

BARS refers to a rating system called _____(56) anchored rating scale.

57. _____
58. _____
59. _____

Multi-person comparison techniques are _____(57) ordering, _____(58) comparisons, and _____(59) distribution.

60. _____
61. _____

A good performance appraisal system includes attention paid to the needs of _____(60) as well as of the _____(61).

62. _____

At a minimum, everyone should receive a formal performance appraisal at least _____(62) a year.

63. _____

It is best to hold the performance and salary reviews _____(63).

Pay and reward systems

64. _____
65. _____
66. _____

An organization's pay and reward systems serve several purposes: (1) _____(64) people to the organization; (2) help motivate employees to exert maximum _____(65); and (3) remind them of the current value of their contributions to organizational _____(66).

67. _____

On the assumption that the individual understands the basis for the allocation of pay and rewards, a framework for performance _____(67) is established.

68. _____

Through self-control or external control for example, high performers can target their efforts on ways to maintain or further improve upon _____(68).

69. _____

A large element of performance control can be realized by simply having the right person assigned to the _____(69) in the first place.

70. _____

A good base compensation scheme increases _____(70) from a staffing perspective.

71. _____

In addition to base compensation, the overall employee _____(71) program of the organization plays a role in the attraction and maintenance of a viable work force.

Employee discipline systems

72. _____

Influencing behavioral control through reprimand is called _____(72).

73. _____

Discipline that ties penalties or punishments to the severity of the employee's infractions, and varies the penalty on any given level of severity according to the number of times it has occurred is called _____(73).

Management by objectives: An integrated planning and control system

74. _____

One useful technique for accomplishing an integration of planning and control is called MBO, Management by _____(74).

75. _____

MBO is a process of joint _____(75) setting between a superior and subordinate.

76. _____
77. _____
78. _____
79. _____

MBO involves a formal agreement between a superior and subordinate concerning: the subordinate's performance _____(76), the _____(s)(77) through which they will be accomplished, _____(78) for measuring whether or not they have been accomplished, and _____(79) for reviewing results.

Making controls effective

80. _____

All control systems share the common goal of helping to insure predictable and coordinated _____(80) contributions by organization members.

81. _____
82. _____
83. _____

Among the human reactions to controls which can lead to such unintended consequences of control systems are resentment of the act of _____(81), _____(82) about one's true performance, and rejection of the _____(83) targets.

84. _____
85. _____
86. _____
87. _____
88. _____
89. _____
90. _____
91. _____
92. _____
93. _____

An effective control system has the following characteristics: strategic and _____(84) oriented, _____(85) based, no more _____(86) than necessary, prompt and _____(87) oriented, _____able(88), _____ible(89), consistent with organization _____(90), designed to accomodate _____-control(91), _____(92) in nature, and fair and _____(93).

TESTING YOUR KNOWLEDGE

True and False Self Test

Directions: Circle the letter (T or F) of the correct response for each of the following statements.

T F   1. The employee innately wants to do good work.

T F   2. To do good work the employee needs to be involved.

T F   3. According to the text, adequate quality control in the U.S. auto industry suffers from an underemphasis on production and poor management.

T F   4. The purpose of the controlling function is to make sure performance is consistent with plans.

T F   5. In the most general sense control actually hinders managerial decision-making.

T F   6. When control is considered as a process, the emphasis is on action.

T F   7. The control process begins with organizing, then planning.

T F   8. Goals and standards should not be seen as a means for evaluating performance.

T F   9. A manager can exercise external control through the direct supervision of subordinates.

T F 10. The role of counseling employees by managers is considered out of line with what is considered management responsibility.

Multiple Choice Self Test

Directions: Circle the letter of the response that best completes each of the following statements.

1. A process of monitoring performance and taking corrective actions to insure desired results is labeled:
   a. planning
   b. organizing
   c. controlling
   d. leading

2. The value of controls is that they:
   a. see to it that the right things happen
   b. help managers make sure employees do what is necessary
   c. help ensure things are done when necessary
   d. ensure things are done the way they should be
   e. all of the above

3. The force that lends importance (necessity) to controlling as a management function is:
   a. uncertainty
   b. complexity
   c. human limitations
   d. delegation and decentralization
   e. all of the above are forces

4. A manager's controlling responsibility entails:
   a. monitoring employee behavior to detect deviations
   b. providing feedback to employees
   c. taking action to correct deviations
   d. all of the above

5. Performance standards are:
   a. comparative
   b. historical
   c. engineered
   d. all of the above are possible

6. The goal of exercising control in organizations is to increase or insure the predictability of:
   a. competitors
   b. the economy
   c. performance
   d. management emotions

7. The first step in the control process is:
   a. staffing
   b. leading
   c. goal setting
   d. organizing
   e. none of the above

8. Performance is appraised in organizations at which level?
   a. individual
   b. group
   c. total organization
   d. could be all of the above

9. Benefits to the organization of effective performance appraisal include:
   a. improved employee performance
   b. more equitable salary rewards
   c. identification of training needs
   d. selection of new employees
   e. all of the above

10. A good performance appraisal needs to be:
   a. relevant
   b. unbiased
   c. significant
   d. practical
   e. all of the above

Matching Self Test

Directions: Write the letter of the description that best fits each numbered item in the blank provided.

_____ 1. Input standards

_____ 2. Management by exception

_____ 3. Precontrols

_____ 4. Steering controls

_____ 5. Output standards

_____ 6. Trust

_____ 7. Leadership

_____ 8. Budget

_____ 9. Information system

_____ 10. Operations control

_____ 11. Evaluation and development

a. Measure results in terms of quantity, quality, cost or time.

b. Specification of appropriate goals and/or input factors.

c. The thing that is an absolute must when management utilizes self-control.

d. The use of power to control employees.

e. Control that allocates financial resources.

f. Measure work efforts put into performance tasks.

g. Controlling on the part of managers that focuses on problems and opportunities.

h. Controls which act in anticipation of problems.

i. Control device that collects, organizes and distributes information.

j. The type of control system that addresses the direct production or service activities of the organization.

k. The purposes served by good performance appraisal systems.

15 Budgetary Control and Management Information Systems

STUDENT LEARNING OBJECTIVES

After completing the chapter material you should be able to:

1. Define the term budget and its role in allocating resources and helping the control function.
2. Express the author's point regarding what managers can expect to find in any organization regarding budgets.
3. Relate budgeting to the notion of "responsibility centers" and list sample centers.
4. List and explain types of budgets and the budgeting process.
5. Identify the long-range budget in terms of what it means and what are long-range programs.
6. Briefly explain steps or procedures listed as part of long-range budgeting.
7. Distinguish the concern of short-range budgeting compared to long-range budgeting, and give examples of short-range budgets.
8. List and explain steps involved in creating the master budget.
9. List and explain three areas of attention in achieving budgetary control.
10. List and explain characteristics of an effective budgetary control system.
11. Define management information systems and how systems facilitate planning and controlling functions.
12. Explain the basic elements of a computer-based MIS, and how to make MIS effective.
13. List some of the common MIS mistakes.

CHAPTER HIGHLIGHTS

Budgets
The budgeting process
Achieving budgetary control
Management information
Management information systems
Making management information systems effective

PROGRAMMED LEARNING

The following statements are drawn from actual textbook content in abbreviated form. The blanks within the statements are numbered to correspond with the answer blanks at the left.

Control systems

1. _____
2. _____
3. _____

Any control system requires communication of the right _____(1) at the right _____(2) and among the right _____(3) if it is to function effectively.

4. _____

A formalized way of allocating resources to specific activities is called _____(4).

5. _____
6. _____

Budgets not only establish _____(5) utilization objectives, but also provide a framework for analyzing _____(6) and highlighting deviations from plans.

7. _____

_____(7) systems collect, organize, store and distribute data regarding activities occurring inside or outside the organization.

8. _____
9. _____

Information systems facilitate planning by assisting in the establishment of _____(8) and _____(9), as well as providing support for the formulation of related budgets.

10. _____

Information systems provide the basis for documenting, disseminating and storing _____(10) results.

11. _____
12. _____

Depending on the level of sophistication, they may also identify _____(11) from plans and even suggest what _____(12) should be taken under the circumstances.

Budgets

13. _____

Budgets help allocate resources to _____(13).

14. _____
15. _____
16. _____
17. _____

In any organization, managers can expect to find that budgets are stated in _____(14) terms; contain an element of management _____(15); are based on _____(16); and can be changed only under specific _____(17).

Budgets and responsibility centers

18. _____

Responsibility _____(18) are work units that are formally charged with budgetary responsibility for carrying out various activities.

19. _____
20. _____
21. _____
22. _____

Four types of responsibility accounting centers are: in _____(19) centers, _____(20) or expense centers, _____(21) centers, and _____(22) centers.

Why budgets are important

23. _____
24. _____
25. _____

Budgets encourage managers to examine their activities _____(23) and creatively relative to available resources; direct management's attention toward the _____(24), and facilitate _____(25).

Types of budgets

26. _____   Budgets based on a single estimate and which do not allow adjustment over time are referred to as _____(26) or static budgets.

27. _____   _____(27) budgets can be adjusted over time to accommodate relevant changes in the environment.

28. _____   _____(28) budgets assign resources to a work unit, manager and his or her immediate subordinates, on a short-term basis.

29. _____   _____(29) budgets are comprehensive short-term budgets for the organization as a whole.

30. _____   Budgets covering periods of more than one year are called _____-_____(30) budgets.

31. _____   A _____-_____(31) budget forces both on-going and newly-proposed programs to compete on an equal footing for available resources.

The budgeting process

32. _____   All budgeting directs attention to both performance _____(32) and
33. _____   anticipated _____(33) requirements.

34. _____   Budgeting for long-range programs should include procedures which each
35. _____   designated organizational unit will use to generate program proposals,
36. _____   procedures for _____(34) program proposals, procedures for _____(35) and reviewing program performance, and procedures for periodic zero-based review of _____-_____(36) programs and new program proposals.

37. _____   The _____(37) budget is the organization's primary short-term budgetary device.

Preparation of the master budget

38. _____   Twelve steps involved in preparing the master budget are: forecasting
39. _____   _____(38), identifying _____(39) patterns for responsibility
40. _____   centers, estimating production _____(40), specifying _____(41)
41. _____   objectives, developing a sales _____(42), developing a production
42. _____   _____(43), developing a purchasing _____(44), developing
43. _____   budgets for _____(45) centers, formulating a _____(46) plan,
44. _____   comparing the profit plan with _____(47) objectives, formulating a
45. _____   projected _____(48) budget, and preparing a projected statement of
46. _____   _____(49) position.
47. _____
48. _____
49. _____

Achieving budgetary control

50. _____

_____-_____(50) analysis in budgetary control is the study of the relationship between budgeted revenues and costs to determine how changes in each affect profit.

51. _____
52. _____

A break-even point occurs where total _____(51) from sales is just sufficient to cover total _____(52).

53. _____
54. _____
55. _____
56. _____
57. _____
58. _____
59. _____
60. _____

In general, successful budgetary controls are: strategic and _____(53) oriented, _____(54) based, simple and _____(55), prompt and _____(56) oriented, _____(57), based on _____(58) factors, fair and _____(59), positive and conducive to _____-_____(60).

Data, information, and information systems

61. _____

_____(61) consists of raw facts such as figures and other symbols used to represent people, events and concepts.

62. _____

_____(62) is data that has been made meaningful or relevant for the recipient.

63. _____

An _____(63) system, accordingly, collects, organizes and distributes data in such a way that it becomes meaningful as information.

64. _____
65. _____

A good information system will serve the needs of both _____(64) and _____(65) users.

Management information systems

66. _____
67. _____

A management _____(66) _____(67), or MIS, collects, organizes and distributes data in such a way that it meets the information needs of managers.

68. _____
69. _____
70. _____

The basic elements which are central to any computer-based MIS are: _____(68), _____(69), and Central _____(70) Unit (CPU).

Making MIS effective

71. _____

An effective MIS creatively integrates computers, organizations and _____(71).

72. _____

The purpose of any MIS is to facilitate the accomplishment of organizational _____(72).

73. _____

The difference between a successful MIS and one that fails often traces to _____(73) factors.

74. _____

A successful MIS is one that is _____(74).

Common MIS mistakes

75. _____
76. _____
77. _____
78. _____
79. _____
80. _____

Any management information system is destined to fail if the designers and users assume: more _____(75) is always better; managers need all the _____(76) they want; that if managers are given all the information they need, their decision making will _____(77); more _____(78) means better performance; managers do not have to _____(79) how a MIS works to use it well; the computer can do _____(80).

TESTING YOUR KNOWLEDGE

True and False Self Test

Directions: Circle the letter (T or F) of the correct response for each of the following statements.

T   F   1.   Budgets establish resource utilization objectives.

T   F   2.   Budgets provide a framework for reporting actual results.

T   F   3.   Information systems facilitate planning by assisting in the initial formulation of objectives and standards.

T   F   4.   Information systems are never able to suggest what actions to take to correct deviations in performance.

T   F   5.   All budgeting involves attention to performance objectives.

T   F   6.   In order to dispense with an annual zero-based budget review management must be satisfied, and (see 7)

T   F   7.   the work environment must be reasonably stable.

T   F   8.   The entire process of budget preparation does not have to be information based.

T   F   9.   Budgets should be flexible.

T   F   10.   Budgets should focus on uncontrollable factors.

Multiple Choice Self Test

Directions: Circle the letter of the response that best completes each of the following statements.

1.   Any control system requires communication of the:
     a.   right information
     b.   timely information
     c.   information to the right people
     d.   all of the above

2.   Information systems facilitate planning by assisting in the:
     a.   formulation of objectives
     b.   formulation of standards
     c.   control process
     d.   identification of deviations from plans
     e.   all of the above

3.   In any organization, managers can expect to find that budgets
     a.   are stated in monetary terms
     b.   contain an element of management commitment
     c.   are based on proposals
     d.   can be changed only under specific conditions
     e.   all of the above

4.   Budgets are important because they:
     a.   encourage management to analyze their own activities
     b.   help to focus on the future
     c.   provide a mechanism through which future problems can be anticipated
     d.   facilitate planning
     e.   all of the above

5. Budgeting for long-range programs should include procedure(s) for:
   a. generating separate department program proposals
   b. evaluating program proposals
   c. monitoring program performance
   d. zero-based review of on-going programs
   e. all of the above

6. To carry out the preparation of a master budget management must:
   a. forecast demand
   b. identify cost patterns
   c. estimate production costs
   d. specify operating objectives
   e. all of the above and more

7. In general, successful budgeting controls are:
   a. strategic and results oriented
   b. information based, but simple to understand
   c. prompt and exception oriented
   d. flexible but controllable
   e. all of the above

8. Over concentration on staying within budget could lead to:
   a. postponement of maintenance
   b. utilization of cheaper raw materials
   c. purchase of inferior quality supplies and materials
   d. all of the above

9. Figures or other inputs that have been made meaningful or relevant for management decision making are called:
   a. data
   b. information
   c. system
   d. numbers

10. A management information system deals with data in what way?
    a. collects data
    b. organizes data
    c. distributes data
    d. none of the above

Matching Self Test

Directions: Write the letter of the description that best fits each numbered item in the blank provided.

_____ 1. Budgets

_____ 2. Managers

_____ 3. Responsibility centers

_____ 4. Revenue centers

_____ 5. Profit centers

_____ 6. Fixed budgets

_____ 7. Master budgets

_____ 8. Zero-based budget

_____ 9. Profit plan

_____ 10. Break-even point

a. Work units within the organization formally charged with budgetary responsibility.

b. Budgetary responsibility is measured on the difference between revenues and expenses.

c. Financial expressions of action plans.

d. Persons in organizations who are responsible for using resources well.

e. Budgets and performance assessments concentrate on product or service outputs.

f. Are based on a single estimate which does not allow adjustment overtime.

g. Forces both on-going and newly-proposed programs to compete on equal footing.

h. Details revenues and costs, and projects net income.

i. Comprehensive short-term budgets.

j. Where total revenue from sales covers total costs.

16 Production and Operations Control

STUDENT LEARNING OBJECTIVES

After completing the chapter material you should be able to:

1. Explain the elements of managing the production/operations activity.
2. List and explain the functions involved in converting raw materials into finished products.
3. Delineate functions in managing production and operations, particularly planning and controlling.
4. List and explain planning production/operations activities, particularly forecasting methods, and resulting planning based on forecasting.
5. Define master scheduling and explain its purpose.
6. List and briefly explain the various types of planning inherent in carrying out production/operations activities.
7. List and briefly explain various types of control inherent in production/operations activity.

CHAPTER HIGHLIGHTS

Production/Operations Management (P/OM)
Making forecasts
Establishing schedules
Controlling inventories
Controlling quality
Production and operations control in managerial perspective

PROGRAMMED LEARNING

The following statements are drawn from actual textbook content in abbreviated form. The blanks within the statements are numbered to correspond with the answer blanks at the left.

The production/operations setting

1. _____
2. _____

Whether an organization manufactures a product or provides a service it must be concerned with the production/operations process that takes raw materials, combines them with _____(1) and _____(2), then produces goods or services.

3. _____
4. _____
5. _____
6. _____

To create a good or service from raw materials, equipment, and people there are several fucntions which any organization must perform: obtaining and storing raw _____(3), scheduling _____(4) and _____(5), creating _____(6) goods and/or services.

Creating finished goods and services

7. _____
8. _____

Obtaining _____(7) materials and scheduling _____(8) and equipment sets the stage for production of the good or service.

9. _____

_____(9) layout requires an assembly line set up with parts and components gathered at the required places along the line.

10. _____

_____-_____(10) layout is used for intermittent production.

Planning production/operations activities

11. _____

The first step in production planning is forecasting expected _____(11).

12. _____
13. _____

The demand forecast is used to develop a _____(12) and _____(13) plan.

Controlling

14. _____

Basically, controlling is used to ensure that the plans are _____(14).

15. _____

Feedback paths are what carry information concerning _____(15) or problems in production or service operations back to the points where decisions can be made and corrective actions taken.

16. _____
17. _____

Production/operations control centers on _____(16) and quality _____(17).

Making forecasts

18. _____

In order to plan production, the first step beforehand is to forecast _____(18).

19. _____

Forecasting based on past data is called _____(19).

20. _____

One way to idenfity patterns in past data is time series _____(20).

21. _____
22. _____
23. _____

The idea behind time-series analysis is to take some past data and break out several individual components. These components are: _____(21), _____(22), _____(23), and random.

24. _____

A forecasting method that follows time, i.e., as new data is obtained and the newest value is added on and the oldest is dropped off, is called _____(24) average.

25. _____

To forecast using moving averages, we just take the most _____(25) average and use that as our forecast for the next time period.

26. _____ The idea behind a weighted moving average is that it puts more weight on _____(26) time periods.

27. _____ In moving average forecasting it is essential to "average out" the _____(27) components.

28. _____ To overcome the data storage problem in doing moving averages, mathematicians have developed a special form of weighted moving average, called _____(28) smoothing.

29. _____ Moving averages and exponential smoothing, two forecasting methods, both work by "averaging out" _____(29) components.

30. _____ However, in the process they also average out _____(30), _____(31),
31. _____ and _____(32) time-series components.
32. _____

33. _____ Moving averages and exponential smoothing are best used for _____-range(33) forecasting.

34. _____ The idea behind time-series analysis is to compare the variation in demand against _____(34).

35. _____ If demand for computer programs is dependent upon the number of computers in use, it is called the _____(35) variable.

36. _____ The essence of _____(36) analysis is to develop a formula which relates demand, the dependent variable, to the independent variable.

37. _____ A mathematical technique that minimizes the deviations from all data points is called _____-_____(37) analysis.

Establishing schedules

38. _____ The purpose of forecasting is to enable us to plan our _____/_____(38) activities.

39. _____ The purpose of scheduling per se is to ensure that the right _____(39)
40. _____ are done at the right _____(40) with the right items and/or
41. _____ _____(41).

42. _____ _____(42) scheduling is a first approximation to the detailed production schedule.

43. _____ The next step in planning after aggregate scheduling is master _____(43).

44. _____ Master scheduling is the detailed planning of those _____(44) or services which will be produced during the short-term.

45. _____ The master schedule is the result of a "_____(45) group's" needs
46. _____ being integrated with _____(46) capabilities and constraints.

47. _____ Marketing needs are viewed by the production-planning analysts in terms
48. _____ of the associated _____(47) needs, _____(48) loads, and
49. _____ _____(49) availabilities.

50. _____ The master schedule plans the _____(50) of each finished product or service.

51. _____ _____-_____(51) planning uses a master schedule to determine when and how many component parts must be ordered to ensure a smooth and sufficient flow of finished products or services.

52. _____ In order to have the most economic amount of capacity available to meet production or service demands, managers need to do _____-planning(52).

53. _____   In manufacturing operations, capacity is usually measured in terms of standard _____(53).

54. _____   Standard time is a measure of work _____(54). To obtain it, several
55. _____   adjustments must be made to clock time. The first adjustment is for
56. _____   _____(55) availability. The second adjustment is for operator _____(56).

57. _____   Standard time measures both resource _____(57) and efficiency of
58. _____   resource _____(58).

59. _____   To determine how much capacity and on which machines, you need two
60. _____   pieces of information. The first, is usually called a _____(59) sheet. The second, a bill of _____(60), indicates how many standard hours are needed on each machine to make one part.

61. _____   A _____(61) chart graphically depicts the routing or scheduling of a production/operations sequence.

62. _____   A network chart that breaks down production/operations into a series of small subactivities is called a _____(62).

Controlling inventories

63. _____   The demand for finished goods inventory is called _____(63) demand.

64. _____   Demand that depends on the production of finished items is called _____(64) demand.

65. _____   Two major costs associated with carrying inventory are the cost of
66. _____   _____(65) the inventory, and _____(66) cost.

67. _____   Two costs, _____(67) and _____(68), are constantly balancing
68. _____   each other.

69. _____   The total of these two costs is minimized when the two are _____(69).

70. _____   The minimum total cost is achieved when the quantity ordered each time is at _____ -order(70) quantity.

71. _____   The EOQ formula is based on _____(71) demand.

72. _____   When planned orders are the same as net requirements, just "offset" by the lead time, the approach is called "_____-_____-_____(72)."

73. _____   Recently, the Japanese have created quite a stir with something called _____(73).

74. _____   "Kanban" means _____-_____-_____(74) delivery of parts.

Controlling quality

75. _____   Meeting customer expectations in products or services is called _____(75) control.

76. _____   Inspection in small batches is called inspection by _____(76).

77. _____   Statistical methods are a good way of checking for _____(77); how-
78. _____   ever, they do not indicate how to _____(78) defects in the first place.

79. _____   _____(79) assurance is the process of preventing the production of defective products or services.

80. _____   A group of employees who meet periodically to discuss ways of improving the quality of their products or services is called a quality control _____(80).

81. _____   The tool that is bringing technology to the fore in control is the
                        _____(81).

82. _____   Whatever the setting, the essential argument is that productivity without
                        effective _____/_____(82) planning and control is not possible
                        for any organization.

TESTING YOUR KNOWLEDGE

True and False Self Test

Directions: Circle the letter (T or F) of the correct response for each of the following statements.

T   F   1. The reason for forecasting expected demand is to get an idea of what will happen in the future.

T   F   2. The demand forecast is used to develop a production/operations plan.

T   F   3. Basically, controlling as a function is used to help whip sluggish employees into action.

T   F   4. In time-series analysis "components" are looked at as a collective whole.

T   F   5. In using moving averages to forecast, all you do is average past data over a specific time period.

T   F   6. The idea behind weighted moving average is to put more emphasis on early, less recent time periods.

T   F   7. In moving average it is essential to "average in" the random components.

T   F   8. We cannot forecast a random component.

T   F   9. Demand can be postponed by backordering.

T   F   10. Aggregate planning is a first approximation to the detailed production schedule.

Multiple Choice Self Test

Directions: Circle the letter of the response that best completes each of the following statements.

1. To generate a good or service from raw material, which function(s) must be performed?
   a. Obtaining raw material
   b. Storing raw material
   c. Scheduling people and equipment
   d. Transforming raw materials
   e. All of the above

2. The first step in production planning is:
   a. organizing equipment
   b. staffing
   c. forecasting demand
   d. ordering raw materials

3. The component(s) to be found in time-series analysis is/are:
   a. trends
   b. seasonal factors
   c. cyclical factors
   d. random factors
   e. all of the above

4. Demand can be legitimately smoothed out by:
    a. inventorying
    b. backordering
    c. shipping low quality goods
    d. having sales people fib about delivery dates
    e. **a** and **b** only

5. In manufacturing operations capacity is usually measured in terms of standard:
    a. kilowatts
    b. units
    c. hours
    d. input/outputs

6. To obtain standard time in production an adjustment may be needed in:
    a. machine availability
    b. operator efficiency
    c. management effectiveness
    d. employee motivation
    e. **a** and **b** only

7. The greatest cost of carrying inventory is:
    a. wasted space
    b. wasted time
    c. capital cost
    d. shrinkage

8. The other "great" cost of inventory is the cost of:
    a. theft
    b. waste
    c. shrinkage
    d. getting enough, on time

9. Recently the Japanese have created quite a stir with Kanban which is:
    a. a new soft drink
    b. a way to quit smoking
    c. "just-in-time" delivery
    d. none of the above

10. Meeting customer expectations in products or services is called:
    a. pampering
    b. "wining and dining"
    c. guesswork
    d. quality control

Matching Self Test

Directions: Write the letter of the description that best fits each numbered item in the blank provided.

_____ 1. Product layout

_____ 2. Process layout

_____ 3. Feedback path

_____ 4. Quality control

_____ 5. Extrapolating

_____ 6. Time-series analysis

_____ 7. Moving average

_____ 8. Weighted moving average

_____ 9. Exponential smoothing

_____ 10. Regression

a. When similar equipment or facilities are grouped together in work centers.

b. Taking past data at intervals to look for trends.

c. When all equipment and people are set up to facilitate flow.

d. Forecasting based on past data.

e. Helps ensure that a good or service is acceptable to the customer.

f. The device that carries information concerning deviations from plans.

g. A way of forecasting that includes past data from several time periods.

h. Puts more emphasis on recent times and data when forecasting.

i. Developing a formula in forecasting which relates demand, the dependent variable, to the independent variable.

j. Taking your constant factor in forecasting (alpha) and mathematically weighing more recent factors.

LEARNING ACTIVITIES — PART 5

Number 1 — Supplemental Reading and Discussion

Directions: Read the following journal article and complete the questions that follow.

LEADERSHIP, MANAGEMENT, AND THE SEVEN KEYS

In recent years a good deal of excitement has grown around the implications and significance of the 7-S organizational framework,[1] stemming both from the insights the system yields into organizational effectiveness and from the explanation it provides for consistently outstanding performance by excellent companies.[2]

In brief, the theory holds that the traditional view of organizations pivots on three axes: *strategy,* which leads almost implicitly to organization *structure,* and *systems* which orchestrate complex functions resulting in performance. The 7-S construct, by contrast, suggests that four additional S's are critical to achieving and understanding the effectiveness of excellent management: *style,* the patterns of action, symbolic and actual, which top management communicates to the organization at large, and which the organization itself ultimately adopts as a cultural orientation; *staff,* meaning the people side of the organization equation, especially the socialization and development process which molds managers into effective, acculturated performers; *skills,* the company's unique competences and dominating attributes; and *superordinate (or shared) goals,* the set of values or aspirations which underpin what a company stands for and believes in.[3]

The significance of the new framework (as others have stated) is in the attention it draws to the "soft," informal facets of organization which formerly were considered insufficiently systematic or "hard" to be of interest. The traditional approach focuses on the relatively easy-to-change strategy, structure, and systems, while the new approach alerts us to the crucial role played by the more elusive features.

The key factors distinguishing the 7-S framework from the traditional approach to organizational effectiveness, in fact, focus on the change levers which leaders, as distinct from managers, have always manipulated to effect organizational change and to achieve superior performance. By extension, much of what the 7-S approach embodies is the direct result of observing organizations run by leaders as opposed to managers.

The implications of this perspective are manifold. For example:

- If one believes that there is a difference between leadership and management, then there is some question as to whether managers can achieve 7-S performance at all.
- Society produces far fewer leaders than it does managers. The socialization process which cultivates managers also reinforces tradition, whereas leaders succeed in making change.
- Some cultures more naturally incline toward utilization of both the hard and the soft levers to effect change and achieve performance. This, in fact, has been called the "art of Japanese management." Does this imply that certain cultures are more naturally adept at creating leaders than others?
- Achieving 7-S management is a long-term undertaking. There is some question as to whether the predominantly short-term orientation of American management can be modified sufficiently to make the transition successfully.
- Finally, our management education system reinforces the traditional view of organization performance. The relative novelty of the 7-S framework makes it unlikely that the approach will be adopted quickly by the educational system.

These issues, while indeed speculative, are worth raising because it is easy to embrace new techniques and approaches as panaceas before fully appreciating their implications. Thus they are put forth as cautions. This having been said, let us return to the distinctions between leadership and management.

The seminal work on the difference between leadership and management is Abraham Zaleznik's 1977 McKinsey award-winning contribution.[4] Zaleznik explores the distinctions in attitudes toward goals, conceptions of work, relations with others, senses of self, and manner of development. Using these basic headings, I will underscore the correspondence between the leader's broad focus on multiple elements of the seven keys, and contrast this with the manager's traditional attention to the more limited set of organization factors.

Attitudes Toward Goals

Goal-setting is a central element in the guidance of organizational achievement. Through setting an overall target on performance and focusing group effort, the executive—leader or manager—implicitly concentrates organizational energies in a given direction.

Zaleznik argues that "Managers tend to adopt impersonal, if not passive, attitudes toward goals. Managerial goals arise out of necessities rather than desires, and, therefore, are deeply embedded in the history and culture of the organization."[5] In contrast, leaders "are active instead of reactive, shaping ideas instead of responding to them. Leaders adopt a personal and active attitude toward goals. The influence a leader exerts in altering moods, in evoking images and expectations, and in establishing specific desires and objectives determines the direction a business takes. The net result is to change the way people think about what is desirable, possible and necessary."[6]

This fundamental distinction in goal-setting attitudes is expressed in the way goals are set in organizations and in the goals which result. The *manager* is more likely to identify threats and opportunities and mobilize to respond to them in a systematic fashion through focus on *strategy*. The *leader,* on the other hand, tends to define a *superordinate goal,* such as product leadership, quality, service, or being number one; in working to achieve that goal, the leader commands outstanding performance. To leaders, strategy is the overall pattern of executing goal achievement. Managers are more likely to see strategy, or a component of it, such as product differentiation or lowest cost, as the overriding issue, rather than the corporate goal itself. Semantics plays a part, but not a big one: lowest cost is a strategy; "number one" is a value.

In McKinsey's studies of excellent companies Thomas Peters states, "The operating principle at well-managed companies is to do one thing well. At IBM, the all-pervasive value is customer service. At Dana it is productivity improvement. At 3M and H-P it is new product development. At P&G it is product quality. At McDonald's it is customer service, quality, cleanliness and value . . . At all these companies, the values are pursued with an almost religous zeal . . ."[7]

Conceptions of Work

Irrespective of how goals are set, organizations must deal, operationally, with the mundane details of getting things done. They must organize and execute the thousands of tasks which, collectively, result in performance, for better or for worse. In the course of this activity, there are decisions made, resources allocated, and positions taken which, in

substance, form the work of the organization. In this context, Zaleznik underscores distinctions between managers and leaders in the areas of choice and risk-taking.

"In order to get people to accept solutions to problems, managers need to coordinate and balance continually . . . The manager aims at shifting balances of power toward solutions acceptable as a compromise among conflicting values."[8] The leader, alternatively, "needs to project his ideas into images that excite people, and only then develop choices that give the projected images substance. Consequently, leaders create excitement in work . . . [U]nless expectations are aroused and mobilized, with all the expectations inherent in heightened desire, new thinking and new choice can never come to light."[9]

These conceptions of work manifest themselves both in managed and in led organizations: Leaders are inclined to make work exciting by encouraging an organizational *style* that is intuitive, highly personal, and tied in closely to the "carrots" that motivate key players to perform. Moreover, the leader's company is more likely to promote entrepreneurial autonomy at appropriately low levels in the organization, as a way of motivating people to make choices for themselves which, collectively, improve the performance of the whole. Peters reports: "Well-managed companies authorize their managers to act like entrepreneurs . . . As a result, these managers develop unusual programs with results that far exceed those of a division or corporate staff."[10] In so doing, leaders use *structure* to advantage as a motivational extension of their leadership style.

Inherent in the decentralized structure is a higher level of risk, since the choices made are more removed from the leader's direct control. A higher degree of remoteness from operating decisions is accepted by leaders, because they tend to "work from high-risk positions, indeed often are temporarily disposed to seek out risk and danger, especially where opportunity and reward appear high."[11] Thus, in the leader's *style* we see an inherent capacity to invest faith in people's desire to respond to excitement, risk and opportunity. This faith can only exist, however, when the leader has assembled appropriate staff and skills necessary to ensure high levels of performance. In consequence, the leader is more comfortable placing his faith in his own or in his key executive's judgment than in analysis, quantitative methods, and other potential assurances. He knows the difference between "computer printout" decisions and "cigar and brandy" decisions and is comfortable with either when he has faith in the people involved or in his own judgement. Because he is willing to take risks on people, the leader depends less on *structure* to dampen the impact of risk, and even less on *systems* to gather information and to make things happen.

Managers, alternatively, in their need to coordinate and balance, place a great deal of faith in *systems* and *structures.* Thus, we see managers' companies *dominated* by planning, forecasting, capital budgeting, and other systems which, at the extreme, can actually supplant judgment.

From the standpoint of risk, Zaleznik points out that for "those who become managers, the instinct for survival dominates their need for risk, and their ability to tolerate mundane, practical work assists their survival."[12] Again we see systems coming to the rescue, with major challenges or unique opportunities continually staffed out for study and analysis, and returned with balanced (read: low-risk) recommendations. Similarly, an overly managerial environment tends to be one in which new ideas wither and die, largely because top management is perceived as so risk-averse that venturesome ideas are viewed as having little chance of approval.

Relations with Others

Human relationships, in one form or another, are the essential ingredients of organization performance. The manner in which these relationships unfold and operate in the organization determines the quality of organizational performance. As expected, managers and leaders see their relations with others differently.

Zaleznik tells us managers seek out activities with people, but at the same time, "maintain a low level of emotional involvement in these relationships . . . The manager's orientation to people, as actors in a sequence of events, deflects his or her attention away from the substance of people's concerns and toward their roles in a process."[13] Leaders, on the other hand, empathize, "Empathy is not simply a matter of paying attention to other people. It is also the capacity to take in emotional signals and to make them mean something in a relationship with an individual . . . The distinction is simply between a manager's attention to *how* things get done and a leader's to *what* the events and decisions mean."[14]

Again, the manager's emphasis is on *systems,* possibly even viewing people as part of a framework of processes, while the leader's focus is on meaning as the foundation of motivation. The ability to empathize, to receive and send signals, and to impute meaning to work are all elements of the leader's *style* and *skill,* constituting his mastery of the soft S's of effectiveness.

Another facet of relationships with others concerns the manager's striving to convert win-lose decisions into win-win situations through compromise. On its face, this seems desirable, but in practice, Zaleznik observes, the result is defective both in the manner of achievement and in the choices which ultimately emerge. Specifically, Zaleznik identifies three tactics by which managers seek to convert win-lose to win-win decisions:

- Focus on procedure, not substance.
- Use of indirect signals rather than direct messages.
- Manipulation of time and delay to reduce the sting of losing.

The ultimate result is an organization steeped in bureaucracy (emphasis on structure) and political intrigue.

The focus of leadership in the face of win-lose decisions stands in sharp relief. Leaders are more apt to cast situations in their worst case form. They are more likely to face reality, make hard decisions, and absorb their consequences. Perhaps because of this, Zaleznik asserts leaders "attract strong feelings of identity and difference, or of love and hate . . . leader-dominated structures often appear turbulent, intense, and at times even disorganized. Such an atmosphere intensifies individual motivation . . . ."[15] Here, again, the leader's style plays a crucial role.

Senses of Self

Much of the distinction between managers and leaders stems from differences in their perceptions of themselves. "Managers see themselves as conservators and regulators of an existing order of affairs with which they personally identify and from which they gain rewards. Perpetuating and strengthening existing institutions enhances a manager's sense of self-worth: he or she is performing in a role that harmonizes with the ideals of duty and responsibility."[16]

The implication of this is that profound change—perhaps even when it is most emphatically needed for the survival of a company—is not normally within the province of managers. This may be one reason why so often a dramatic shift in corporate focus is accompanied by a wholesale management change, as well. Conversely, when organizations achieve desired levels of performance—for example, after a turnaround or following a period of rapid growth—they appoint managers to install systems, procedures and structures designed to consolidate their positions. Managers, in the traditional sense, are not sought out to make change.

In contrast, Zaleznik sees leaders as working in, but never belonging to, organizations. "Their sense of who they are does not depend upon memberships, work roles, or other social indicators of identity . . . [They] search out opportunities for change. The methods to bring about change may be technological, political, or ideological, but the object is the same: to profoundly alter human economic and political relationships."[17]

In summary, these differences imply that leaders have an inherent inclination to utilize the soft S's of style, skills, staff and shared goals. Managers, alternatively, tend toward reliance on the traditional triad of strategy, structure, and systems. Organizationally, the extreme result is likely to be leader-run companies high in performance, energy, focus and motivation, in contrast to manager-run companies with mediocre performance, bureaucratic structures, and ponderous decision-making systems.

Conflict, Convergence and Culture

Ironically, the 7-S framework offers two contrasting perspectives on the future potential of management.

• First, if the points made in this article are valid, 7-S management is the province of leaders, and managers per se will not ordinarily be capable of achieving sufficicient mastery of all seven keys to attain consistently superb performance.

• Alternatively, the framework suggests that the effects of leadership (or, at least, its visible instruments) can possibly be *developed consciously and applied systematically by managers* to beneficial effect, by paying attention to the soft as well as the hard S's.

Proponents of the new framework say it is indeed possible to make managers more effective by focusing attention on the soft seven keys. Conversely, the point can equally be made that leaders can become more effective managers by focusing more effort on the traditional strategy, structure, and systems. In this sense, the 7-S framework underscores the importance of balance, of attention to style, shared values, systems, structure, and so forth equally, in the enlightened interplay of the hard and the soft. The whole can become larger than the sum of the parts; management and leadership can be made to converge.

In practice, the best performing companies have, or have had, leaders at the top reinforcing values, lending style, molding staff, and developing unique skills. At the same time, in rare cases, these leaders also possess superior traditional managerial skills. Where both facets are not present in the same individual, hierarchy assumes great significance. For example, where the leader occupies high position, managers below him are likely to be well-motivated and the organization's performance correspondingly impressive. By contrast, when leader personalities work under traditional managers, there is likely to be friction and frustration, ultimately resulting in high turnover. The key complaints of those leaving are an inability to get ideas heard, perception of threats or opportunities unheeded by the firm at large, and a prevailing managerial attitude prone to delusions about competitive realities or internal capabilities.

It is in countering the negative impact of these potential conflicts that particularly creative organizations are apparently successful. Excellent companies encourage ideas from all quarters. They keep structures lean and simple and encourage operational autonomy.[18]

On the issue of culture and its impact (whether Japan, for example, is more likely to produce leaders than the West), the 7-S framework offers important insights. First good management does not depend on the presence of leadership, although in many cases, it is enhanced by leadership qualities. What is crucial is the presence of the soft and the hard instruments in balance. Second, the Japanese are, apparently, more inclined to use the soft tests of management—as an extension of their cultural norms—than are Western managers whose culture stresses different values.[19] Third, managerial performance is multivariate. Culture certainly plays a part, but what is more significant is that excellent performance in organizations in Japan or in the West depends upon achieving harmony among all seven keys to organization.

The awareness created by the 7-S approach to organizational effectiveness should benefit organizations run by either leaders or traditional managers, as we have used the terms. Outstanding companies are distinguished not by the leaders who head them or by the managers who run them, but rather by the manner in which leadership and management are harmonized to create a climate in which work is both uncommonly meaningful and unusually effective.

Source: Craig M. Watson, "Leadership, Management, and the Seven Keys," *Business Horizons,* March-April 1983, pp. 8-13.

Notes to the article:

[1]Robert H. Waterman, Jr., Thomas J. Peters, and Julien R. Phillips, "Structure Is Not Organization," *Business Horizons,* June 1980: 14-26.

[2]See, for example, Thomas J. Peters, "Putting Excellence Into Management," *The McKinsey Quarterly,* Autumn 1980: 31-41, and Anthony G. Athos and Richard Pascale, *The Art of Japanese Management* (New York: Simon & Schuster, 1981).

[3]Each of the seven S's is defined more fully in "Structure Is Not Organization" (see note 1). Also, see Robert H. Waterman, Jr., "The Seven Elements of Strategic Fit," *The Journal of Business Strategy,* Winter 1982: 69-73.

[4]Abraham Zaleznik, "Managers and Leaders: Are They Different?" *Harvard Business Review,* May-June 1977: 67-78.

[5]Zaleznik: 70.   [6]Zaleznik: 74.   [7]Peters: 88.   [8]Zaleznik: 72.   [9]Zaleznik.   [10]Peters.

[11]Zaleznik.   [12]Zaleznik: 73.   [13]Zaleznik.   [14]Zaleznik: 74.   [15]Zaleznik.   [16]Zaleznik: 75.

[17]Zaleznik.   [18]Peters: 32.   [19]Athos and Pascale.

Questions for Discussion

1. The traditional view of organization is based on a theory that suggests organizations pivot on three axes. List the three axes.

2. The 7-S construct, by contrast, suggests that four additional S's are critical to achieving and understanding management. List these four S's.

3. What is the significance of the new framework of the four additional S's? Explain.

4. Under the 7-S theory differences are cited between "manager" and "leader." Define the differences and what is meant by using "soft levers" by leaders.

5. Cite differences in goal-setting attitudes between the traditional manager and a true leader.

6. Cite differences between managers and leaders in terms of their conceptions of work.

7. Cite differences between managers and leaders in their relations with others.

8. Cite differences between managers and leaders in terms of their image of self.

9. What is meant in the statement that leaders in contrast to managers work in the organization, but never belong to it?

10. What are the implications for the future for managers and leaders in utilizing the 7-S's of framework of management?

Number 2 — Exercise: Budgeting

Introduction: Businesses cannot operate effectively without budgeting as a planning and controlling function. This statement is appropriate for individuals as well, and yet consumer advisers estimate that perhaps as many as 50% of adult wage earners do not budget their income. Do you? If not, this following exercise can be an important first step in getting control of your own financial affairs.

Directions: Given your present income, set up a budget for one short-term fiscal period, either a week or month. Do this budget as follows:

1. List in a tabular format, your major expenditure areas as shown below: food, clothing, housing, transportation, etc. Should you also list savings?
2. At the start of the fiscal period, list the budgeted dollar amount you intend to spend for each area.
3. During the fiscal period keep track of every expenditure by listing it under the appropriate budget column. Do this "religiously."
4. At the end of the fiscal period, add actual expenditures and compare with the original budgeted amounts.
5. Finally, identify problem areas, take steps to correct problems, and do another budget.

See chart on following page.

Number 3 — Exercise: Monitoring Interruptions; Getting Control

Introduction: One of the most common out-of-control problems people face both in their personal lives and their formal organization lives is interruptions. An interruption is defined as anything that halts us from doing an on-going activity, particularly one that is planned and goal-oriented. Interruptions are so commonplace that you probably don't even recognize the subtle ones and don't realize how much time they usurp from your life.

Directions: Use the interrupter chart below to monitor your interruptions for at least one "normal" day. Then summarize the results, identify correctable problems, and suggest solutions via the questions that follow the exercise. Note, under "reasons for the interruption" you may need to alter column headings to be more descriptive of your present situation. Also, "real time" refers to not just the time of the interruption, but how long it took to get back to your planned activity.

Interrupter Chart

Name of interrupter		Real time consumed by interrupter	Reason for the interruption		If for business, was the interruption necessary?	
Interrupter (self)	Interrupter (name)	List minutes	Personal/social ( )	Business ( )	yes ( )	no ( )

Budget Form

	Food Budget	Clothing Budget	Housing Budget	Transportation Budget	Education Budget	Recreation Budget
A. Budgeted at start of fiscal period						
B. Actual expenditures during fiscal period	Date	Date	Date	Date	Date	Date
	1.	1.	1.	1.	1.	1.
	2.	2.	2.	2.	2.	2.
	3.	3.	3.	3.	3.	3.
	4.	4.	4.	4.	4.	4.
	5.	5.	5.	5.	5.	5.
	6.	6.	6.	6.	6.	6.
	7.	7.	7.	7.	7.	7.
	8.	8.	8.	8.	8.	8.
	9.	9.	9.	9.	9.	9.
	10.	10.	10.	10.	10.	10.
	11.	11.	11.	11.	11.	11.
	12.	12.	12.	12.	12.	12.
	13.	13.	13.	13.	13.	13.
	14.	14.	14.	14.	14.	14.
	15.	15.	15.	15.	15.	15.
	16.	16.	16.	16.	16.	16.
	17.	17.	17.	17.	17.	17.
	18.	18.	18.	18.	18.	18.
	19.	19.	19.	19.	19.	19.
	20.	20.	20.	20.	20.	20.
	21.	21.	21.	21.	21.	21.
	22.	22.	22.	22.	22.	22.
	23.	23.	23.	23.	23.	23.
	24.	24.	24.	24.	24.	24.
	25.	25.	25.	25.	25.	25.
	26.	26.	26.	26.	26.	26.
	27.	27.	27.	27.	27.	27.
	28.	28.	28.	28.	28.	28.
	29.	29.	29.	29.	29.	29.
	30.	30.	30.	30.	30.	30.
	31.	31.	31.	31.	31.	31.
Total Expenditures						

Questions for Discussion

1. Who or what is your predominant interrupter source?

2. What is the total of "real time" lost column? What percent of the day does it represent?

3. Summarize the reasons for the interruptions columns, and even for the business or other seemingly important interruptive reasons, list how many were nevertheless really unnecessary.

4. How often were you the interrupter? You might find it interesting to repeat questions 1-3 with you being the ER.

5. Identify which interruptions in the exercise are definitely unnecessary and controllable. List at least one thing you might do to stop, or at least limit some of the "problem" interruptions above.

Number 4 — Exercise: Controlling Interruptions

Introduction: In the previous exercise you were provided a means of monitoring interruptions, an important aspect of gaining greater control of your life. Monitoring is not enough, however. You need to take corrective action regarding the meaningless interruptions that waste your time and throw you out of control.

Directions: Clarify your interruption problems through the following interruption analysis exercise. There are three boxes in the interruption correction process in which you need to both analyze current problems and to suggest solutions.

Interruption Analysis

Three Boxes in the Interruption Correction Process

Antecedent: The things in the setting that went on before that allowed the interruption to occur.	Interruption: The description of what actually took place in the process.	Reinforcement by you: Any positive or even neutral feedback that you are giving ER which encourages the interruptive behavior.

Antecedents	Interruption description	Reinforcement
1. List antecedents.	1. List or describe the interruptive scenario.	1. List what reinforcements you are giving.
2. List needed alterations in the antecedent setting.	2. Identify any controllables here that you could use to reduce the time consumed.	2. List ways to provide negative reinforcement.

Now, go on to the next page for "tips" on handling interrupters, and add your own ideas to the list.

Tips on Handling Interrupters

<u>Altering antecedents and the favorable climate</u>

1. Hang "Do not disturb!" signs on your desk
2. Hide
3. Wear ear muffs
4. Move away from heavy traffic areas
5. Turn your desk to avoid eye contact
6. Make your interrupter chart visible

<u>When it's too late, and you are trapped</u>

1. Vomit on the ER's shoes (not very elegant)
2. Tell ER that you have been exposed to a very contagious disease
3. Rise immediately when ER starts to talk and move into the doorway
4. Don't develop eye contact
5. Don't smile or nod approvingly
6. Place a button under your desk which you can press to simulate your own phone ring so as to interrupt yourself
7. Hand the ER something heavy to hold while you continue your work

<u>Closing on the ER</u>

1. After one minute of listening to ER, summarize in 10 words or less what s/he has said, and add that you have already heard the same thing twice
2. Walk out of the room
3. Introduce a second approaching ER to the first, and let them converse while you go on with what you need to do
4. Politely tell the ER to leave
5. After 10 minutes present a bill to ER for your consultative services

<u>Number 5 — Matching Wits with the Experts</u>
  (Matching time wasters with professional managers)

Introduction: One aspect of control comes under the heading of time management. Managers are under continuous pressure to manage their time well and thereby stay in control.

Directions: Write down your list (perhaps 10 to 15 things) of major time wasters below; then turn the page and compare your list with four different groups of professional managers.

<u>Your List of Time Wasters</u>

1.	11.
2.	12.
3.	13.
4.	14.
5.	15.
6.	16.
7.	17.
8.	18.
9.	19.
10.	20.

Time Wasters of Four Groups of Top Managers*

Group A: German Managers
Group B: College Presidents
Group C: Canadian Military Officers
Group D: Black Leaders of a Religious Organization

Group A

Unclear objectives
Poor information
Postponed decisions
Procrastination
Lack of information
Lack of feedback
Routine work
Too much reading
Interruptions
Telephone
No time planning
Meetings
Beautiful secretaries
Lack of competent personnel
Lack of delegation
Lack of self-discipline
Visitors
Training new staff
Lack of priorities
Management by crisis

Group C

Trash mail
Socializing
Unnecessary meetings
Lack of concentration
Lack of mangerial tools
Peer demands on time
Incompetent subordinates
Coffee breaks
Crisis management
Unintelligible communications
Procrastination
Lack of clerical staff
Poor physical fitness
Red tape
Pet projects
Lack of priorities

Group B

Scheduled meetings
Unscheduled meetings
Lack of priorities
Failure to delegate
Interruptions
Unavailability of people
Junk mail
Lack of planning
Outside (civic) demands
Poor filing system
Fatigue
Procrastination
Telephone
Questionnaires
Lack of procedure for routine matters

Group D

Attempting too much at once
Lack of delegation
Talking too much
Inconsistent actions
No priorities
Span of control
Usurped authority
Can't say no
Lack of planning
Snap decisions
Procrastination
Low morale
Mistakes
Disorganized secretaries
Poor communications
Overoptimism
Responsibility without authority

---

*Source of Time Wasters: Alec R. Mackenzie, *The Time Trap*, McGraw-Hill Book Company, 1975.

Discussion

1.   List your time wasters that overlap with those of experienced managers.

2.   Explain why these time wasters occur: that is, what control mechanisms are missing in your setting.

3.   Regarding some of the common time wasters among the four lists and your own, what specific ideas from the control chapters do you feel would help overcome certain time wasters? List and discuss.

Number 6 — Experiential Learning Exercise

The Out of Control Small Group

(Dealing with a Tardy Party)

Introduction: The following organizational control problem can be done either as an individual exercise or an in-class experiential activity. Read the situation and become familiar with the individuals involved, and then follow the directions at the end of the descriptive material.

The Out of Control Small Group

(Role Play)

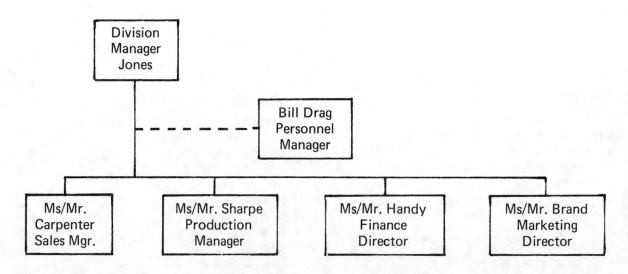

Bill Drag, a very productive employee, has just arrived at the weekly staff meeting ten minutes late again for the third week in a row. Everyone else has been on time, if not a few minutes early. The staff consists of those people illustrated in the above chart showing four people in traditional line configuration and Bill Drag in a staff slot as personnel manager.

Bill's routine excuse includes something to the effect that he cannot break away at a precise time when he is involved in his personnel work. Supervisor Jones has privately chided Drag for being late, but this has not changed Drag's behavior pattern.

The other four members have become increasingly concerned and irritated with Drag's tardiness, especially since he was the one who earlier set up the time management program in which they all participated.

Lateness is sort of ironic since the agenda passed out to the group for today's meeting included the list of discussion questions below regarding what ways control might be improved.

Character Descriptions for Role Playing

Division Manager Jones: You are very open, a nonauthoritarian manager, and this style has worked very well with your line and staff personnel. Drag's lateness has been an issue not previously aired in the group since you felt before today that it was between him and you. Having failed to get Drag's behavior pattern altered by twice mildly scolding him you are now open to group discussion. However, you will not open such discussion. It must come from someone in the group, and it must be handled constructively without name-calling.

Drag has been highly productive in your division in personnel matters, especially in bringing in new training ideas. His ideas, however, have not always been fully appreciated by the busy line people who, in the face of short-term deadlines, have disliked participating in time-consuming training.

You feel that the once-per-week meetings are necessary and productive. No one has challenged you on the frequency of these meetings.

Bill Drag: As Personnel Manager you feel very strongly that you should be treated as "staff," not "line." This position relates uniquely to line people. While equal to others on the organization chart, "Staff" means that you serve in an advisory and/or service roll to the line departments shown. Therefore, if your division manager lets the group discuss lateness as a control topic you will object strongly.

One reason that you will object to group discussion is that the matter really should be between you and Jones. Secondly, you feel that if the line members query you on lateness or attempt to direct you on ways to improve, they will be undermining your effectiveness as a staff person.

Your role, then, is to jump in early and suggest to Jones (if indeed lateness is aired) that this matter is between you and him.

Facts regarding your lateness are:

1. Three weeks ago you were late when you arrived after an overextended lunch meeting with another personnel representative from another division of your company.
2. Last week you were late after getting caught with one of your own recruiters who stopped you in the hall about some important business.
3. This week you simply weren't watching the clock.

Carpenter—Sales Manager: You supervise fifteen sales people who you feel were productive before Drag ever introduced such training ideas as time management. However, now that you and your sales force are on a time program, you aren't going to let Drag get by with this lateness. You are going to insist that:

1. The group does air the matter and tell Drag how you feel.
2. Drag apologize properly for his tardiness.
3. Drag ensure the group that he'll correct his ways or face discipline.

Since you once wanted the personnel job held by Drag, but were bypassed when Drag was hired, you aren't going to hold back at this time.

Sharpe—Production Manager: You don't particularly like Drag, although you must admit that some of his ideas in training have improved production.

You have always felt somewhat intimidated by Drag's forcefulness and verbal articulation. Great gift with the gab! You are not sure how the tardiness issue should be handled, but if one of the other people wants to push the issue, you will be a willing participant. Drag always seems to be getting some company or community recognition. Just once you would like to see the guy revealed as human, who isn't any better than anyone else!

Hardy—Finance Director: As a finance and accounting person you enjoy balancing accounting ledgers, but you strongly dislike these staff meetings. You see no reason that meetings should be held weekly, and this seems to be a good time to raise the issue. You feel that these meetings could be held less frequently, and you can sympathize with Drag, and readily overlook his tardiness. You've been tempted to skip entire meetings. Sure, they are productive meetings, but you feel they could be held less frequently. You intend to:

1.   Raise the issue of too many meetings.
2.   Suggest substituting memos for meetings.
3.   Compliment Drag on his oustanding work in the company.

Brand—Marketing Director: As the newly-hired marketing director, you are primarily here to listen and learn as much as you can about the company and these key colleagues. Getting to know personalities will be helpful to you as you make your way in the company. You will not criticize Drag, and you will support Jones on whatever stance he takes. You intend to:

1.   Clarify issues.
2.   Arbitrate differences.
3.   Avoid taking sides.

Directions: First you should try to role play this scenario using the brief personality sketches and roles ascribed to each person. Of course, each personality gets revealed here in print, and it might be more interesting to let each role player create his/her own perspective within the context of the case so that the interacting styles won't be quite so predictable.

Groups of six people should be set up and each member assigned a role. Once the division manager is identified he or she can actually go through the organizing of a meeting, establishing an agenda, and encouraging discussion regarding ways to improve control.

The discussion questions below can be used. Of course, the role group should begin minus Bill Drag so that his late arrival is actually done after the group has started the discussion. His late arrival, therefore, should be somewhat interruptive.

A seventh person can be assigned to each group as a recorder of events that take place in the groups. In particular, make note of out-of-control symptoms either of members or of the group or both.

Discussion Questions

Answer the following discussion questions which are appropriate for either the role play group or for using the situation above as an individual case.

1.   Why is controlling an important management function?

2.   In what ways is controlling related to other management functions such as planning, organizing, and leading?

3.   What specific controlling methods and tools can organizations use to improve operations?

4.   Which of the text's "forces" in controlling are particularly germane to the case situation above?

5.   Regarding the case situation, in what ways would the text's "four basic elements in the control process" be helpful in dealing with the group's various out-of-control symptoms? More specifically, cite examples of what performance goals and standards might be used here, and how actual monitoring of performance might be done.

6.   Regarding Bill Drag's behavior, how might performance appraisal concepts be utilized here?

LOOKING BACK; LOOKING AHEAD

Part 5 dealt with the last of the major management functions, controlling, the process of monitoring performance and taking corrective action to insure desired results. It was stressed by the author that control is needed to make sure that actual performance is consistent with intentions and that organizational objectives are met. The text offered methods for managers to execute control, and linked other key functions such as planning and organizing to the controlling function. In other words, good planning and organizing to the controlling function. In other words, good planning and organizing as well as managerial leadership are ingredients in the formula for control.

Particular emphasis was put on budgeting as a critical managerial tool, and "management information systems" served to link controlling to the last chapter in Part 5 dealing with production and overall operations.

In Part 6, your attention will be turned to a variety of management challenges under the "contemporary" time frame. Is the challenge of managing today and in the late eighties and beyond a different challenge than managing in the near or distant past? How so?

The author starts the "contemporary" theme by focusing on the managing of conflict, change, and organization development. You should find interesting the author's notion that conflict—constructive conflict—is not only a positive factor in organizations but perhaps necessary for maintaining organization vitality and individual development.

People and organizations resist change, and the material on change agentry on the part of managers is an interesting extension of previous material on leadership.

Labor-management relations in terms of such areas as collective bargaining and the traditional adversarial relationship between labor and management are carefully developed topics in Chapter 18. You may want to ponder the future of organized labor in the U.S. in terms of such developments as the rise of the service-oriented economy and fewer so-called "blue collar" jobs. In the future will nonmanagement employees in new high technology fields find it necessary to organize into unions?

The author explores for you the prospects of working in, perhaps managing in, the international arena. How is it different? How do different cultures and traditions impact upon business managers' decision making?

In covering the international setting, particularly where in certain countries payoffs and other questionable practices are done, the author leads into his last Part 6 chapter, on ethics and social responsibility. What is managerial ethics and what is managerial social responsibility? Does the U.S. and/or international business arena need a written formal code of ethics? These and other issues are adroitly addressed by your author in Part 6.

PART VI

PRODUCTIVITY IN
THE CONTEMPORARY ENVIRONMENT

INTRODUCTION – PART 6

(Chapters 17 – 20)

<u>Highlights</u>

Part 6 places the challenges of management in a "contemporary" perspective. This attempt to make management material very current is not an easy task since we live and work in a world that is rapidly changing in some respects, yet standing still in others. In the U.S., for example, there is productive capacity in agriculture to feed many additional third world nations, yet starvation for many of these countries continues decade after decade. Thus, there is change in a contemporary sense, but no change in a historical sense, depending upon your birth place.

In Chapter 17, the author begins Part 6 of the text by writing about managing of conflict, change, and organizational development. The author's thesis statement emphasizes that organizations and managers must continually adjust and adapt to changing situations if they are to prosper and survive over time. To make change happen from the organization perspective requires innovation, creativity, and a marketing orientation. In Chapter 17 you will also learn that conflict is part of every organization, and that certain types of conflict breed the needed changes that help organizations survive. How have you changed over the past five years? What inner motivational factors have influenced your change, and what external factors? A personal orientation to this change topic seems inevitable since we are all change agents in one respect or another.

In Chapter 18, the text covers labor-management relations. To help you understand Chapter 18 you should recall the previous material on organizing and note the collective bargaining unit is also an organization. How does the collective bargaining unit fit within the managerial organization structure? Does it make organization life more complex? Yes, of course! And through this chapter you will learn about reasons nonmanagement people unite on their own even though as individuals they are already part of a formal work unit. Why are unions necessary? How do they function? How do labor and management relate and negotiate differences? These questions as well as many others get covered in the labor-management material.

Chapter 19 throws management into the international arena, and whether you want to be or not, you are part of this broader scenario. You are part of this international arena perhaps in what you drive, eat, or wear. Businesses today, large or small, must be conscious of the world at large as their managers make decisions for tomorrow. Of course, employees as well as managers of tomorrow's thriving organizations should have an understanding of the international business arena and comparative managerial styles. For example, are you aware of theory Z which has been ascribed to the Japanese style of managing? Why is it apparently successful? Would the Japanese style of consensus problem-solving work here in the U.S.?

What about other aspects of international business? Chapter 19 covers a variety of international issues—cultural values, economics, legal-political implications—which will broaden considerably your managerial knowledge.

A natural conclusion to Part 6 is the chapter on ethics and social responsibility related to managerial decision making. The author explains managerial ethics in the context of standards and principles and gives examples of ethical dilemmas faced by managers. You will find this chapter intriguing particularly if you put your own values and ethics in the context of your being an organizational representative. Do you have a "price," as someone once suggested about any one of us for which you would "sell your soul"? How strong are you in your convictions? Would you compromise them in terms of personal or corporate gain? Keep these questions in mind as you go through Chapter 20.

<u>Chapter Titles for Part 6</u>

Chapter 17 – Managing Conflict, Change, and Organization Development
Chapter 18 – Managing Industrial and Labor Relations
Chapter 19 – Managing in an International Arena
Chapter 20 – Managing With Ethics and Social Responsibility

CAREER PERSPECTIVE — PART 6

How Will Change Affect You and Your Career?

Change at an increasing rate seems certain for the future as various countries pursue economic growth and stability and thereby compete, and, in some cases, cooperate in terms of utilizing resources. The U.S., for example, finds itself challenged by the Japanese in high technology industries. China seems ready to open its walls to trade with the West. These are major trends, sometimes referred to as megatrends, that have important implications for you, particularly in terms of jobs and careers.

To what extent have you pondered megatrends in terms of their likely impact on your career and life style? The following list of megatrends and projected trends should be read by you and then responded to by you through two questions: (1) "In what way will this trend affect my career and life style?" and (2) "What, if anything, can I do now to take advantage of the trend?"

Megatrends *(current or conjectured)*	*In what way will the trend affect my career and life style?*	*What, if anything, can I do now to take advantage of the trend?*
1. Change itself will render much of one's education obsolete in just a few years.		
2. The U.S. is moving away from an industrial society toward being a service and information society.		
3. Manual labor will be replaced by robots.		
4. Unemployment for the unprepared will run 25% of the work force and be a lifelong experience for large portions of the population.		
5. Sharper socio/economic class distinctions between employed and not employed will develop.		
6. Crime rates will increase rendering some major cities unsafe in which to live.		
7. Pollution will "kill" major geographic sections of the U.S. rendering these areas unfit for humans as well as other life.		
8. Life spans will increase to the extent that perhaps 50% of the population will be over 65 years.		

Megatrends *(current or conjectured)*	*In what way will the trend affect my career and life style?*	*What, if anything, can I do now to take advantage of the trend?*
9. A nuclear accident will occur.		
10. People who work will no longer be employees but self-employed independent contractors.		
11. People won't "go" to work; they'll function employment-wise within their own dwelling.		
12. World wide trade, particularly with China and the Soviet bloc, will become commonplace.		
13. Half the working parents will be single.		
Others. You list and comment.		

17 Managing Conflict, Change, and Organization Development

STUDENT LEARNING OBJECTIVES

After completing the chapter material you should be able to:

1. Explain the importance of organizations and managers recognizing the need for and having the ability to change.
2. Define creativity and innovation and how they play a role in organizational change.
3. Contrast the difference between destructive and constructive conflict in organizations, and how each affects the development and change opportunities of the organization.
4. List and explain types of conflict that develop within the business/organizational environment, and describe ways management might deal with each type.
5. Define three different ways managers can address conflict: (a) nonattention, (b) suppression, (c) resolution.
6. Compare and contrast the text's two conflict management styles, cooperativeness and assertiveness.
7. Explain the manager's role as change agent, particularly in a planned change environment.
8. List and explain the planned change process, and what change strategies managers have at their disposal.
9. Explain resistance to change and how managers can deal with such resistance.
10. Define organizational development (OD) and the behavioral science principles which management must recognize.
11. Explain the text's OD model and OD interventions.

CHAPTER HIGHLIGHTS

Creativity and innovation in organizations
Conflicts in organizations
Conflict management
Organizational change
Managing planned change
Organizational development (OD)

PROGRAMMED LEARNING

The following statements are drawn from actual textbook content in abbreviated form. The blanks within the statements are numbered to correspond with the answer blanks at the left.

Creativity and innovation in organizations

1. _____

Organizations and managers must continually adapt to changing situations and be willing to initiate change if they are to prosper and even _____(1) over time.

2. _____
3. _____
4. _____

A healthy organization provides for and stimulates a free flow of information and interchange of _____(2), _____(3), and _____(4) among its members.

5. _____
6. _____

Managers must establish conditions for _____(5) and _____(6).

7. _____

Organizational _____(7) is the process of taking a new idea and putting it into practice as part of the organization's normal operating routines.

8. _____
9. _____
10. _____

From a practical perspective, an innovative organization is one that is able to: maintain a continuing influx of new _____(8); modify new ideas to fit organization _____(9); and _____(10) and reinforce new ideas as part of day-to-day operating routines.

Conflict in organizations

11. _____
12. _____
13. _____

Substantive conflicts in organizations involve disagreements over such things as _____(11), the allocation of _____(12), distribution of _____(13), policies and procedures, and job assignments.

14. _____

_____(14) conflicts result from feelings of anger, distrust, dislike, fear, and resentment, as well as from personality clashes.

15. _____

The type of conflict that works to the disadvantage of the individual(s) and/or organization(s) involved is called _____(15) conflict.

16. _____
17. _____
18. _____
19. _____
20. _____

Constructive conflict results in benefits rather than disadvantages for the individual(s) and/or organization(s) involved, such as: increased _____(16) and _____(17), increased _____(18), increased _____(19), and reduced _____(20).

Types of conflict situations

21. _____
22. _____
23. _____
24. _____

Typical managerial situations in which conflicts occur are: conflict within the _____(21), _____(22) or individual-to-individual conflict, _____(23) conflict, and _____(24) conflict.

25. _____
26. _____
27. _____
28. _____

Four individual conflict situations are: _____-_____(25) conflict, _____-_____(26) conflict, _____-_____(27) conflict, and _____(28) (multiple) approach-avoidance conflict.

29. _____
30. _____

Interpersonal conflict occurs among one or more individuals. It can be either _____(29) or _____(30) in nature, or both.

31. _____

Interorganization conflict is often referred to by the term _____(31).

32. _____
33. _____

Whether conflict works beneficially for the organization or not depends on two factors: the _____(32) of the conflict, and how well the conflict is _____(33).

Understanding conflict situations

34. _____
35. _____
36. _____
37. _____

Key factors to be considered in any conflict situation include differences over: _____(34), _____(35), _____(36), and _____(37).

38. _____
39. _____
40. _____
41. _____
42. _____

Stages of conflict include: _____(38) conditions, perceived and _____(39) conflict, _____(40) conflict, conflict _____(41) or supression, and conflict _____(42).

43. _____
44. _____
45. _____
46. _____

The antecedents of conflicts are often found in role _____(43), competition for scarce _____(44), task _____(45), communication _____(46), unresolved prior conflicts, and individual differences in perceptions, personality needs, values, and goals.

47. _____
48. _____

When conflict is felt, it achieves meaning in the sense that sufficient _____(47) exists such that there is a desire to reduce the _____(48).

49. _____

Conflict that is openly expressed is said to be _____(49).

50. _____

Manifest conflict can be resolved by correcting _____(50) conditions.

Conflict management

51. _____
52. _____
53. _____

Conflict can be addressed through: _____(51), _____(52), or _____(53).

54. _____

Conflict resolution only occurs when the _____(54) reasons are removed.

55. _____
56. _____

A person's "style" or approach to a conflict situation can be described in terms of relative emphasis on _____(55) and _____(56).

57. _____
58. _____
59. _____
60. _____
61. _____

There are five conflict management styles that result from various combinations of cooperativeness and assertiveness in conflict situations: _____(57), _____(58) or authoritative, _____(59) or smoothing; _____(60), _____(61) or problem-solving.

62. _____

Lose-lose conflict occurs when noone achieves his or her time _____(62).

63. _____

In _____-_____(63) conflict, one party achieves its desires to the exclusion of the other party's desires.

64. _____
65. _____

Win-win conflict is achieved by _____(64) of the issues and the use of _____-_____(65) to reconcile differences.

66. _____
67. _____

_____-_____(66) and _____(67) are often the most successful approaches to conflict resolution.

The manager as mediator

68. _____
69. _____
70. _____
71. _____

Managers can do a variety of things to actively intervene in an attempt to resolve conflict situations: appeal to _____(68) goals; expanding the _____(69) available to everyone; altering one or more _____(70) variables in a situation; and altering _____(71) variables.

Organizational change

72. _____

Managers who make things happen can be called _____(72) agents.

73. _____

Planned change is a direct response to someone's perception of a _____(73) gap.

74. _____

Formally speaking, _____(74) change involves some modification in the various components that constitute the essence of the organization itself.

75. _____
76. _____
77. _____
78. _____

Targets of organizational change, as shown in Table 17.5, include organizational purpose and _____(75), _____(76) tasks, _____(77), _____(78) and structures.

Managing planned change

79. _____
80. _____
81. _____

Kurt Lewin, a noted psychologist, recommends that any planned change effort be viewed as a three-phase process: _____(79), _____(80), and _____(81).

82. _____
83. _____
84. _____

Managers' strategies for getting other persons to adopt a desired change include: _____-_____(82), _____-_____(83), and _____-_____(84).

85. _____

When people resist change, they are defending something important which appears _____(85) by the change attempt.

86. _____
87. _____
88. _____
89. _____

Six general approaches to resistance to change include: education and _____(86), _____(87) and involvement, facilitation and _____(88), negotiation and _____(89), manipulation and co-optation, and explicit and implicit coercion.

Organization development (OD)

90. _____

The OD process begins with _____(90).

91. _____

Diagnosis leads to active _____(91) wherein change objectives are pursued through a variety of collaborative and specific activities.

92. _____

In the _____(92) stage of OD, changes are monitored, reinforced, and evaluated.

93. _____

OD _____(93) are activities initiated by consultants or managers in support of a comprehensive OD program.

94. _____
95. _____
96. _____
97. _____
98. _____
99. _____
100. _____

Interventions to improve individual effectiveness include: _____(94) training; management training, _____(95) negotiation, job _____(96), _____(97) planning, _____ _____(98), process _____(99), and inter-group _____ _____(100).

TESTING YOUR KNOWLEDGE

True and False Self Test

Directions: Circle the letter (T or F) of the correct response for each of the following statements.

T F 1. Organizational innovation is the process of taking a new idea and putting it into practice as part of the organization's normal operating routines.

T F 2. Destructive conflict results from feelings of anger, distrust, dislike, fear, and resentment.

T F 3. Conflict can enhance creativity and innovation in organizations.

T F 4. Whether conflict works beneficially for an organization or not depends on **who** is in conflict with each other.

T F 5. An example of inter-group conflict would be a disagreement between unions and organizations.

T F 6. Key factors to be considered in any conflict situation include differences over facts, methods, goals, and values.

T F 7. A force-coercion strategy uses the power bases of legitimacy, rewards, and punishments as primary inducements to change.

T F 8. Change agents using a normative-reeducative strategy attempt to bring about change through persuasion backed by special knowledge and rational argument.

T F 9. "Resistance" is viewed as something to be overcome in order for change to be successful.

T F 10. Organizational development interventions are activities initiated by consultants or managers in support of a comprehensive program.

Mulitple Choice Self Test

Directions: Circle the letter of the response that best completes each of the following statements.

1. A healthy organization provides for and stimulates a free flow interchange from its members of:
   a. criticisms
   b. suggestions
   c. ideas
   d. all of the above

2. From a practical perspective, an innovative organization is one that is able to:
   a. maintain a continuing influx of new ideas
   b. modify new ideas to fit organization needs
   c. implement and reinforce new ideas
   d. all of the above

3. Whenever disagreements exist in a social situation over issues of substance you are likely to have:
   a. conflict
   b. emergence of leadership
   c. game playing
   d. team building

4. Constructive conflict can result in which of the following:
   a. increased creativity and innovation
   b. increased employee effort
   c. increased group cohesion
   d. reduced interpersonal tension
   e. all of the above

5. When a person is forced to make a choice between equally unattractive goals this is labeled which type of conflict?
   a. approach-approach
   b. avoidance-avoidance
   c. approach-avoidance
   d. double (multiple) approach avoidance

6. An individual refusing to do a new assignment because of fear of failing is probably experiencing which type of conflict?
   a. individual
   b. interpersonal
   c. inter-group
   d. inter-organizational

7. The key factor in any conflict situation is:
   a. facts
   b. methods
   c. goals
   d. values
   e. text lists all the above as "key"

8. A role ambiguity is an example of which stage of conflict development?
   a. antecedent conditions
   b. perceived and felt conflict
   c. conflict suppression
   d. conflict aftermath

9. An example of an antecedent from which conflicts develop is:
   a. role ambiguities
   b. competition for scarce resources
   c. task interdependencies
   d. communication barriers
   e. all of the above

10. Managers can address conflict through:
    a. nonattention
    b. suppression
    c. resolution
    d. all of the above

Matching Self Test

Directions: Write the letter of the description that best fits each numbered item in the blank provided.

_____ 1. Organizational innovation

_____ 2. Substantive conflicts

_____ 3. Change agent

_____ 4. Planned change process

_____ 5. Explicity and implicit coercion

_____ 6. Normative-reeducative strategy

_____ 7. Organization development process phases

_____ 8. Action research

_____ 9. Facilitator role

_____ 10. Conflict resolution

a. Unfreezing, changing, and refreezing.

b. Taking a new idea and putting it into practice.

c. Diagnosis, intervention, reinforcement.

d. Involves disagreements over such things as goals, resources, rewards, etc.

e. Process of systematically collecting data on an organization.

f. Person or group who changes things.

g. Use of force to get people to accept change.

h. Identifies or establishes values and assumptions from which support for a proposed change will naturally emerge.

i. Interpersonal in nature and requires successful use of communication skills.

j. Occurs when underlying reasons are removed and no lingering conditions or antagonisms remain to rekindle the same conflict in the future.

18 Managing Labor-Management Relations

STUDENT LEARNING OBJECTIVES

After completing the chapter material you should be able to:

1. Define the terms "labor union," "labor-management relations," and "collective bargaining."
2. Briefly review the evolution of the labor movement, its purpose and impact on business and society.
3. Distinguish between various types of unions and union organization types and structures.
4. Explain the legal environment of labor-management relations and how organizations become unionized.
5. Explain collective bargaining issues and processes and labor contract components.
6. List and explain managerial implications of collective bargaining, particularly its impact on managerial decision making.
7. Explain the traditional adversarial relationship between management and labor, and why there is a new trend toward cooperation.
8. Explain in what ways managers can improve labor-management relations.

CHAPTER HIGHLIGHTS

Labor unions in society
The legal environment of labor-management relations
How organizations become unionized
Collective bargaining
Managerial implications of collective bargaining
Improving labor-management relations

PROGRAMMED LEARNING

The following statements are drawn from actual textbook content in abbreviated form. The blanks within the statements are numbered to correspond with the answer blanks at the left.

Labor unions in society

1. _____

An organization to which workers belong and which collectively deals with employers on their behalf is called a labor _____(1).

2. _____

_____-_____(2) relations is the ongoing relationship between a group of employees represented by a union and management in the employing organization.

3. _____

The foundation for any labor-management relationship is collective _____(3).

4. _____
5. _____

Although the first American unions were established around the year _____(4), the labor movement remained small until the decade of the _____(5).

6. _____
7. _____
8. _____
9. _____

The early resistance of workers to unionization is generally attributed to several factors related to the social, political, and economic environments of the day. These included: the absence of a well-entrenched _____(6), the massive influx of _____(7), relatively _____(8) wages and standards of living, employers' _____(9) to unions.

10. _____
11. _____

The growth period in unions after 1935 is attributed to the transformation of the American economy from agriculture to one based on heavy _____(10) and _____(11) creating an industrial working class which was conscious of limited opportunities for upward mobility.

12. _____

Declining _____(12) and the passage of time increased the number of workers who spoke a common language and shared a cultural heritage.

13. _____

_____(13) pressures of the depression added impetus to unionization as a result of increased worker discontent and a tarnished image for business.

14. _____

Changes in public policy created a _____(14) environment more supportive and protective of unions.

15. _____
16. _____
17. _____

Reasons for decline in union membership since World War II include _____(15) changes and changing _____(16) of the work force; plus unions have been slow to _____(17) to changing social and economic conditions.

Purposes of unions

18. _____

U.S. unions focus almost exclusively on the _____(18) concerns of their members.

19. _____

U.S. unions are generally supportive of the _____(19) system.

20. _____

The primary purpose of labor unions remains, in the eyes of most union leaders, the _____(20) of the employee in the workplace.

21. _____

The earliest U.S. labor organizations were composed exclusively of persons in skilled _____(21).

22. _____

Labor unions that typically serve a single industry and represent both skilled and less skilled workers across a wide variety of occupations are called _____(22) unions.

23. _____   Some unions are organized in a variety of unrelated industries. They are referred to as _____(23) unions because they lack a specific craft or industry focus.

Unions as organizations

24. _____
25. _____   The basic organizational unit of the U.S. labor movement is the _____(24) or _____(25) union.

26. _____   Most are affiliated with the _____-_____(26) labor federation.

27. _____   The AFL-CIO is an _____(27) which provides services to its affiliated but independent unions.

28. _____   Among other things, the AFL-CIO is active in the_____(28) arena.

29. _____   Unions affiliated with the AFL-CIO retain _____(29) in negotiating contracts and administering their internal affairs.

30. _____   The building block of virtually all national and international unions is the _____(30).

31. _____   The local president and other officers of locals are normally assisted by _____(31), local union officials present in the employing organizations and who represent workers in resolving disputes with management.

32. _____
33. _____   Two management problems relating to the administration of national and local unions which have plagued the U.S. labor movement over the years are organized _____(32) and excessive _____(33) on the part of the union organization.

The legal environment of labor-management relations

34. _____   The Act which specifically gives employees the right to join or form unions, to bargain collectively, and to undertake "concerted" activities is the _____(34) Act.

35. _____   Under the Wagner Act, the _____ _____ _____(35) Board was created to conduct representation elections through which employees decide whether or not to unionize, investigate any unfair labor practice charges, and generally administer the provisions of the act.

36. _____   The Act that allows individual states to enact "right-to-work" laws which prohibit union membership from being used as a condition for employment is called the _____-_____(36) Act.

37. _____   The unfair labor practices defined by the NLRA are not _____(37).

38. _____   But when an unfair labor practice is alleged to have occurred, the NLRB _____(38).

39. _____   If the allegation is substantiated, it will prescribe _____(39) action.

40. _____   The most common order by the NLRB is for the offending party to _____(40) from such actions in the future.

How organizations become unionized

41. _____   The most common way that organizations become unionized is through a group of _____(41) concerned about wages or other employment conditions, and they approach a union and request help in forming a local union and obtaining collective bargaining rights.

42. _____   They usually do so with a specific issue or goal as their rallying point such as comparable _____(42).

43. _____   Economists have shown that union growth is related to the business _____(43).

44. _____   Other things equal, unions tend to grow more in periods of high
45. _____   _____(44) and economic _____(45).

46. _____   Psychological studies find employee attitudes toward unions to be more favorable when job _____(46) is low.

47. _____   White collar and professional workers are more likely to favor unionization when dissatisfied with _____(47) rewards of their jobs.

48. _____   Blue collar workers are more likely to favor unionization when dissatisfied with the _____(48) rewards of their jobs.

49. _____   In addition employees are more likely to favor unionization when: they
50. _____   perceive of themselves as having little _____(49) to change work con-
51. _____   ditions for the better; they expect a union to be effective in changing work _____(50); and they have only limited _____(51) opportunities elsewhere.

52. _____   Emerson Electric has followed a particularly successful nonunion strategy in which the central ingredient is good _____(52).

53. _____   Firms successful in resisting unionization have implemented modern
54. _____   _____(53) systems, with considerable emphasis on employee
55. _____   _____(54) (e.g. quality circles), progressive _____(55) and benefits
56. _____   programs, employment _____(56), and promotion from
57. _____   _____(57).

58. _____   The process of certifying a union begins when a _____(58) for an election is filed with the NLRB.

59. _____   Prior to any election, the NLRB may have to determine if the employees in the proposed unit share a "community of _____(59)" and if all of them fall under the jurisdiction of the law.

60. _____   The NLRA requires that a union establish its "_____(60) status" in order to be recognized.

Collective bargaining

61. _____   The process of negotiating, interpreting, and administering a labor contract establishes the conditions of employment under which managers and their subordinates work together in the unionized setting is called collective _____(61).

62. _____   The collective bargaining process and the labor agreement will, at a mini-
63. _____   mum, generally address the following issues: union _____(62),
64. _____   management _____(63), wages and _____(64), and _____(65)
65. _____   security.

66. _____   Most bargaining begins with a statement of _____(66) by both management and the union on a given issue.

67. _____   A _____(67) is a complaint from an employee regarding treatment he or she has received in respect to a condition of employment.

68. _____   Most grievances charge that a manager or management in general has violated some provision of the labor _____(68).

69. _____   _____(69) is the process by which parties to a labor-management dispute agree to abide by the decision of a neutral and independent third party called an arbitrator.

70. _____   In the negotiation process called _____(70), the third party only makes suggestions to the parties in the hope that concession and compromise will result.

Managerial implications of collective bargaining

71. _____   Collective bargaining places limits on managerial _____ _____(71).

72. _____   For example, the presence of a union and collective bargaining generally reduces the ability of managers in an organization to tie worker performance to _____(72).

73. _____   Unions also tend to look unfavorably on merit pay plans in which wage or salary increases are tied to performance _____(73).

74. _____   _____(74) rather than performance may be the governing criterion for promotion in unionized settings.

75. _____   Conflicts over work assignment most often arise in craft union settings in the form of _____(75) disputes.

76. _____   In industrial union settings, conflicts over work assignments are most likely to result from management decisions to _____(76) to outsiders work that traditionally is done by union members.

77. _____   The principle of _____(77) cause is central to employee discipline in collective bargaining situations.

78. _____   Job _____(78) as a possible result of increased automation and other forms of technological change is a continuing concern of organized labor.

Improving labor-management relations

79. _____   The traditional view of labor-management relations is reflected in an _____(79) relationship.

80. _____   Presently there is a trend toward _____(80) between management and labor.

81. _____   Specific steps to improve labor-management relations include: effective
82. _____   _____(81), respect for the _____(82) contract, support for the
83. _____   _____(83) procedure, and sponsorship of the labor-management
84. _____   _____(84).

TESTING YOUR KNOWLEDGE

True and False Self Test

Directions: Circle the letter (T or F) of the correct response for each of the following statements.

T F 1. Union membership has increased from World War II to a level of about 47% of today's work force.

T F 2. Women, professional workers, and white collar workers have historically been less apt to belong to unions.

T F 3. The earliest American labor organizations were composed of persons in skilled trades.

T F 4. The AFL-CIO is one of the biggest trade unions today.

T F 5. The National Labor Relations Board has been set up to investigate labor crimes.

T F 6. The National Labor Relations Board requires that a union must establish at least 62% of the votes cast in order to become certified as the employees' bargaining agent.

T F   7. In industrial union settings, conflicts over work assignments most often arise in the form of jurisdictional disputes.

T F   8. Collective bargaining is the process of negotiating, interpreting, and administering a labor contract.

T F   9. In craft unions, the union may select a job candidate and refer him/her to a prospective employer.

T F   10. The process by which parties to a labor-management dispute agree to abide by the decision of a neutral and independent third party is called arbitration.

Multiple Choice Self Test

Directions: Circle the letter of the response that best completes each of the following statements.

1. The early resistance of workers to unionization is generally attributed to:
    a. the absence of a well entrenched class system
    b. the massive influx of immigrants
    c. relatively high wages
    d. employer resistance
    e. all of the above

2. The growth period for unions after 1935 is attributed to:
    a. The accelerated industrialization of America
    b. declining immigration with accompanying rise in U.S. citizenship and culture
    c. economic pressures
    d. a more supportive legal environment
    e. all of the above

3. A major distinction between American labor unions and those in most other countries is:
    a. structure or organization
    b. who can belong
    c. focus of American unions primarily on economic issues
    d. all of the above

4. Labor unions that typically serve a wide variety of occupations in a single industry are called:
    a. trade
    b. industrial
    c. general
    d. commercial

5. The Act that allows states to enact "right-to-work" laws is:
    a. Taft-Hartley
    b. Wagner
    c. NLRB
    d. Smith-Wesson

6. Other things equal, unions tend to grow more in periods of:
    a. high immigration
    b. recession
    c. high inflation and economic expansion
    d. depression

7. Psychological studies have shown that employees' attitudes towards unions are more positive when:
    a. job satisfaction is low
    b. they perceive themselves as having little power
    c. they expect that unions can improve working conditions
    d. all of the above

8. Firms successful in resisting unionization have done so through:
   a. utilization of employees' decision making
   b. progressive compensation
   c. employment security
   d. all of the above

9. The NLRA requires that in order to be certified under petition for an election, _____ percent of employee signatures is needed:
   a. 20
   b. 30
   c. 51
   d. 70

10. A step to improve labor-management relations would be:
    a. effective communication
    b. respect for the labor contract
    c. support for the grievance procedure
    d. sponsorship of the labor-management "team"
    e. all of the above

Matching Self Test

Directions: Write the letter of the description that best fits each numbered item in the blank provided.

_____ 1. Local

_____ 2. Collective bargaining

_____ 3. Closed shop

_____ 4. Agency shop

_____ 5. Grievance

_____ 6. Arbitration

_____ 7. Conciliation

_____ 8. Mediation

_____ 9. Wagner Act of 1935

_____ 10. Labor contract

a. Requires all employees to pay a service fee to the union even though they don't officially have to join.

b. Process of negotiating, interpreting, and administering a labor contract.

c. Process by which parties to a labor-management dispute agree to abide by decision of a neutral party.

d. Person must be a union member in good standing before hired as an employee.

e. Neutral third party tries to keep the parties to a dispute focused on the issues of disagreement.

f. An administrative unit which services at the local level a particular group of workers represented by the union.

g. Complaint from an employee regarding treatment he or she has received in respect to a condition of employment.

h. Neutral third party engages in substantive discussions with union and management negotiators in separate meetings.

i. Gave employees the right to collective bargaining.

j. Formal written agreement stipulating wages, hours, and other terms of employment for union members.

19 Managing in an International Arena

STUDENT LEARNING OBJECTIVES

After completing the chapter material you should be able to:

1. Define international business and multinational corporations.
2. List reasons businesses go international, and what "forms" they choose.
3. Describe home country and host country relations in terms of international and MNC business, particularly concerns and benefits.
4. Explain "moral" act as an important concept in international business.
5. List and explain environmental constraints in conducting international business.
6. List and explain economic, legal-political, educational, and cultural differences to anticipate in the international business setting.
7. Explain in what ways the basic management functions, planning and controlling, are affected by the international arena.
8. Review organization structures, and add the author's two more adaptable structures for worldwide operations.
9. Discuss some of the complexities of staffing for MNCs.
10. Define "comparative management practices" as a field of inquiry and give some examples of areas of management which need research and managerial attention in practice.

CHAPTER HIGHLIGHTS

International management
International business
Multinational corporations (MNCs)
Environmental constraints on international operations
Management functions in an international perspective
Comparative management practices

PROGRAMMED LEARNING

The following statements are drawn from actual textbook content in abbreviated form. The blanks within the statements are numbered to correspond with the answer blanks at the left.

International business

1. _____ The conduct of for-profit transactions of goods and services across national boundaries is called _____(1) business.

2. _____
3. _____ Business firms engage in international activities for many possible reasons: _____(2), _____(3) markets, _____(4) materials, _____(5) resources, and _____(6) labor costs.
4. _____
5. _____
6. _____

7. _____ The number of foreign firms establishing sizeable operations in the U.S. is _____ing (7).

8. _____ Forms of international business activity include: _____/_____(8)
9. _____ of goods and services; _____(9) agreements for producing or offering
10. _____ goods or services in another country, _____ _____(10) for
11. _____ operating foreign companies or facilities, joint _____(11) through
12. _____ mutual ownership with foreign partners which establish operations in a foreign country, and _____(12) subsidiaries or branches.

Multinational corporations (MNCs) and the world economy

13. _____ A business firm with international operations in two or more (and usually several) foreign countries is called a MNC, _____ _____(13).

14. _____ Decision-makers in MNCs bear a responsibility that moves beyond the productivity of their business operations to encompass issues of major _____(14) significance.

15. _____ Among the critics of MNCs are those who are concerned that MNCs have an _____(15) impact on the foreign or host countries in which they operate.

16. _____ Ideally speaking, the goals of the MNC and host country _____(16) rather than contradict one another.

17. _____ Among the more general concerns are fears that MNCs will operate in
18. _____ host countries in ways that: extract excessive _____(17); fail to help
19. _____ _____(18) firms develop; divert the most talented of local _____(19)
20. _____ from domestic enterprises; fail to transfer advanced _____(20) and
21. _____ know-how into local hands; fail to respect local _____(21), needs,
22. _____ and government objectives; dominate the local _____(22); and inter-
23. _____ fere with the local _____(23).

24. _____ One of the most provocative and emotional of the themes in the prior
25. _____ list is the suspicion that MNCs exercise too much influence over the internal _____(24) and _____(25) affairs of their host countries.

26. _____ Even in their home countries, however, MNCs are subject to criticism.
27. _____ Among those are concerns that MNCs: export _____(26); divert
28. _____ _____(27) investments away from domestic opportunities to those
29. _____ abroad; lose touch with domestic _____(28) and priorities; and allow and even encourage _____(29) practices in their overseas dealings.

30. _____
31. _____

For those doing business in other cultures, the author proposes this definition of a "moral" act: that which persons of good _____(30) and honorable _____(31) in the host country recognize as proper conduct.

32. _____

This approach to morality parallels the "_____(32) concept" which calls for researching the needs of target consumers, in order to devise an appropriate response.

Environmental constraints on international operations

33. _____
34. _____
35. _____
36. _____
37. _____

A framework for looking at the external environments of organizations and singling out important factors for managerial attention is called the _____(33) environment and includes: the _____(34) values, _____(35), _____-_____(36), and _____(37) conditions common to a given geographical region.

38. _____

International management must accommodate environmental _____(38) to achieve performance success.

39. _____
40. _____
41. _____

Among developing countries there exist three fundamental economic concerns: quality-of-_____(39) concerns, technological _____(40), and capital _____(41).

42. _____

Another more basic economic issue from one country to the next relates to the nature of the foreign _____(42) system itself.

43. _____
44. _____

In broadest terms the economic systems of the world fall on a continuum of two extremes— _____(43) market economies and _____(44) planning economies.

45. _____

Free market economies characterize most _____(45) nations such as the U.S.

46. _____
47. _____

They operate under an economic system governed by laws of _____(46) and _____(47).

48. _____

Although government policies will influence the free market system, they do so to a far lesser extent than in _____(48) planning economies.

49. _____

_____(49) is a shared set of beliefs, values, and patterns of behavior common to a group of people.

50. _____
51. _____
52. _____
53. _____

Hofstede studied national culture in four dimensions briefly described as: _____(50) distance, _____(51) avoidance, _____-_____(52), and _____(53).

54. _____
55. _____

Based on the results of Hofstede's study, he argues that management practices must be _____(54) to fit local cultures, and that management _____(55) developed in one culture should be seriously questioned when being transferred to another.

56. _____
57. _____

Even if you question Hofstede's research findings, the author says that in a foreign culture, one should at least be prepared for _____(56) differences and _____(57) and custom differences.

The management functions in international perspective

58. _____
59. _____

Central to the text's strategic planning model when applied to international planning is analysis of the _____(58) environment and the organization's internal strengths and _____(59).

60. _____

Planning in the international arena requires a _____(60) perspective.

61. _____   Another effort that can assist planning and controlling in the international
62. _____   arena is global _____(61), particularly those involving _____(62)
                        risk analysis.

63. _____   Political (or country) risk analysis involves forecasting the probability of
                        various events which can threaten the security of a foreign _____(63).

64. _____   Among the basic factors that would be considered in a political risk
65. _____   analysis for operations in a particular foreign country are the following:
66. _____   social _____(64), foreign _____(65), _____(66) system, and
67. _____   _____(67) climate.

68. _____   A basic principle of organization design holds in the international as well
69. _____   domestic setting—structure should match _____(68) and _____(69)
                        (size, technology, strategy, and people).

70. _____   Two structures more adapted to worldwide operations are the multi-
71. _____   national _____(70) and _____(71) structures.

72. _____   Each encourages _____(72) and _____(73) in responding to
73. _____   varying needs and conditions on a worldwide basis.

74. _____   Organizations operating internationally should have some home country
                        _____(74) in foreign locations.

75. _____   Any firm that is truly international in orientation should have people with
                        _____(75) experience in key decision-making positions within the cor-
                        porate headquarters staff.

Comparative management practices

76. _____   A central research question of primary interest is whether or not a
                        _____(76) practice that works well in one country or culture can
                        be successfully transferred to another country or culture.

77. _____   Some propositions based on Hofstede's research regarding organization
78. _____   design in foreign countries include greater _____(77) and greater
                        _____(78).

79. _____   Some specific Japanese practices that are viewed with special interest in
80. _____   terms of having potential for use in the U.S. are: _____(79) employ-
81. _____   ment, job _____(80), _____(81) decisions, and quality-control
82. _____   _____(82).

TESTING YOUR KNOWLEDGE

True and False Self Test

Directions: Circle the letter (T or F) of the correct response for each of the following statements.

T F 1. Management which involves the conduct of business or other operations in foreign
          countries is called international management.

T F 2. Basic management functions, planning, organizing, leading, and controlling also apply to
          international markets.

T F 3. Leadership in the international setting should fit all aspects of the organization's per-
          spective.

T F 4. Multinational corporations face a variety of external environmental constraints such as
          political, educational, and cultural differences.

T F 5. Comparative management is the study of how management practices differ and transfer
          across cultures.

T F   6. Japanese practices in management should be initiated into management practices of other cultures.

T F   7. The legal-political system internationally is separate from the organizational system.

T F   8. International management must accommodate environmental constraints to achieve performance success.

T F   9. Profit is a major reason for organizations becoming global in operation.

T F   10. Centralized planning economies are a characteristic of the western nations such as the U.S.

Multiple Choice Self Test

Directions: Circle the letter of the response that best completes each of the following statements.

1. A reason a business might go international is to:
    a. improve profits
    b. expand markets
    c. obtain new raw materials
    d. secure additional financial help
    e. all of the above could be good reasons

2. Which of the following is considered a form of international business?
    a. licensing agreements
    b. management contracts
    c. joint ventures
    d. subsidiaries
    e. all of the above could be

3. One of the most provocative and emotional fears of host countries regarding MNCs is that they will:
    a. extract excessive profits
    b. exercise too much influence over economic and political affairs
    c. fail to help domestic firms
    d. fail to share advanced technologies

4. In their home countries MNCs are subject to which of the following criticisms? They will:
    a. export jobs
    b. divert capital away form domestic opportunities
    c. lose touch with domestic needs
    d. allow corrupt practices
    e. all of the above

5. A framework for looking at the external environments includes:
    a. cultural values
    b. economic
    c. legal-political
    d. educational
    e. all of the above

6. Free market economies operate under an economic system governed by:
    a. centralized governmental planners
    b. laws of supply and demand
    c. fraudulent practices
    d. excess regulation

7. According to Hofstede, a national society culture which focuses on groups as resources for work and problem-solving would be labeled by the term or dimension:
    a. power distance
    b. uncertainty avoidance
    c. individualism-collectivism
    d. masculinity

8. To facilitate planning in the international arena management should:
   a. use a worldwide perspective
   b. do global forecasts
   c. conduct political risk analysis
   d. all of the above

9. A basic factor(s) that would be considered in a political risk analysis is/are
   a. social instability
   b. foreign conflict
   c. governmental system
   d. economic climate
   e. all of the above

10. A basic principle of organization holds in the international as well as the domestic setting—structure should match:
   a. goals and strategies
   b. inputs and outputs
   c. environment and context
   d. size and shape
   e. none of the above

Matching Self Test

Directions: Write the letter of the description that best fits each numbered item in the blank provided.

_____ 1. Comparative management

_____ 2. MNCs

_____ 3. Free market economies

_____ 4. Japanese management characteristics

_____ 5. Culture

_____ 6. Planning, organizing, leading, and controlling

_____ 7. Basic factors to consider in political risk analysis for operations in a particular foreign country

_____ 8. Multi national geographic and product structures

_____ 9. International management

_____ 10. International business

a. Study of management practices from one country or culture to the next.

b. Characterize most western nations such as U.S.

c. Lifetime employment, job rotation, collective decisions, quality circles.

d. Management functions that apply to the international arena.

e. Set of beliefs, values, and patterns of behavior common to a group of people.

f. A business firm with international operations in two or more foreign countries.

g. Encourage decentralization and flexibility in responding to varying needs and conditions on a world wide basis.

h. Used to describe management which involves the conduct of business or other operations in foreign countries.

i. Social instability, foreign conflict, governmental system, economic climate.

j. Conduct of for-profit transactions of goods and services across national boundaries.

20 Managing Ethically and with Social Responsibility

STUDENT LEARNING OBJECTIVES

After completing the chapter material you should be able to:

1. Define ethical behavior and relate its meaning to morality and individual norms and values.
2. Explain managerial ethics and the related terms, standards and principles.
3. Summarize some of the text examples of ethical dilemmas faced by managers, and from what relationships these dilemmas seem to originate.
4. List and explain the text's three key forces representing the social context within which the manager must perform.
5. Cite trends in managerial ethics, and what blocks exist to the exposure of unethical behavior.
6. Explain why behavior of superiors is often cited by organization members as the single most important factor influencing unethical decisions.
7. Cite what your text says would be the value of a formal code of business ethics.
8. Define corporate social responsibility, levels of responsibility, and list major areas in which organizations should be socially responsible.
9. List and discuss text arguments for and against assumption of social responsibility.

CHAPTER HIGHLIGHTS

What is ethical behavior
Managerial ethics
Maintaining high ethical managerial standards among managers
Corporate social responsibility
Government regulation of business
Ethics, social responsibility, and the manager's challenge

PROGRAMMED LEARNING

The following statements are drawn from actual textbook content in abbreviated form. The blanks within the statements are numbered to correspond with the answer blanks at the left.

What is ethical behavior

1. _____
2. _____

Ethics is the code of _____(1) of a person or group that sets _____(2) as to what is good or bad, or right or wrong in one's conduct.

3. _____
4. _____

To really establish whether a given behavior is ethical or not, we must inquire beyond its _____(3) and probe into whether it is right or wrong in a broader _____(4) sense.

5. _____
6. _____

The social context of ethical behavior is the source of the _____(5) and _____(6) that give meaning to a moral code.

7. _____
8. _____

It can be argued that the ethical standards of business practice should be congruent with the _____(7) and _____(8) of society as a whole.

Managerial ethics

9. _____
10. _____

Managerial ethics are _____(9) and _____(10) guiding the actions and decisions of managers.

11. _____

Managerial ethics influence managers' actions and decisions which influence _____(11) impacts of organizational behavior.

Ethical dilemmas faced by managers

12. _____
13. _____
14. _____

Most ethical dilemmas develop in the manager's relationships with _____(12), _____(13), and _____(14).

15. _____
16. _____
17. _____

The most frequent ethical dilemma involves honesty in _____(15) through _____(16) as well as the receipt of special gifts, entertainment, and _____(17).

18. _____
19. _____
20. _____

Managerial ethics are influenced by three key forces representing the social context in which the manager must perform: the manager as a _____(18), the _____(19) organization, and the _____(20) environment in which both exist.

Maintaining high ethical standards among managers

21. _____
22. _____
23. _____

Three important organizational blocks to exposing unethical behaviors are: strict chain of _____(21), task group _____(22), and _____(23) priorities.

24. _____

When surveyed on business ethics, executives point to the behavior of their _____(24) as the single most important factor influencing unethical decisions.

25. _____

The implication is that top management sets a _____(25) tone for the organization as a whole.

26. _____

Top managers must maintain high ethical standards and communicate to employees similar _____(26).

27. _____

A supervisor may unknowingly encourage unethical practices by exerting too much pressure for the accomplishment of _____(27).

A managerial code of ethics

28. _____

Executives who favor ethical codes see them as a means for clarifying _____(28) regarding goal accomplishment.

29. _____
30. _____
31. _____

Arguments against the codes include fears that it will be impossible to specify _____(29) to cover all situations and actions, fears that codes will overly restrict individual _____(30) to act, and that ethical codes are difficult to _____(31).

Corporate social responsibility

32. _____
33. _____

A socially responsible company delivers _____(32) and _____(33) products to its customers.

34. _____
35. _____
36. _____
37. _____
38. _____
39. _____

Major areas of social responsibility according to Table 20.3 include: ecology and _____(34) quality, _____ism(35), community _____(36), governmental _____(37), corporate giving, minorities and disadvantaged persons, labor _____(38), stockholder relations, and _____(39) activity.

40. _____
41. _____
42. _____

Organizations may respond with three different degrees of commitment to their external social obligations: social _____(40), social _____(41), and social _____(42).

43. _____

The level at which corporate behavior anticipates and even takes a lead in longer-run movement beyond current expectations, or takes preventative action to avoid adverse social impacts from company activities is called social _____(43).

44. _____
45. _____
46. _____
47. _____
48. _____
49. _____
50. _____

Major arguments against business assumption of social responsibility include: loss of _____(44) maximization; _____(45) of business, lack of _____(46) of employees to deal with social issues, dilution of _____(47), expansion of corporate _____(48), lack of _____(49), and lack of broad _____(50).

51. _____
52. _____
53. _____
54. _____
55. _____
56. _____
57. _____
58. _____
59. _____
60. _____
61. _____

Major arguments supporting the assumption of social responsibility for business include: public _____(51), long-run _____(52), public _____(53), better _____(54), avoidance of government _____(55), balance of _____(56) and power, let business _____(57), business has the _____(58), problems can become _____(59), prevention is better than _____(60), and stockholder _____(61).

62. _____

Among the trends in government legislation in recent years is a growing interest in quality-of-_____(62) issues.

63. _____
64. _____
65. _____
66. _____
67. _____

Five ways in which businesses attempt to influence government include: _____(63) contacts, public relations _____(64), _____(65), direct _____(66) support, and _____(67) acts.

Emerging managerial values

68. _____ The underlying beliefs and attitudes which help determine individual behavior are called _____(68).

69. _____ The three historical phases of managerial values are identified as: Phase I:
70. _____ _____ maximizing (69) managers, Phase II: _____(70) managers,
71. _____ and Phase III: "quality-of-_____(71)" managers.

72. _____ Managers should apply the basic management functions of _____(72),
73. _____ _____(73), and _____(74) in administering its social responsibility.
74. _____

TESTING YOUR KNOWLEDGE

True and False Self Test

Directions: Circle the letter (T or F) of the correct response for each of the following statements.

T F 1. Values are a code of morals of a person or a group that sets standards as to what is right or wrong in one's conduct.

T F 2. A social audit is a systematic assessment and reporting of an organization's resource and action commitments and accomplishments in areas of social responsibility.

T F 3. Interest in an organization's social responsibility has been declining very slowly.

T F 4. How socially responsible an organization chooses to be is dependent on the personal value system of its managers.

T F 5. Ethical behavior by managers both meets legal obligations and conforms to guiding social principles of what is "right or wrong" or "good or bad."

T F 6. There are many guidelines that exist when determining ethical standards.

T F 7. Social auditing will increase in popularity and sophistication in the future.

T F 8. Audit programs help management translate vague ideas about social performance into hard realities.

T F 9. If a particular action is illegal, our society dictates that the behavior is most likely unethical.

T F 10. Ethical behavior is behavior that is morally accepted as "right or good" in the context of governing moral code.

Multiple Choice Self Test

Directions: Circle the letter of the response that best completes each of the following statements.

1. Managerial ethics are affected by:
   a. family influences
   b. personal standards
   c. personal needs
   d. religious values
   e. all of the above can influence ethics

2. An organizational block to exposing unethical behavior was cited by the text as:
   a. too strict chain of command
   b. task group cohesiveness
   c. ambiguous priorities
   d. all of the above
   e. none of the above

3. Regarding firms' quests for profit and social responsibility:
    a. A ceiling should be put on profitability since anything higher than 30% return is thought to be irresponsible.
    b. Meeting social responsibilities is usually detrimental to the profit goals.
    c. Nonprofit firms are inherently more likely to be socially responsible than are profit seeking firms.
    d. There is no reason why profits and social responsibility can't go hand in hand.

4. The level of corporate social responsibility at which there is merely compliance with basic legal requirements is called:
    a. social obligation
    b. social security
    c. social responsibility
    d. social responsiveness

5. An argument cited in the text against social responsibility was:
    a. potential loss of profit maximization
    b. high cost of carrying out social responsibility
    c. lack of employee skills
    d. extending of organization power
    e. all of the above

6. On the positive side of arguing for government regulation of business, which of the following was cited as a positive regulatory intervention:
    a. occupational and public safety
    b. pollution protection
    c. fair labor practices
    d. consumer protection
    e. all of the above

7. The government agency that protects your food and drug quality is:
    a. FDP
    b. FDR
    c. FDA
    d. EPA

8. PACs, a political tool of business, is the acronym for:
    a. Policing Actions of Congressmen
    b. Presidents Against Corruption
    c. Political Action Committees
    d. Payoffs Awarded to Congressmen

9. In the evolution of managerial values, the text suggests that in our society managers can be characterized as in what stage?
    a. profit maximizing phase
    b. trustee phase
    c. "quality of life" phase
    d. none of the above

10. Social responsibility is related to which of the functional areas of management?
    a. planning
    b. organizing
    c. controlling
    d. leading
    e. all of the above

Matching Self Test

Directions: Write the letter of the description that best fits each numbered item in the blank provided.

_____ 1. Values

_____ 2. Historical phases of managerial values

_____ 3. Social audit

_____ 4. Strict chain of command, task group cohesiveness, ambiguous priorities

_____ 5. Ethical dilemma

_____ 6. Managerial ethics

_____ 7. Ethical behavior

_____ 8. Effective control

_____ 9. Personal value systems

_____ 10. Lobbying

a. Reports of an organization's resource and action commitments of social responsibility.

b. Standards and principles guiding the actions and decisions of managers.

c. Underlying beliefs and attitudes which help determine individual behavior.

d. Something accepted as "right" or "good" in the context of a governing moral code.

e. Determine how well managers' decisions and actions satisfy performance, ethical and social responsibility criteria.

f. Profit maximizing, trusteeship, "quality of life."

g. Organizational blocks to expose unethical behaviors.

h. Occurs when a manager must decide whether or not to pursue a course of action which is illegal or unethical in the broader social context.

i. The result of evaluations and information feedback that help managers to make decisions that maintain or even enhance the organization's social contributions.

j. A way business can influence government.

LEARNING ACTIVITIES — PART 6

Number 1 — Supplemental Reading and Discussion

Directions: Read the following journal article and answer the discussion questions that follow:

SURVIVING THE SECOND INDUSTRIAL REVOLUTION

(Where we are heading in the age of *Automation*)

I've always been fascinated by the Industrial Revolution. One of the questions it always raises—as it did when I was doing my student work—is why was it a revolution? Was it the machines? The steam engine, the cotton gin, the railway, and the power loom were all extraordinary inventions. But the conclusion I eventually came to was that they were revolutionary because they were agents for great social change. They took people out of the fields and brought them into factories. They gave us mass production and, through mass production, the first society in which wealth was not confined to a few. The Industrial Revolution produced a sense of hurry, a sense of time, a sense of goal that simply hadn't existed before. It changed human society, and that was what was revolutionary—not the machines themselves.

Looking at what is happening today, I think the same is true. If you had asked Richard Arkwright or James Watt whether they thought they were changing society, they certainly would not have thought so. They were simply concentrating on what they were doing. One of our problems is that we are today changing society with much of our new technology. It's very important to be conscious of that fact and to think much more widely, as many of our leading scientists are doing, of what the social consequences and the human meaning will be as new technological strides are made.

The Electronics Revolution

We are now engaged in an electronics revolution, but we have to see this revolution in a long-term perspective to understand its significance. As I noted in my book, "Automation will appear as a distinct phase in industrial progress, but it is nevertheless a part of the long continuum of man's mechanization of his work. The economic and social effects of the new technology should be viewed in this perspective."

It is very easy to get swept up in publicity about revolutionary technological changes. In fact, we are making revolutionary progress in the sense that we are moving ahead and in new directions from a very substantial base. However, our current electronics revolution is building on a heritage of technological revolutions that enables us to adjust to change almost un-

consciously. This also enables us to proclaim widely that there is a revolution—and then to virtually ignore the complex business, economic, and social issues we must master before we can say that we have succeeded with our revolution.

It seems to me that some of the really interesting developments have not yet started or, if they have, are not yet recognized. Either way, they will be very important.

The computer industry has developed and grown in the last 30 years to what is today a big industry, but it has already started to shift. No longer only a capital industry producing capital goods, it has also become a consumer-product industry, a shift that is going to be very significant in the years ahead. Computers are now involved in producing not only products but services, and not only direct products but indirect products—the incorporation of chips into automobiles and consumer and capital products of all kinds.

Many important consequences will derive from this change, because it means that international economic competitiveness in almost every other service and product area will be determined more and more by computers and the information industry. Consumers will increasingly judge the quality of the goods and services they buy on the basis of the computer support that they get with them.

What we see emerging is a technology that has increasingly embedded itself in our economic infrastructure. The availability of computer resources is becoming as crucial to national economic viability as the availability of energy and raw materials. If the success of the Japanese tells us anything, it should tell us that. That computers are becoming a consumer field, and that they are going to change materially the productivity of virtually all other businesses and affect the kinds of products and services they offer is of utmost importance to our nation's well being.

Greater Productivity

Productivity growth is stimulated by new technology, not only because automation streamlines work, but, more important, because it gives us an opportunity to analyze the jobs we do as individuals, as work groups, and as large systems at the enterprise level. The process of rethinking is truly difficult, a fact we are learning as we struggle to find ways to measure the productivity of our own actions, especially in the office of today.

It has long been felt that the essence of any definition of productivity was the idea of more efficient operations, defined narrowly. On the basis of this paradigm, an entire school of thought in productivity examination was born. Now, however, with the increasing penetration of office automation into the workplace, the definition of productivity in its classical sense is being challenged.

At the heart of this transformation in thinking lies the realization that office automation not only will change the efficiency with which work is performed but also will change the nature and definition of work itself. In other words, people are beginning to move into the second phase of change.

It is useful to consider an analogy with general systems theory. General systems are known to operate using a defined set of criteria and rules of interaction and structure until the feedback throughout the system becomes of such proportions as to cause a fundamental disequilibrium in the system. When this occurs, a "state change" is effective. This is what is happening as we automate information in the office environment.

In its narrowest sense, information productivity can be thought of as a means to achieve profits through improvement in measureable output. Increasingly, however, we are finding that a completely output-oriented measurement is not adequate for understanding the effects of office automation. By thinking of the office environment as a system, certain rules governing the operating efficiency of its units can be derived. Using such rules, we can make progress in identifying criteria for measuring and improving efficiency.

However, just as with a general system, an office will also undergo a fundamental transformation when subjected to a certain amount of stress. When this occurs in the office environment, not only will structural relationships change, but human and conceptual relationships will change, too.

At the individual level, the changes will start to spill over from one person to another and one office to another, and unless we focus our attention on the whole process, we lose control of what is happening to the system as a whole. Thus no matter whether or not we can prove changes in productivity, it is an essential part of managing to strive continually to analyze productivity.

Right now too much attention is being focused on simplistic cost/benefit equations to improve organizational productivity. Instead, measuring productivity should be a process of analyzing the quantity and quality of what we do. It should enable us to better choose our own destiny as we strive to employ new technology in the ways best suited to what we intend to do.

Improving Life for All

The changes occurring in technology involve extraordinary technical steps that lead to material decreases in costs. This means that the machine can begin to do more and more complex tasks that will make work easier for human beings. Basically, the human/machine interface is getting much easier—and that is what I believe is the real meaning of technological changes.

The intertwining of technological and biological developments is going to be formidable. And, far from undermining our appreciation for life, automation is enabling us to gain a new appreciation of just how much complexity there is and how much latent potential there is in the biological realm.

The late Vannevar Bush, developer of the first analog computer, said we would end up with computers implanted in each of us. We already have chips in heart devices, and we will have a multiplicity of increasing human involvements with electronic circuitry.

Changing the Nature of What We Do

Up to now, automation has been used mostly to mechanize work—how we have done and are doing things now. To a certain extent, a second and enormously important phase has started—and that is to change **what** we do. The parameters of competition in business are being completely changed as a result of imaginative use of our advancing technology.

All around us major corporations have begun to encroach on each other's territory, generating entirely new and exciting forms of competition. A salient example is, of course, the battle forming between the titans of telecommunications and computing, but other exciting, creative, and less confrontational kinds of crossbreeding are also occurring. For example, retailers are finding that they can offer extensive financial services that used to be the highly regulated preserve of banks. At the same time, banks and similar institutions can offer a wide variety of financial services directly to the home as well as sell merchandise over the wires.

A financial service finds retail business opportunities in cable television for home entertainment, and the same kind of wires are starting to provide internal networks for major corporations. Newspapers and publishing houses are moving into electronic publishing and suddenly find themselves head to head with giants of the aerospace industry, which have turned their research libraries into on-line information services. In each of these areas new business opportunities have developed because technology has enabled major enterprises to reassess their potential and rethink what they do. For example, the computer game industry which didn't even exist a few years ago, already is twice the size of the U.S. movie industry. Everywhere we see astonishing progress in electronic funds transfer, cash-flow management, electronic tellers, and global communications. Banking at home is poised to move well beyond the pilot stage. Only a few years ago these services were peripheral to banking activities, but now they mark the competitive edge that one institution has over another.

A similar phenomenon has occurred in the retail industry with the spread of bar codes and point-of-sale (POS) terminals. POS technology contributes to effective inventory management and sales strategy, and opens new opportunities for improved customer service.

Initial steps are being taken toward establishing information links between retail business' information systems and those of suppliers and manufacturers, opening the way to the electronic exchange of purchase orders, invoices, stock-on-hand reports, and other advances that point to savings of time and labor and greater efficiency for both the retailer and supplier.

In addition to these and other opportunities for better computing and communications within and between companies and industries, we are also starting to hear more and more about automated environments—automated buildings and computerized climate controls. It is now becoming cheaper to install controls and wires than to use energy that benefits no one. These same wires and controls can supply computer tools to white collar workers at all levels and run a complex assembly line. We have even seen the introduction of a robot operated by the same brand of personal computer that managers use for their own work.

It is in this final area that we are really starting to see significant change. The work that managers do is being radically restructured. Working with words and numbers, or meeting and communicating with people, is where almost all the activities of managers and professionals take place. Computers are doing more and more of the filing, formatting, and reformatting of work that used to be supported by numerous underlings and secretaries. Such machines are transforming our business environment.

Capitalizing on Change

We are totally changing the structure of industries as a result, not of mechanizing what we did yesterday, but of doing something quite new—providing services that weren't provided previously. This will be the dominant characteristic of the years ahead: providing services and products that simply didn't exist before.

I have long believed that any important technological innovation brings about three phases of change. First you mechanize what you did yesterday; second, you find that, what you do changes; and third, you find that a result of these changes, the greatest change of all occurs in society.

When my first book, *Automation*, was first published 30 years ago, many important advances in technology were just being made, or were just beginning to move into the first phase of mechanizing what had been done before. By now we are into the second and third phases, actually doing different work and coping with the changes that automation technology has brought about in society.

These changes are hard to recognize while you are living through them, but that is precisely what we must do to capitalize on change. In the first stage we see time and again that success goes to a few companies in each industry that seize market share or increase profits by recognizing how technology can change what they have been doing. However, it inevitably follows that the entire industry moves to a new level of competition or finds itself in new businesses, and what it does changes. Finally, and most important, these changes do not and cannot occur in a vacuum. Society is adjusting to these changes, too. People as individuals are moving into new occupations, they find new work relationships, and their leisure changes. There is increased social mobility, and our rights and freedoms are adjusted to conform to a new reality.

This is not just a national phenomenon. It is worldwide. And what is especially fascinating is that society is also molding the technology to make it more suitable for people.

A few years ago the stereotype was that developments in automation and computers meant rigid systems: highly centralized, monolithic types of structures that were dehumanizing. Today it's exactly the reverse. Systems are becoming highly decentralized, very flexible, very human, increasingly friendly, and very easy to adapt in any way wanted by the people who are using them. This leads to the ability to unleash human imagination—the most important force we have. And what imagination will lead us to is something we can hardly begin to guess. That is what is really happening in this field.

We Need a Guiding Vision

During the period immediately ahead, an increasing array of public policy problems will be related to technology. What is a branch of a bank? Is a terminal a branch? What should our country's communications policy be, let alone the world's? This question is currently being debated in Washington, perhaps not with the degree of perspective that many of us would like to see, but that is characteristic of virtually all our public policy considerations.

The process we use to set public policy reflects the fragmented structure of our government. We are therefore ill-equipped to deal cohesively with the increasing number of problems that involve many areas at once. One example is antitrust. It would be a fascinating irony if the information stolen from IBM, for which two Japanese companies have been indicted, is precisely the information that the European Economic Community is trying to obtain through its antitrust actions. The EEC's proposed remedy in the antitrust action would give it precisely the information that the Japanese are charged with stealing.

Another pressing question confronting us is how we in the United States can maintain our ability to innovate, which is what put us in the leadership position in the technology of automation. Our great strength in innovation comes from various sources—the mobility of a highly educated population, the American belief in backing small enterprises, the ability to get things started. But how do we now ensure that the marvelous cornucopia of new technology and inventions will continue to yield the things that our society rests on? Will, indeed, Silicon Valley, Route 128, the Hudson Valley, and other hi-tech strongholds continue to contribute so enormously to technology?

We have a society in which an increasing number of factors work against taking risk. How do we maintain one in which there is a value system that fosters risk? This issue merits much attention and will determine much of what happens next.

We have gradually built up a system in which there are thousands of places in which you can veto doing something. But we have no really organized method of going about setting priorities, no system of tradeoffs. We can block things all over the place, and every year we invent new ways, either legislatively or with the massive numbers of lawyers we're turning out. At some point society has to be able to say we want to do all of these things we can't, that this is more important than that, or that we can go so far here and so far there. It's easy to find an authoritarian solution to setting priorities, but it's very tough to find a democratic solution.

Furthermore, we ought to be innovating in our attempts to understand the impact of discernible future change on current planning decisions. Some years ago I suggested that we create autonomous "institutes of the future" that would be publicly funded but not tied to current budgets, and insulated with public boards not related to the political administration in office. Having a number of such institutions would permit some to take contradictory positions on issues relating to the current impact of future change and for the future impact of current decisions.

We need a guiding vision. It was extremely interesting to note that French President Francois Mitterrand has stated that the future determinant of French society and its economy will be the computer and automation. Recent statements from the Ministry for Information of International Trade in Japan also said that the main determinant of international competitiveness in all fields will be the computer. Singapore officials have made statements along the same lines. This common element is very interesting. They at least have some guiding vision and a view of how to draw together all the various elements. We need to invent a way to do that without decreasing our ingenuity or individual initiatives, and without getting us into a structure that is undemocratic or that goes against history.

Source: John Diebold, "Surviving the Second Industrial Revolution," *Management Review*, March 1983.

Discussion Questions

1. What is the value of history, for example, the Industrial Revolution, in studying management for today?

2. What kinds of "revolutions" are being experienced by U.S. businesses?

3. What are the implications of the computer industry becoming a consumer-product industry?

4. What does the author mean when he says that we measure productivity too simplistically? What additional criteria need be added?

5. What does the author mean when he says that we need a "guiding vision" in the U.S.?

6. Up to now, automation has been used mostly to mechanize work—how we do things. The next phase is using computers to change what we do. Explain this difference in "how we do" versus "what we do" through some of the article's examples.

7. Technological innovation brings about three phases of change according to the article. List the three and briefly explain.

8. In summary, what does the writer contend that new technological systems unleash?

Number 2 — Exercise: Collective Bargaining

Introduction: Imagine being considered an employee in your role as student. In other words, getting paid wages to pursue your education. That's exactly the assumption made in the collective bargaining exercise below. Students have organized themselves into a collective bargaining unit and have demanded that a formal contract be negotiated. As a result of their organized effort, management, the administration, has offered below their "first and final" offer.

Directions: Assume that the setting is your own institution and you are a student representative who will be negotiating a "better" contract.

Have a little fun with this, and make counter demands for each part of the proposal offered. For each item, you may want to stretch your demands to levels which later you might be willing to drop depending upon the give and take that might occur over each contract item.

This exercise could be culminated in a class negotiating session after you've make your counter proposals. Set up a small group with members representing both management and labor, and negotiate a final contract.

Statement of Position

The following proposal has been offered by your administrators in establishing the new employee program:

Administration Proposals	*Student Counter Proposals*
1. Student/employee work week: 40 hours	1.
a. 20 hours in class attendance	
b. 20 hours in a monitored library study station or similar formalized setting.	

Administration Proposals	_Student Counter Proposals_

2. Attendance: Mandatory
   a. maximum of two class hours per class in absences per term allowable with no deduction in pay.
   b. suspension from classes when three or more absences occur. Return allowable the next year.

2.

3. Tardiness: One dollar per minute assessed per each minute late; funds go to faculty recreation pool.

3.

4. Wages: By grade level
   a. freshmen, 4.00
   b. sophomores, 4.50
   c. juniors, 5.00
   d. seniors, 6.00

4.

5. Dress code: Formal
   a. men, sport coats, and ties or suits and ties.
   b. women, sport suits, and appropriate accessories.

5.

6. Grade performance: To advance from one level to another, i.e., freshman to sophomore, requires maintaining a 2.5 GPA (c being 2.0).

6.

7. To begin each class, students must sing, "Good morning dear professor" in harmony.

7.

8. Men and women will have separate classes. No coed classes.

8.

9. Work quality: All work typed; no lates.

9.

10. Performance assessment: No objective exams. Evaluation is subjective based entirely on the impressions of the professor.

10.

Collective Bargaining Discussion Questions

1. In the contract above, what items were missing that you feel such a potential contract might have?

2. Did the original seem to be a sincere effort (minus the "good morning" song) by administration?

3.   While it may seem like a good idea to become paid student/employees, what kinds of obligations are formed on the part of students when they become employees? You might recall the "psychological contract" from an earlier chapter in responding to this question.

4.   Presently in your setting, what student rights seem most neglected by faculty or administration? Do you feel some sort of collective activity by students regarding these neglected rights might help remedy the neglect? Explain.

5.   Why do organizations resist unionization efforts? Do you feel your administrative personnel would be receptive to a strong collective group of students wanting to make major changes in areas of academia that affect them? Explain.

6.   How would the actual collective bargaining process be done in your setting? Explain using such terms as negotiation, conciliation, mediation, and arbitration.

7.   In general how might student/administration and student/faculty relations be improved? What material from the "improving labor-management relations" section of the chapter might be helpful here?

Number 3 — Matching Wits with the Experts

Where We Stand: The U.S. Vis-a-Vis Other Major Industrial Nations

Introduction: Andrew Cross in an article entitled "Where We Stand: The U.S. Vis-a-Vis Everyone Else," makes interesting comparisons of the U.S. with France, West Germany, United Kingdom and Japan. Four categories of comparison, economics-business, culture-society, technology-medicine and politics-law, are set up in the table below with six measures listed for each category. Based on a variety of data sources, the writer deliberately picked two measures for each of the six categories in which the U.S. is definitely "better off." Similarly, he listed two measures as criteria for each of the four categories in which the U.S. is about even with the other countries. Similarly, he listed two measures for each of the four categories in which the U.S. is "worse off" than the other countries used in the comparison.

Directions: For each of the categories, A, B, C, and D below and the respective six measures for each category, do your own estimation of how the U.S. compares by checking the respective columns of "better off," "even," or "worse off" depending on your choice. Remember, when you're done with each category, there should be two answers each for the choices "better off," "even," and "worse off."

Table

Comparative Indicators, U.S. Versus France, West Germany, United Kingdom and Japan

		Better off	*Even*	*Worse off*
A.	**Economics-Business**			
1.	Government spending as a percent of gross national product (GNP)	( )	( )	( )
2.	Change in social security pension payments	( )	( )	( )
3.	Labor productivity (absolute level and growth trend)	( )	( )	( )
4.	Share of national income going to the lowest 20 percent	( )	( )	( )
5.	Misery index = unemployment rate + inflation rate	( )	( )	( )
6.	Individual savings rate as a percent of disposable personal income	( )	( )	( )
B.	**Culture-Society**			
1.	Rooms per dwelling and persons per room	( )	( )	( )
2.	Speed at which long distance telephone calls can be completed	( )	( )	( )
3.	Book production per 1,000 persons	( )	( )	( )
4.	Speed of urban traffic and timing of traffic lights	( )	( )	( )
5.	Women in medicine and engineering	( )	( )	( )
6.	Full-time enrollment rates of 20 to 24 year olds in college	( )	( )	( )
C.	**Technology-Medicine**			
1.	Research and development spending as a percent of GNP	( )	( )	( )
2.	Scientists and engineers as a proportion of total labor force	( )	( )	( )
3.	Public health expenditures as a percent of GNP	( )	( )	( )
4.	Noise pollution from road traffic and aircraft (55+ decibels)	( )	( )	( )
5.	Energy use per capita in kilograms of coal equivalent	( )	( )	( )
6.	Number of months needed for testing and review of new drugs	( )	( )	( )
D.	**Politics-Law**			
1.	Political stability (lack of coups, investment climate ratings)	( )	( )	( )
2.	Pollution control spending as a percent of GNP and of investment	( )	( )	( )
3.	Political campaign contribution ceilings	( )	( )	( )
4.	Extent of zoning laws and applications	( )	( )	( )
5.	Voter participation rate in major elections	( )	( )	( )
6.	Aid to less developed countries as a percent of GNP	( )	( )	( )

When you have finished your ratings, turn the page to see how you match with Cross's findings.

Source: Andrew Cross, "Where We Stand: The U.S. Vis-a-Vis Everyone Else," *Business Horizons,* March—April 1983.

Cross's Findings

A. Economics-Business
    1. Government spending as a percent of gross national product (GNP)   +
    2. Change in social security pension payments   +
    3. Labor productivity (absolute level and growth trend)   0
    4. Share of national income going to lowest 20 percent   0
    5. Misery index = unemployment rate + inflation rate   —
    6. Individual savings rate as a percent of disposable personal income   —

B. Culture-Society
    1. Rooms per dwelling and persons per room   +
    2. Speed at which long distance telephone calls can be completed   +
    3. Book production per 1,000 persons   0
    4. Speed of urban traffic and timing of traffic lights   0
    5. Women in medicine and engineering   —
    6. Full-time enrollment rates of 20 to 24 year olds in college   —

C. Technology-Medicine
    1. Research and development spending as a percent of GNP   +
    2. Scientists and engineers as a proportion of total labor force   +
    3. Public health expenditures as a percent of GNP   0
    4. Noise pollution from road traffic and aircraft (55+ decibels)   0
    5. Energy use per capita in kilograms of coal equivalent   —
    6. Number of months needed for testing and review of new drugs   —

D. Politics-Law
    1. Political stability (lack of coups, investment climate ratings)   +
    2. Pollution control spending as a percent of GNP and of investment   +
    3. Political campaign contribution ceilings   0
    4. Extent of zoning laws and applications   0
    5. Voter participation rate in major elections   —
    6. Aid to less developed countries as a percent of GNP   —

Discussion: The theme of the article is that these times demand moderation, perhaps even cut backs, on the part of many major economic powers. The question of where to cut back is more interesting when you can see comparatively how each country already stands. Regarding the U.S., in which categories do you feel we could cut back? What negative effects would result? Explain.

Number 4 — Experiential Learning Exercise

Introduction: In Chapter 20 of your text ethics is defined as the code of morals of a person or group that sets standards as to what is right or wrong in one's conduct. In work settings, your ethics can be challenged in terms of others wanting you to compromise them as illustrated in the following vignettes.

Directions: First role play the following by having two class members pair up and recite the role lines provided. Then discuss what should be done when these kinds of "favors" or compromises are requested of you.

The Hustle

Role Player A: Boss
Role Player B: Employee
Setting:　　　Small office

Boss: I have a potential customer who is close to signing an extremely lucrative contract with us. S/he is coming to town this evening, and is looking for a "fun" night out on the town.

This person is very important to our future business. I want you to be her/his host/ess and make sure s/he has a "fun" evening.

Employee: (Response open to individual reaction)

Discussion Questions

1. Why is this situation sort of double jeopardy for the employee?

2. Besides the request itself which sounds like the boss is asking for nonjob-descriptive favors, what tactic is the boss using that also seems ethically questionable?

3. How would you respond as the employee?

Free Lunch

Role Player A: Old employee
Role Player B: Newly-hired employee, a cashier
Setting:　　　Large restaurant

Old Employee: Welcome to the gang. I see you've met most of the other restaurant employees. Listen to me! We never pay for goodies around here. I'm helping myself to the salad for today but don't ring it up. Management won't miss it. It's only $2.95 on the menu anyway!

Newly-hired employee: (Response open to individual reaction)

Discussion Questions

1. Why is this request from a peer member potentially difficult for any new employee?

2. What rationale is the old employee using to make the "free lunch" seem okay?

3. If the newly-hired employee accedes even once, how does this affect trying to say no in the future?

4. Should the newly-hired employee go to management, or instead confront the employee in resolving this apparent theft by an insider?

The Write Off

Role Player A: West coast executive
Role Player B: East coast executive
Situation: **B** just recently made a lot of money from **A**'s company in a legitimate business deal, and more business is likely, although there is nothing in terms of immediate prospects. Quite surprised, **B** receives a call and request from **A** as follows:

   Role Player A: (on a phone) Hello Mr. B. Look, my wife and I want to vacation in your city, but I want to write the expenses off as business expenses. Please write me a letter requesting my consultative expertise on whatever you can dream up. I'll need a letter in my file in case the IRS challenges me regarding the veracity of the trip. Thanks for your help.
   Role Player B: (Response open to role player's reaction)

Discussion Questions

1.   Is this type of write-off a common practice? Wouldn't it be okay, if A did confer with B when in B's city even if it were for a very short time?

2.   How should B handle this?

3.   Is there any responsibility on B's part to try to affect ethical behaviors of members of other firms?

LOOKING BACK; LOOKING AHEAD

   In Part 6 you had an opportunity to view the role of the manager in a contemporary perspective. The challenge of managing for change in situations of conflict, for example, was emphasized. There can be conflicts between individual needs and the demands organizations make on individuals. There can be conflicts between managers' values and morals and those of employees. There can be conflicts between demands of organized labor and management. Conflict, thus, can be thought of as a hurdle to overcome in bringing about change. However, you also learned that positive types of conflict can lead to positive change, and from this perspective, conflict in organizations is a virtue. You also found that you **are** part of the international arena, and that you will benefit by expanding your own thinking in business and management in terms of this global perspective. Very likely your own career will involve you in some way beyond the borders of your own country.
   Part 7 has but one, culminating chapter. Brevity, however, is not its only virtue. Part 7, Chapter 21, "Management for Productivity: A Career Perspective," offers you the opportunity to, indeed, put the entire course and subject into a career perspective for yourself. Have your opinions or feelings about business and management changed since you began the text and course? If so, in what ways? Was your interest regarding a career in management reinforced, for example? Are there new directions that you learned about from various subtopics that were covered?
   What about the future? The author reviews certain trends such as those of environmental changes, people, and technology. He deals with stress and stress management as important factors in having a positive career experience. Then, very appropriately the author covers the "managing" of your own career from start to finish. Have you thought about applying various management functions and skills to managing your own career? You should find this last chapter of the text an interesting finishing chapter.

INTRODUCTION – PART 7

(Chapter 21)

Highlights

Part 7 has but one concluding chapter focusing on managing as a career area. This final chapter in the text helps put the many ideas, theories and concepts of the book into a final perspective, and the author asks you, the reader, to look ahead into your managerial future to try to anticipate the challenges, excitement, and opportunities to come.

What kind of future will managers and employees face? The chapter starts with some trends in the managerial environment to help project the future. For example, the author speculates that inflation will probably continue to be a problem as will energy shortages. In terms of people trends, the author cites the desire for self-determination which will carry over into the work environment in terms of employees wanting more control over how and when they do their jobs, more individual rights, security, and a high quality of life overall. Of course, the future for managers entails stress, and the text explains sources of stress and some ways that managers might manage stress.

An excellent section of the chapter entitled "Managing a Management Career" focuses on the importance of planning your career. Career planning, according to the text, is the process of systematically matching individual career goals and capabilities with opportunities for fulfillment. The author points out that how you plan your career may differ from how others do it. Nevertheless, career planning is important, and you will find Chapter 21 helpful in ways to plan your career and manage it from initial career entry to retirement.

Finally, as a recap to the entire text, the author summarizes the productivity theme and the managerial skills, functions, and roles that help in achieving productivity.

CAREER PERSPECTIVE — PART 7

Introduction

Chapter 21, Figure 21.5, provides steps in formal career planning. Now that you have come to the final chapter of the text and the end of the course, it is timely to put your own career plans into perspective.

Directions

Repeated below are the text's five formal career planning steps, A—E. You should do at least the first three steps which can be answered on paper at this time in your life. The other two steps may also be done now although they are steps that go beyond paper tasks.

Steps in Formal Career Planning

A.   Personal Assessment
  1.   List your major strengths

  2.   List your major weaknesses

  3.   List your aptitudes and abilities

  4.   Identify your work/career preferences

B.   Analysis of Opportunities
  1.   Summarize current economic conditions and what the prospects are for the next 12-18 months.

  2.   Translate economic conditions into labor market situations. That is, what is the relative supply and demand of people in your job/career interests areas. How does employment opportunity seem in the short and long term? Explain.

  3.   In general what occupational areas seem to be the growth areas of the future? Which ones seem to be shrinking? List.

C.   Selection of Career Objectives
In terms of your own personal assessment and analysis of opportunities, steps A and B, complete this career perspective exercise by answering the following:
1.   What is your short-term (1-3 years) career objective? Briefly explain.

2.   Do you have an intermediate (3-5 years) career objective? Explain.

3.   Do you have a long-term career goal? Try to state it even if general.

D.   Selection and Implementation of Plan
1.   Explain how you would conduct a job search.

2.   How does one succeed in gaining initial entry into a job and career, even those with large supplies of job seekers?

3.   In what ways will you continue your own personal development once you have finished your current formal education? List ways.

E.   Evaluation of Results and Revision of Plans as Necessary
1.   In what ways will you monitor your own progress in your career? For example, do you have particular goals you are trying to achieve? Levels you are trying to reach? Explain.

2.   How can you get feedback regarding your own growth and career progress?

3.   In what ways will you be comparing actual growth with your desired growth?

21 Management for Productivity:
A Career Perspective

STUDENT LEARNING OBJECTIVES

After completing this chapter material you should be able to:

1. List and explain what seem to be the "values" that hold an organization together.
2. List the text trends that suggest key factors managers will have to contend with in the future.
3. Quote Robert Fulmer's paradoxes to come, and explain how these paradoxes bear on management.
4. Define job stress and the managerial role in dealing with stress.
5. Distinguish between constructive and destructive stress.
6. Explain the "expanded view" of the social responsibility of the managerial role regarding job-related influences on employee health.
7. List and briefly explain negative stress sources in the work setting.
8. Define and explain effective stress management including stress prevention and coping.
9. Explain career planning and what might be the manager's responsibility in his or her own career development as well as in helping their employees.
10. Express agreement or disagreement with the career tactics advice offered in the latter part of the career discussion.
11. Review by relisting the factors involved in managerial productivity—managerial skills, functions, and roles.

CHAPTER HIGHLIGHTS

A manager's look into the future
Job stress and the manager's role
Mangement for productivity: A recap

PROGRAMMED LEARNING

The following statements are drawn from actual textbook content in abbreviated form. The blanks within the statements are numbered to correspond with the answer blanks at the left.

A manager's look into the future

1. _____
2. _____
3. _____
4. _____

Based on Ralph Sorenson's "lifetime of learning to manage effectively," he added several additional traits or skills that good managers must possess: ability to _____(1) oneself, _____(2) skills, managers must be _____(3) human beings, and have _____(4) and a strong sense of integrity.

A manager's look into the future

5. _____

Regarding future employment opportunity, many of the new jobs will go to persons in _____(5) industries.

6. _____
7. _____
8. _____
9. _____

Supervisor-subordinate relationships of the future, in particular, are likely to reflect the following specific changes among the people in the work force over time: pressures for self-_____(6), pressures for employee _____(7), pressures for _____(8), and pressures to achieve and maintain a high quality of _____(9).

10. _____

Another undeniable aspect of our environment is the emergence of high _____(10) as a dominant force in our lives.

11. _____
12. _____
13. _____

Without doubt, the greatest technological forces of the present decade are the _____(11), _____(12) information processing, and the _____(13).

14. _____
15. _____
16. _____
17. _____
18. _____
19. _____
20. _____
21. _____
22. _____
23. _____

Robert Fulmer offers the following paradoxes as potential complications in the managerial experience that you may well have to face up to in the future: the incentives that once encouraged people to work, namely _____(14) and _____(15), are less effective today than in the past; but just as financial incentives seem to be losing some of their prior clout, Fulmer points out that interest in the more _____-oriented(16) occupations is growing; increased competition for _____(17), but more _____(18) in work positions; more ability and need to _____(19) decisions, but more pressure to _____(20); the triumph of worker _____(21), yet a revival of _____(22) management; more people working, yet higher _____(23).

24. _____

Even though the phrase is well used, it is appropriate to say the future is sure to be an "age of _____(24)."

Job stress and stress management

25. _____

_____(25) is a state of tension experienced by individuals facing extraordinary demands, constraints or opportunities.

26. _____
27. _____
28. _____
29. _____

Work stress can result from excessively high or low _____(26) demands, _____(27) conflicts or ambiguities, poor _____(28) relations, or _____(29) progress that is too slow or too fast.

30. _____
31. _____

The _____(30) orientation, impatience, and perfectionism of individuals with Type A _____(31) may create stress for them in work circumstances other persons find relatively stress free.

32. _____
33. _____
34. _____
35. _____

_____(32) stress acts in a positive way for the individual and/or the organization. Low to moderate levels of stress act in a constructive or energizing way that increases _____(33), stimulates _____(34), and encourages _____(35) in one's work.

36. _____

_____(36) stress is dysfunctional for the individual and/or the organization.

37. _____
38. _____

Excessive stress from life-style and/or environmental sources can reduce resistance to _____(37) and increase the likelihood of physical and/or mental _____(38).

39. _____
40. _____
41. _____
42. _____

The expanded view of the manager's role includes helping employees maintain good health. Organizational responsibility for health maintenance can be defended on the basis of: _____(39), _____(40), _____(41), and return on _____(42).

43. _____

Destructive stress management can reduce _____(43).

44. _____
45. _____

Effective stress management is the ability to _____(44) stress, _____(45) with stress, and maintain personal wellness.

46. _____
47. _____
48. _____

Among work factors with the greatest potential to cause excessive stress are role _____(46), _____(47) and maintain personal _____(48).

49. _____

Among work factors with the greatest potential to cause excessive stress are role _____(49), conflicts, and overloads.

50. _____
51. _____
52. _____

Stress coping can be done through the following: control the situation, open up to _____(50), _____(51) yourself, exercise and _____(52).

53. _____

Personal _____(53) is a term used to describe the pursuit of one's physical and mental potential through a personal health promotion program.

Managing a managerial career

54. _____

A _____(54) is a sequence of jobs and work pursuits constituting what a person does for a living.

55. _____

A _____(55) path is a sequence of jobs held over time during a career.

56. _____

Career _____(56) is the process of systematically matching individual career goals and capabilities with opportunities for their fulfillment.

57. _____

A fundamental requirement of successful career planning is _____-_____(57).

58. _____

The essence of any successful career, no matter how well planned, is for a person to be good at his or her _____(58).

59. _____

The potential to advance most frequently arises through a record of _____(59) accomplishment.

60. _____
61. _____
62. _____

Three adult life stages are: _____ _____(60) transition, _____(61) transition, and _____ _____(62) transition.

63. _____

A career _____(63) is a position from which someone is not likely to move to a higher level of work responsibility.

64. _____
65. _____
66. _____

Three reasons account for many career plateaus: _____(64) choice, limited _____(65), and limited _____(66).

67. _____ By way of final advice, consider the following suggested career tactics:
68. _____ _____(67), stay _____(68), be willing to _____(69), find a
69. _____ _____(70), manage your _____(71), and continue your
70. _____ _____(72).
71. _____
72. _____

Management for productivity: A recap

73. _____ In the practice of management, performance can be achieved by developing
74. _____ essential managerial _____(73), implementing management
75. _____ _____(74), and enacting managerial _____(75).

TESTING YOUR KNOWLEDGE

True and False Self Test

Directions: Circle the letter (T or F) of the correct response for each of the following statements.

T F   1. "Future Shock" is a term used to describe society's feelings on nuclear arms.

T F   2. Incentives that encourage people to work, such as money and fear, are more effective today than ever.

T F   3. Effective stress management requires the ability to prevent stress, cope with stress, and maintain personal wellness.

T F   4. Essential managerial skills include technical, human, and conceptual skills.

T F   5. The author predicts that future employment will most likely be found in the service and informational areas.

T F   6. The Daniel Yankelovich poll has found that money and job security motivate 44% of the work force.

T F   7. By 1990, there will be greater competition for jobs because more than half of the labor force will be between the ages of 25 and 44.

T F   8. Harlan Cleveland, a successful executive, states that a career as a successful executive must be carefully planned.

T F   9. Today, the essence of any successful career is for a person to obtain good political contacts.

T F   10. A career plateau occurs during midlife just before one enters into another career.

Multiple Choice Self Test

Directions: Circle the letter of the response that best completes each of the following statements.

1. The "values" that hold organizations together include:
   a. team spirit
   b. prudent action
   c. sense of justice
   d. fortitude and challenge
   e. all of the above

2. Trends in people in the work force are likely to include:
   a. pressures for self-determination
   b. pressures for individual and group rights
   c. pressures for security
   d. pressures to achieve a high quality life
   e. all of the above

3. Regarding the question of the decline in value of traditional workplace factors, which statement below accurately reflects the text:
   a. Money and fear are just as effective as in the past in influencing employees.
   b. College enrollments in the liberal arts are rapidly increasing.
   c. Greater competition for jobs particularly in the age group 25—44.
   d. Less employee interest in decision-making.

4. Work stress results from:
   a. excessively high or low work demands
   b. role conflicts of ambiguities
   c. poor interpersonal relations
   d. all of the above

5. Constructive stress is stress that:
   a. you can cause the "enemy", the competition
   b. is used to test the strength of buildings
   c. you can cause to happen just for the heck of it
   d. stimulates creativity and encourages diligence in one's work

6. It has been determined that excessive stress can:
   a. reduce resistance to disease
   b. increase likelihood of mental illness
   c. cause heart attacks
   d. cause problems such as hypertension, ulcers, and depression
   e. all of the above

7. The best way to deal with stress is to:
   a. prevent it
   b. cope with it
   c. deny it exists
   d. suppress it

8. The way to cope with stress is to:
   a. control the situation
   b. open up to others
   c. pace yourself
   d. exercise and relax
   e. all of the above can help cope

9. The point in one's adult transition within career where there is a "settling in " and mellowing of goals:
   a. early adulthood
   b. midlife transition
   c. later adulthood
   d. near retirement

Matching Self Test

Directions: Write the letter of the description that best fits each numbered item in the blank provided.

_____ 1. Job-sharing, permanent part-time

_____ 2. "Quality of Life" concerns

_____ 3. Constructive stress

_____ 4. MBO

_____ 5. Personal wellness

_____ 6. Career planning

_____ 7. Career plateau

_____ 8. Essential managerial skill

_____ 9. Managerial roles

_____ 10. Management functions

a. Movement toward worker participation in affairs and decisions of the workplace.

b. Stimulates creativity and encourages diligence in one's work.

c. Future employment programs aimed at accommodating pressures of work and family life.

d. An opportunity for a superior to spot stressors and take the opportunity to reduce or eliminate them.

e. More art than science and highly individualized.

f. Technical, human, conceptual.

g. Pursuit of one's physical and mental potential through a personal health promotion program.

h. Position from which someone is not likely to move to a higher level of work responsibility.

i. Planning, organizing, leading, and controlling.

j. Interpersonal, informational, and decisional.

LEARNING ACTIVITIES — PART 7

Number 1 — Supplemental Reading and Discussion

Introduction: Chapter one addresses the changing environment as one of the aspects with which management must deal in order to facilitate the productivity of employees. Environment can be viewed in the external sense that business operates in the universe of social-political-economic forces with the potential to influence organizations and their members. This broader view of environment was the focus of the entire text.

Another view of environment is internal, or the immediate job surroundings in which employees work. The following article deals with this issue of the internal environment and its impact on employees.

Directions: Read the following reprint of a journal article and complete the discussion questions which follow:

"THE PRODUCTIVITY VALUE OF ENVIRONMENT"
(In Offices of the Future)

Many fear that the office of the future will be a forbidding high-tech world, where the computer reigns triumphant and human beings are no longer of any real use. The truth, however, is quite the opposite, for the business of business is ideas, and ideas are produced by people—not machines. Human work input can never be dispensed with no matter how technologically "advanced" the workplace becomes. The white collar worker is here to stay. The success of the office of the future depends on their expertise and productivity.

Not long ago, BOSTI (Buffalo Organization for Social and Technical Innovation), a New York research firm, did a study on increased productivity as a result of good office environment. It showed that satisfaction with work space created an extra $1,600 of productivity annually in a white collar worker.

How do we make sure that any given environment will satisfy the people who live in it? At my architectural firm we start with the basic tool: market research. My wife, Jane, is in the advertising business, and I've learned from her that advertising expertise has a direct translation to architecture and interior design. "Start with market research," she suggests. "That will tell you what is important to people and what is not. The research leads the way to a strategy and then to the execution itself. If your research is sound, your execution will work."

What do people want?

We start out with the assumption that each business is unique. We conduct extensive interviews with personnel at all levels; we usually talk to one out of every seven employees. We have to look at such things as "adjacencies" (who should be near whom);

the behavioral aspects of work station locations, lighting, acoustics and—another new word in the design vocabulary—"ergonomics" or human factors of comfort.

We also look at the issues of spatial relations, color, texture, relief spaces, and places for idea exchange. Then we look at how best to accommodate the machine into the design. Historically, when computers were first introduced into the office environment, they were housed in separate rooms. Now they have moved from the back room into the president's office.

Finally, we discuss with our clients the ways in which they wish to distinguish their organization in the marketplace. To borrow another phrase from the advertising world, what do they want their "brand image" to be?

Interactional distances

In Texas, people drive 100 miles to a barbecue without giving it a second thought. But 101 miles might just keep them home by their own fire. We have discovered, through research, that workers in different businesses have certain distances beyond which they will not go to react with others (this phenomenon is the "interactional distance").

One engineering company, for example, knew very well that engineers produced more ideas when they talked together. However, the engineers would not walk more than about 90 feet. The company installed "coffee nooks" with high stools at appropriate distances so the engineers could perch (research also showed that sitting in comfortable chairs made them feel guilty about wasting time), and put ceramic graph paper on the walls and supplied lots of magic markers for easy doodling. The design resulted in more interaction and more ideas.

Adjacencies

It must be very clear, before a pencil touches the sketch pad, who should be next to whom in the office, and why. We set up a "Departmental Proximity Matrix" with a rating key from 3, meaning it is absolutely necessary for two people or functions to be near each other for their mutual benefit, down to zero, an indication that proximity is undersirable.

At another company, we discovered it was essential for the general counsel to be near the patents department. On the other hand, it was definitely not a good idea for the highly sensitive tax department to be located near personnel, where many nonemployees were coming in and out for interviews.

Probably the most important result of studying adjacencies is the focus on planning and the savings that so often result. Most companies simply do not think about how they are utilizing space, unless they move into new space or renovate existing space. We help them focus on their needs by asking questions. Is a certain department going to grow in ten years? Or shrink? Can two departments that are now relying on two sets of support facilities share the same facilities? Our matrix is a kind of marketing plan for the most cost effective use of space. When a CEO sees the impact this kind of planning can have on the bottom line, it becomes very important.

Lighting

What are we to make of a recent study in *The New York Times* about the strong effects of office lighting on emotional and even sexual well-being? Or studies of the secretion of enzymes which affect behavior when employees look at certain colors? Our interest in these issues has led us to some independent research in conjunction with the University of California at San Diego. We've assessed the impact of some factors my architectural colleagues and I simply never considered before.

Human beings, like plants, thrive on natural light. So even when we design large enclosed spaces, we try to incorporate areas where people can enjoy sunlight. Our design for the corporate headquarters of Schering-Plough created interior atria with skylights and lots of greenery; natural environments for relief space and time. One nearly certain prediction for the office of the future is that lighting will have to accommodate around-the-clock work shifts. Lighting levels must then possess the capacity to adjust to the presence of absence of natural light. It all comes back to our main theme: making people comfortable and productive. How do we make it pleasant for them to work or take a lunch break at 3:00 a.m.?

Conventional fluorescent lighting in open office areas is traditionally far brighter than it need be. A single level throughout is too bright, too "flat" and adds to fatigue. The new thinking leads us to "task/ambient" lighting. Task lighting simply illuminates the specific work area or work surface. Ambient lighting illuminates the room. We have seen productivity in our drafting room increase 14 percent when we changed from general fluorescent to task-directed fluorescent.

Like so many aspects of the office of the future, changes in lighting take some getting used to. At Chemical Bank's office in downtown New York, where we installed lower ambient levels than most people were accustomed to, first reactions were: "too dark." However, as staff members became used to the non-institutional environment, reactions became extremely positive.

The combination of low-level ambient lighting and appropriate task-lighting levels help to personalize the work environment and make the employee feel more at home. It is simply one more way to make the office more human.

Man versus machine

Many companies that have recently added new automated equipment to their offices were shocked to find increased absenteeism, especially on Mondays; longer breaks and longer lunch hours; increased employee turnover in affected departments; and inflated salary demands.

New studies are quantifying what some of us have long suspected. The introduction of automated equipment into the office faces tremendous hostility from employees. The poor performance of unhappy workers can negate the productivity benefits of the new machinery.

What seems to have gone wrong? Machines have created feelings of anxiety. Some people fear they will be replaced by the machines. Others are concerned that they are being monitored, measured in "keystrokes." Some organizations, particularly those lobbying on behalf of women office workers, complain that automation makes the secretary's job more routine and reduces her status.

I am convinced that it has also created a generation gap between those executives comfortable with using equipment like desktop computer terminals and those who are not. One large financial company installed such equipment on the desks of all its senior people, only to discover most of the older professionals simply turned the screens to the wall. They had to bring in a batch of young MBAs to start hitting the keyboards, demonstrating the ease of the machines to their own conventional peers.

Of course, time will solve the generation problem. The kids now growing up with Apple computers helping them do homework in third grade won't be threatened. In fact, they'll demand more. A recent study of student satisfaction at Bucknell University revealed the single greatest desire of the student body: more computer terminals at more places on campus.

The problem does not lie with the computer, but rather with the environment that neither comforts the user nor gives him assurances of his personal worth. The proliferation of pivots, gears, tilts, glare and noise eliminators and other gadgetry (which most computer operators never use) increases the feeling of an alien, computer-like environment.

Management must remind its workers that they remain the company's greatest asset. The simplification of the computer environment, for one thing, correctly postures the equipment as a tool, not a usurper. And management must remember that perks added to the environment at the same time as machines make the office more a "people place" and help the employees accept the new changes.

Need for flexibility

There's a lot we don't know about the office of the future. One thing is for sure, however: Things will keep changing. And changing more rapidly than ever. So the key to office planning is **flexibility**.

Installation of a raised floor system, with removable tile for easy access to component systems wiring that can be snapped into place delivers maximum flexibility. It means that office components, including the office itself, can be changed overnight, with a minimum use of skilled labor.

Says John J. Collins, who as general manager for New York Telephone, has responsibility for accurately forecasting the future use of that company's office space throughout New York State: "Open planning will continue to be the wave of the future."

William M. Hogan, senior vice-president of the E. F. Hauserman Company, one of the largest makers of open plans systems components, agrees. "Human values and needs are often seen in conflict with growing productivity requirements and technology," he says. "We believe technology, as a productivity facilitator, includes both automated machines and the work environment. The challenge to all of us is to coordinate and integrate the people, the space, and the technology of the office."

Source: Michael Mass, "The Productivity Value of Environment," *Management Review,* March 1983.

Discussion Questions

1. For what reason does the writer say we need not fear that the office of the future will be a forbidding, high-tech place—thus cold and unwelcome?

2. To what extent does employee satisfaction with work space translate into productivity?

3. What does the author say is the starting point in making sure any given environment will satisfy those who live in it? Do you agree? Why? Explain.

4. List the environmental factors that the writer of the article considers before designing office space. What would you add to the list?

5. What do environmental terms such as behavioral aspects of the work station and ergonomics mean? Define and put them in a work context.

6. What is the last factor that is asked of clients in determining appropriate environments? To what extent can any one office reflect a company image? Explain.

7. What is "interactional distance" and how does it influence office design?

8. What are "adjacencies" and how do they affect office design?

9. What is "task/ambient" lighting?

10. In what ways has the addition of computers or other high-tech machines affected those executives who must live with them?

11. In summary, what environmental factors seem most important for you in contemplating work in an office setting?

Number 2 — Exercise: Rewards and Employee Transition

Introduction: The text speaks about employees' needs and values relating to the point at which they are in their careers. In other words, as employees move from career entry to early adulthood, to mid-life transition, and later to middle and late adulthood, their work behaviors will be predicated by their present life circumstances. Furthermore, each phase of life and work often presents a new and different set of circumstances for them, and managers need to be sensitive to employees and the particular life/career phase they are in.

Directions: Given the text's four phases of career and career transition below, you are to explain what particular types of work-related factors, particularly rewards, are of greatest importance to employees in each category.

Career phase	*Rewards that would be particularly attractive. (Rewards in salary, benefits, etc.)*
A. Career entry	
1. Describe things of importance in general.	1. Example: Tuition for additional education.
	2.
	3.
	4.
	5.
B. Transition to and through early adulthood	
1. Describe things of importance in general.	1. Example: Paternity leave for dads.
	2.
	3.
	4.
	5.

Career phase	*Rewards that would be particularly attractive. (Rewards in salary, benefits, etc.)*
C. Transition to and through mid-life	
1. Describe things of importance in general.	1. Example: Retraining opportunity for career change.
	2.
	3.
	4.
	5.
D. Transition to and through later adulthood	
1. Describe things of importance in general.	1. Example: Extended leaves or time off.
	2.
	3.
	4.
	5.

Number 3 — Exercise: Paradoxes in the Manager's World

Introduction: Robert Fulmer is cited in the text for identifying paradoxes in trends under the areas of environment, people, and technology. He offered the following paradoxes as potential complications for managerial personnel of the future:

1. Decline of traditional incentives, but increased popularity of financially rewarding careers.
2. Increased competition for promotions, but more flexibility in work positions.
3. More ability and need to centralize decisions, but more pressure to decentralize.
4. The triumph of worker participation, yet a revival of scientific management.
5. More people working, yet higher unemployment.

Directions: Expand upon the five paradoxes listed by Fulmer by listing five apparent paradoxes that you see in the social/economic/political environment in which you live. Then make a brief response to what each paradox implies to those managing.

Your List of Paradoxes in Trends

1. Example: Independence in the form of single parents, yet more dependence on nonfamily support systems of our society.

Management Implications:

2.

Management Implications:

3.

Management Implications:

4.

    Management Implications:

5.

    Management Implications:

6.

    Management Implications:

7.

    Management Implications:

8.

    Management Implications:

9.

    Management Implications:

10.

    Management Implications:

Number 4 — Matching Wits with the Experts

    Introduction: There is a Social Readjustment Scale* that is sometimes used to help explain stress levels in people's lives. Drs. Tom Holmes and Richard Rahe developed this scale and assigned stress units to each of 43 factors below.

    One hundred units would be the maximum stress points that would be assigned on their scale, for example, to death of a spouse. There are 42 additional items below that are from the "Social Readjustment Scale" the stress units or points.

    Directions: Assign what you perceive is the relative stress value of the 43 items listed below. The range of possible units or points is 1 to 100. Second, turn the page to compare your perception of relative stress factors with theirs. Third, using their stress units, circle the items that have affected you in the recent past, add the stress points to get a total.

*Source: Holmes, T.H. and Rahe, R.H.: "The Social Readjustment Rating Scale," *Journal of Psychosomatic Research 11,* pp. 213-218, Copyright 1967.

Social Readjustment Scale

1.   Student Perception of Relative Stress value of factors listed 1–43.

Rank	Life event	Mean value
1.	Death of spouse	___
2.	Divorce	___
3.	Marital separation	___
4.	Jail term	___
5.	Death of close family member	___
6.	Personal injury or illness	___
7.	Marriage	___
8.	Fired at work	___
9.	Marital reconciliation	___
10.	Retirement	___
11.	Change in health of family member	___
12.	Pregnancy	___
13.	Sex difficulties	___
14.	Gain of new family member	___
15.	Business readjustment	___
16.	Change in financial state	___
17.	Death of close friend	___
18.	Change to different line of work	___
19.	Change in number of arguments with spouse	___
20.	Mortgage over $10,000	___
21.	Foreclosure of mortgage or loan	___
22.	Change in responsibilities at work	___

Rank	Life event	Mean value
23.	Son or daughter leaving home	___
24.	Trouble with in-laws	___
25.	Outstanding personal achievement	___
26.	Wife begins or stops work	___
27.	Begin or end school	___
28.	Change in living conditions	___
29.	Revision of personal habits	___
30.	Trouble with boss	___
31.	Change in work hours or conditions	___
32.	Change in residence	___
33.	Change in schools	___
34.	Change in recreation	___
35.	Change in church activities	___
36.	Change in social activities	___
37.	Mortgage or loan less than $10,000	___
38.	Change in sleeping habits	___
39.	Change in number of family get-togethers	___
40.	Change in eating habits	___
41.	Vacation	___
42.	Christmas	___
43.	Minor violations of the law	___

Now, turn the page and compare your assignment of stress points with those by Holmes and Rahe, and assess your own stress level.

Social Readjustment Scale

2.   Holmes and Rahe Scale and Student Self Assessment of Stress.

Rank	Life event	Mean value	Student self-assessment
1.	Death of spouse	100	
2.	Divorce	73	
3.	Marital separation	65	
4.	Jail term	63	
5.	Death of close family member	63	
6.	Personal inury or illness	53	
7.	Marriage	50	
8.	Fired at work	47	
9.	Marital reconciliation	45	
10.	Retirement	45	
11.	Change in health of family member	44	
12.	Pregnancy	40	
13.	Sex difficulties	39	
14.	Gain of new family member	39	
15.	Business readjustment	39	
16.	Change in financial state	38	
17.	Death of close friend	37	
18.	Change to different line of work	36	
19.	Change in number of arguments with spouse	35	
20.	Mortgage over $10,000	31	
21.	Foreclosure of mortgage or loan	30	
22.	Change in responsibilities at work	29	
23.	Son or daughter leaving home	29	
24.	Trouble with in-laws	29	
25.	Outstanding personal achievement	28	
26.	Wife begins or stops work	26	
27.	Begin or end school	26	
28.	Change in living conditions	25	
29.	Revision of personal habits	24	
30.	Trouble with boss	23	
31.	Change in work hours or conditions	20	
32.	Change in residence	20	
33.	Change in schools	20	
34.	Change in recreation	19	
35.	Change in church activities	19	

Rank	Life event	Mean value	Student self assessment
36.	Change in social activities	18	_____
37.	Mortgage or loan less than $10,000	17	_____
38.	Change in sleeping habits	16	_____
39.	Change in number of family get-togethers	15	_____
40.	Change in eating habits	15	_____
41.	Vacation	13	_____
42.	Christmas	12	_____
43.	Minor violations of the law	11	_____

Scoring: 300 points or more is considered high stress level leading to a strong likelihood of developing illness related to stress. 150—300 points or units indicate a fair chance of illness.

Discussion Questions:

1. What do your stress units total? If above 150 points, can you attribute stress that you've had to any health problems? Explain.

2. Regarding the scale itself and the assigned units or points, aren't these quite subjective? That is, 50 points for marriage might be considerably high or low depending upon each individual. What items on the scale were you 20 points or more in disagreement? Explain from your own perspective.

3. Based upon the text coverage of stress, in what ways can you deal with your own stress? Explain.

Number 5 — Experiential Learning Exercise

Introduction: Some jobs by their very nature are stressful for employees who occupy them. An example would be flight controller for the FAA. Other jobs are much less stressful, but on occasion have stress inducing moments or situations which if not handled well, continue to put stress on the employees involved.

Directions: Below are three stress inducing situations which could develop in a variety of employment settings and jobs. You can role play them, and/or write responses and discuss how to handle the situation so as to alleviate the apparent problem and also reduce the stress on yourself.

The Angry Customers

Situation:

Your retail store ran a colorful ad in the Sunday Newspaper claiming that the first 100 customers through your doors today would receive fishing hats. You noticed before you opened that a lineup of perhaps 200 people were already jostling in line. Unfortunately top management failed to get the special el cheapo hats to your store, and you have now opened the store offering rain checks to those who qualify as part of the first 100.

Role Play or Situation for Discussion:

Customer A: "Rain check, baloney! I drove 30 miles and came two hours early. I want my hat!"

You: (Your own role response or written response as Floor Manager.)

Customer A: (Dialogue can be continued, if role playing.)

Continuation of fishing hat problem:

Customer B: "I see lots of fishing hats on the shelf here, and I'm taking this blue one. Your ad promised a free hat, and I'm taking mine" (one that is much more expensive than are the giveaway hats).

You: Your own role or written response.

Customer B: (Dialogue can be continued, if role playing.)

The "Rah Rah" Gung Ho Supervisor

Situation:

As a new college grad, you landed a selling job with a major soap company. Interestingly, you are being tutored and managed by a nondegreed person who says he made it the hard way—lots of good old fashioned work. He or she also is a "fire em up" and "give em hell" type so that when you are in this person's presence you are constantly being exhausted with pep talks, either positive or negative, depending upon the situation. Here are some of your recent statements, followed by some of his/her own one-liners which you are to react to. Not being a rah rah type you are feeling stress in the presence of the boss.

1a.   You, as Sales Person: "The customer just wouldn't buy our brand."

1b.   Your Sales Manager: "Never take no for an answer!"

1c.   Your response: (Open for role play or written response.)

2a.   You, as Sales Person: "Well, I didn't have a very good sales day."

2b.   Your Sales Manager: "Winners always have good days; start thinking like a winner!"

2c.   Your response: (Open for role play or written response.)

3a.   You, as Sales Person: "I don't know if I'm well enough informed about this customer to make the sale."

3b.   Your Sales Manager: "It's all in your attitude; you're only as good as you want to be. Fire up!"

3c.   Your response: (Open for role play or written response.)

LOOKING BACK; LOOKING AHEAD

It is appropriate now to look back not only to Part 7 of the text, but also to the entire text. The author set the theme of productivity for this management text, and throughout the book, attention was placed on the manager's role in facilitating organizational productivity.

The author in Part 1 sets productivity in motion by explaining it in the context of what management is and how managers get work done through subordinates. He provided us a brief historical perspective on the evolvement of management as a science and art.

In Part 2, the first function of management, planning, was developed so that productivity was linked to goals and strategies.

In Part 3, four chapters were devoted to organizing for productivity. You learned about the fundamentals of organizations, their structures, and how authority and responsibility are reflected in structure. You also learned how important organizations are in terms of job designing. Job designs leading to formal job descriptions become a legal basis on which people are evaluated in terms of performance and for which they are paid.

Of course, informal groupings take place so that besides formal organization charts, you saw that employees form their own networks which help fulfill some of their social needs, but may not contribute much to organizational output. Managers must learn to manage both formal and informal groups. In the staffing phase of Part 3, you learned that getting potentially productive new-hires is a major step in achieving overall organizational productivity. The challenge in staffing, of course, lies with developing valid and reliable selection tools.

Part 4 carried you into and through yet another key managerial function, leading. You learned that not all managers are leaders, and that leadership goes beyond simple personal traits.

You learned that effective leadership is done through skills of communication and influencing employee behavior in terms of motivation toward organizational goals. Finally, you learned more about the "sociology" of the group in terms of group dynamics. Group interplay can be conducive or harmful to overall productivity.

Part 5 offered the final functional area of management entitled controlling. You found that controlling is a negative or necessarily restrictive word. Controlling is a natural functional role of managers and it is linked to planning, in particular, where targets of performance are set. Budgets and management information systems in particular serve as control mechanisms for managers.

Part 6 put management and productivity in a contemporary environment which includes change. Change is inevitable, and must be a planned activity in most organizations. You saw that change breeds conflict since it can be a threat to the security of employees. For organizations to develop both change and conflict must be managed well. If organized labor is part of the organizational setting, then additional challenges exist for managers in terms of dealing with yet another unit and their contractual rules and procedures.

In the international arena, you learned that management skills are needed, but that each different socio-economic-cultural setting requires special managerial attention so that employees will be dealt with appropriately.

The author gave you "food for thought" in raising questions about the manager's role in conducting an ethical and sociably-responsible organization whether it be locally, nationally, or internationally.

Finally, your author offered you in Part 7 a concluding chapter that gave you the opportunity to put the subject of management in your own career perspective. Has your understanding of what management is and what managers do changed since the outset of the book? Do you understand the preparation necessary in terms of knowledge and skills if you aspire to be a manager? Has the text influenced your thinking regarding managing as a career choice? How so?

Of course, there are no additional chapters toward which to "look ahead." However, it is appropriate to advise you to look ahead in several ways. One way is to encourage you to determine what would be next in course work in management or related content areas. Your present text might have given you some direction already in separate chapters. A variety of management-related topics were covered—planning, organizing, and controlling; problem solving and decision making; communicating, leading, and motivating. Any one of these topics has considerably more material which you could explore through formal courses or on your own.

Another way to look ahead is have you identify current journals and newspapers which should become your regular reading and help keep you current in management and the environment in which organizations must operate. Of course, the *Wall Street Journal* is one, but what others are readily available in your closest library?

ANSWERS

CHAPTER 1

Programmed Learning

1. work	24. purpose	46. performance
2. work	25. environment	47. subordinates
3. manager	26. effort	48. productivity
4. resource	27. human	49. productivity
5. material	28. division	50. time
6. performance	29. authority	51. effectiveness
7. human	30. command	52. efficiency
8. material	31. authority	53. accomplishment
9. people	32. goals	54. outputs
10. managers	33. plans	55. inputs
11. organizations	34. action	56. management
12. people	35. middle	57. academic
13. labor	36. conduits	58. inquiry
14. purpose	37. implement	59. controlling
15. essential	38. judgment	60. leading
16. individual	39. interpersonal	61. planning
17. people	40. line	62. organizing
18. purpose	41. staff	63. leading
19. labor	42. general	64. skill
20. authority	43. administrators	65. technical
21. good	44. subordinates	66. conceptual
22. service	45. superiors	67. learning
23. open		

Testing Your Knowledge

True and False	Multiple Choice	Matching
1. T	1. A	1. C
2. T	2. D	2. I
3. F	3. C	3. A
4. T	4. A	4. B
5. T	5. D	5. D
6. T	6. C	6. F
7. T (a total of 4 functions exists)	7. C	7. J
8. F	8. E	8. G
9. F	9. D	9. H
10. T	10. C	10. E

CHAPTER 2

Programmed Learning

1. theory
2. mangement
3. theories
4. managerial
5. art
6. science
7. art
8. science
9. analyzed
10. verbalize
11. vocabulary
12. techniques
13. profession
14. professionals
15. art
16. science
17. professionalism
18. knowledge
19. scientific
20. specialization
21. labor
22. industrial
23. mass
24. rational
25. economic
26. management
27. administration
28. bureaucratic
29. prosperity
30. prosperity
31. "science"
32. abilities
33. incentives
34. planning
35. motion
36. simplification
37. standards
38. incentive
39. organizing
40. leading
41. controlling
42. bureaucracy
43. productivity
44. structures
45. bureaucracy
46. technical
47. designs
48. management
49. organizational
50. social
51. self-actualizing
52. atmosphere
53. participatory
54. physical
55. technical
56. social
57. human
58. needs
59. attitudes
60. behaviors
61. satisfied
62. progression
63. needs
64. tension
65. behavior
66. productivity
67. X
68. Y
69. dislike
70. control
71. participation
72. freedom
73. responsibility
74. requirements
75. variety
76. systematically
77. mathematical
78. optimum
79. decision
80. economic
81. mathematical
82. computers
83. productivity
84. technical
85. implement
86. situation
87. rational/economic
88. social/self-actualization
89. contingency
90. complex
91. variable
92. needs
93. change
94. demands
95. strategies
96. cooperation
97. "system"
98. environment
99. environmental
100. situational
101. environmental
102. technological
103. characteristics
104. functions
105. environment

Testing Your Knowledge

True and False

1. F
2. F
3. T
4. F
5. T
6. F
7. T
8. T
9. F
10. T

Multiple Choice

1. D
2. E
3. C
4. A
5. A
6. D
7. D
8. B
9. D
10. D

Matching

1. D
2. H
3. J
4. G
5. A
6. B
7. F
8. I
9. E
10. C

CHAPTER 3

Programmed Learning

1. right
2. choice
3. problem
4. solving
5. desired
6. anticipate
7. action
8. rational
9. analytical
10. intuitive
11. intuitive
12. systematic
13. problem
14. solutions
15. course
16. action
17. action
18. desired
19. actual
20. actual
21. desired
22. programmed
23. decisions
24. expected
25. nonroutine
26. nonprogrammed
27. nothing
28. creativity
29. perceptual
30. cultural
31. brainstorming
32. nominal
33. certainty
34. risk
35. uncertainty
36. creativity
37. inventory
38. decisions
39. choice
40. made
41. who
42. easy
43. resolve
44. decision
45. classical
46. perceive
47. uncertainty
48. information
49. group
50. participative
51. implement
52. evaluate

Testing Your Knowledge

True and False

1. T
2. T
3. T
4. F
5. T
6. F
7. F
8. F
9. T
10. T

Multiple Choice

1. A
2. C
3. C
4. B
5. E
6. C
7. D
8. C
9. E
10. D

Matching

1. C
2. E
3. D
4. H
5. J
6. B
7. F
8. G
9. A
10. I

CHAPTER 4

Programmed Learning

1. planning
2. future
3. objectives
4. anticipatory
5. decisions
6. states
7. plan
8. organize
9. lead
10. control
11. plan
12. planning
13. how
14. when
15. where
16. whom
17. objective
18. strategic
19. operational
20. tactical
21. single
22. strategic
23. strategic
24. standing
25. single
26. policy
27. directions
28. constraints
29. procedures
30. rules
31. action
32. discretion
33. budgets
34. schedules
35. fixed
36. zero
37. schedules
38. whom
39. objectives
40. objectives
41. premises
42. alternative
43. implementing
44. inside out
45. outside in
46. inside-out
47. bottom-up
48. direction
49. lower
50. participate
51. assumptions
52. inputs
53. alternatives
54. commitment
55. control
56. follow through
57. forecasting
58. premise
59. qualitative
60. delphi
61. quantitative
62. time-series
63. econometric
64. statistical
65. human
66. error
67. stability
68. adaptability
69. contingency
70. contingency
71. fate
72. means-ends
73. purpose
74. objectives
75. priorities
76. organizational
77. external
78. control
79. routines
80. information
81. internal
82. resistance

Testing Your Knowledge

True and False

1. T
2. F
3. F
4. F
5. T
6. T
7. T
8. T
9. F
10. T

Multiple Choice

1. A
2. D
3. E
4. E
5. E
6. E
7. C
8. B
9. C
10. D

Matching

1. H
2. D
3. C
4. E
5. G
6. A
7. B
8. F
9. J
10. I

CHAPTER 5

Programmed Learning

1. strategy	25. strategic	49. strategic
2. strategy	26. goods	50. human
3. decision making	27. services	51. strengths
4. behavior	28. methods	52. weaknesses
5. direction	29. targets	53. values
6. framework	30. strategy	54. corporate
7. programmed	31. opportunities	55. values
8. retrenchment	32. weaknesses	56. culture
9. survival	33. alternatives	57. strategic
10. effectiveness	34. strategy	58. guidelines
11. society	35. action	59. implement
12. employees	36. mission	60. intuition
13. objectives	37. objectives	61. incrementalism
14. organizational	38. opportunities	62. changes
15. strategies	39. values	63. substance
16. official	40. culture	64. process
17. operating	41. weaknesses	65. process
18. identification	42. mission	66. checklist
19. integration	43. opportunities	67. people
20. collaboration	44. results	68. good
21. adaptation	45. problems	69. process
22. revitalization	46. opportunities	70. stone
23. hierarchy	47. perspective	71. success
24. strategic	48. capabilities	

Testing Your Knowledge

True and False	Multiple Choice	Matching
1. F	1. C	1. B
2. F	2. C	2. A
3. T	3. D	3. D
4. F	4. E	4. I
5. T	5. D	5. J
6. T	6. E	6. H
7. T	7. D	7. C
8. F	8. D	8. E
9. T	9. A	9. F
10. T	10. E	10. G

CHAPTER 6

Programmed Learning

1. perform	31. managerial	61. anarchy
2. people	32. efforts	62. group
3. labor	33. create	63. cost
4. together	34. strategy	64. coordinate
5. purpose	35. technology	65. authority
6. organizing	36. environment	66. vertical
7. resources	37. people	67. command
8. flow	38. size	68. scalar
9. guidelines	39. specialization	69. unity
10. planning	40. design	70. span
11. controlling	41. departmentation	71. flat
12. communication	42. coordination	72. tall
13. decision making	43. vertical	73. delegation
14. effort	44. horizontal	74. duties
15. specialized	45. departmentation	75. authority
16. coordinated	46. authority	76. obligation
17. structure	47. communication	77. accountability
18. resources	48. control	78. authority
19. structure	49. decisions	79. responsibility
20. chart	50. function	80. responsibility
21. work	51. labor	81. decentralized
22. relationships	52. stable	82. horizontal
23. work	53. problems	83. functional
24. subunits	54. matrix	84. personnel
25. management	55. diverse	85. staff
26. informal	56. decision making	86. advisory
27. work	57. cross	87. functional
28. gaps	58. growth	88. divide
29. communicate	59. dynamic	89. coordinate
30. change	60. power	

Testing Your Knowledge

True and False	Multiple Choice	Matching
1. F	1. E	1. A
2. T	2. E	2. C
3. T	3. E	3. B
4. F	4. E	4. D
5. F	5. D	5. F
6. T	6. D	6. E
7. T	7. D	7. K
8. T (also specialization of job design)	8. E	8. G
9. T	9. B	9. I
10. T	10. A	10. H

CHAPTER 7

Programmed Learning

1. design
2. structure
3. environment
4. technology
5. size
6. strategy
7. bureaucracy
8. diversion
9. hierarchy
10. technical
11. standards
12. bureaucratic
13. change
14. size
15. complexity
16. behavior
17. rigid
18. unwieldy
19. initiative
20. system
21. inputs
22. contingency
23. bureaucratic
24. organic
25. stable
26. organic
27. strategic
28. environment
29. situation
30. context
31. organic
32. mechanistic
33. rate
34. predictability
35. general
36. specific
37. organizational
38. technology
39. size
40. strategy
41. people
42. strategic
43. technology
44. productivity
45. intensive
46. mediating
47. long-linked
48. organic
49. mechanistic
50. mechanistic
51. mechanistic
52. organic
53. organic
54. mechanistic
55. task
56. routine
57. discretion
58. variety
59. subsystem
60. subenvironments
61. environmental
62. strategic
63. subsystems
64. integration
65. differentiation
66. time
67. goal
68. interpersonal
69. structure
70. differentiation
71. coordination
72. differentiation
73. forces
74. teams
75. matrix
76. differentiation
77. integration

Testing Your Knowledge

True and False	Multiple Choice	Matching
1. T	1. B	1. H
2. T	2. E	2. G
3. F	3. A	3. A
4. T	4. E	4. B
5. T	5. E	5. I
6. T	6. C	6. J
7. T	7. A	7. E
8. T	8. D	8. F
9. T	9. D	9. C
10. F	10. E	10. D

CHAPTER 8

Programmed Learning

1. jobs
2. departments
3. organizations
4. job
5. value
6. psychological
7. psychological
8. values
9. contributions
10. inducements
11. balance
12. work life
13. productivity
14. satisfaction
15. context
16. hygiene
17. conditions
18. interpersonal
19. policies
20. supervision
21. salary
22. dissatisfaction
23. context
24. dissatisfaction
25. hygiene
26. satisfiers
27. content
28. performance
29. performance
30. psychological
31. performance
32. rewards
33. performance
34. performance
35. satisfaction
36. design
37. content
38. context
39. what
40. setting
41. scope
42. tasks
43. specialization
44. enlargement
45. rotation
46. satisfaction
47. performance
48. enrichment
49. depth
50. planning
51. evaluating
52. enrichment
53. variety
54. identity
55. significance
56. autonomy
57. feedback
58. work
59. responsibility
60. results
61. growth
62. psychological
63. high-order
64. technology
65. enriched
66. autonomous
67. compressed
68. flexible
69. job
70. absenteeism
71. tardiness
72. turnover
73. performance

Testing Your Knowledge

True and False
1. T
2. F
3. T
4. T
5. F (not necessarily)
6. T
7. T
8. T
9. T
10. F

Multiple Choice
1. B
2. C
3. C
4. E
5. C
6. E
7. C
8. C
9. A
10. E

Matching
1. E
2. I
3. C
4. D
5. H
6. G
7. B
8. J
9. A
10. F

CHAPTER 9

Programmed Learning

1. staffing
2. support
3. effort
4. structures
5. jobs
6. leadership
7. ability
8. people
9. jobs
10. performance
11. planning
12. recruitment
13. selection
14. orientation
15. training
16. human resource
17. staffing
18. availabilities
19. job
20. description
21. specifications
22. specifications
23. needs
24. supply
25. growth
26. budget
27. turnover
28. technology
29. supply
30. audit
31. equal
32. affirmative
33. recruitment
34. selection
35. advertisement
36. contact
37. screening
38. internal
39. realistic
40. selection
41. application
42. interviewing
43. testing
44. reference
45. physical
46. hire
47. application
48. information
49. test
50. performance
51. valid
52. reliable
53. specification
54. time
55. assessment
56. socialization
57. orientation
58. performance
59. satisfaction
60. commitment
61. training
62. needs
63. objectives
64. methods
65. program
66. evaluating
67. learn
68. reinforcement
69. job
70. coaching
71. apprenticeship
72. modeling
73. off-the-job
74. mentoring
75. replacement
76. promotions
77. transfers
78. terminations
79. retirements
80. outplacement
81. firing

Testing Your Knowledge

True and False

1. T
2. T
3. T
4. F
5. T
6. T
7. T
8. T
9. T
10. F

Multiple Choice

1. A
2. B
3. C
4. E
5. A
6. B
7. C
8. E
9. A
10. D

Matching

1. D
2. F
3. G
4. B
5. C
6. E
7. J
8. A
9. H
10. I

CHAPTER 10

Programmed Learning

1. leading	33. followed	65. style
2. communication	34. power	66. circumstance
3. interpersonal	35. position	67. contingency (or situa-
4. motivation	36. personal	tional)
5. group	37. formal	68. leadership
6. leadership	38. obligation	69. situations
7. power	39. dependence	70. style
8. manager	40. expertise	71. situation
9. formal	41. identify	72. leader-member
10. informal	42. trait	73. task
11. chain	43. behavioral	74. position
12. power	44. contingency	75. path-goal
13. manipulative	45. personal	76. structured
14. reward	46. traits	77. unstructured
15. coercive	47. supervisory	78. achievement-oriented
16. legitimate	48. achievement	79. capable
17. reward	49. intelligence	80. characteristics
18. coercive	50. decisiveness	81. decision
19. legitimate	51. self-assurance	82. consensus
20. expert	52. behaviors	83. quality
21. reference	53. style	84. accepted
22. expert	54. task	85. efficient
23. reference	55. people	86. power
24. personal	56. task	87. leadership
25. behavior	57. people	88. performance
26. acceptance	58. decisions	89. satisfaction
27. directive	59. orders	90. expertise
28. capable	60. people	91. mechanistic
29. organization	61. task	92. routine (or repetitive)
30. personal	62. participative	93. technology
31. psychological	63. democratic	94. style
32. indifference	64. laissez-faire	95. situations

Testing Your Knowledge

True and False	Multiple Choice	Matching
1. T	1. C	1. C
2. T	2. C	2. D
3. T	3. C	3. A
4. F	4. D	4. J
5. T	5. B	5. B
6. T	6. E	6. I
7. T	7. A	7. F
8. T	8. C	8. G
9. F	9. A	9. H
10. T	10. D	10. E

CHAPTER 11

Programmed Learning

1. communication
2. communicate
3. decision making
4. desires
5. intentions
6. infuence
7. oral
8. planning
9. organizing
10. leading
11. controlling
12. sender
13. encoding
14. message
15. channel
16. decodes
17. meaning
18. intended
19. perceived
20. cost
21. noise
22. semantic
23. feedback
24. channels
25. physical
26. cultural
27. status
28. feedback
29. time
30. historical
31. simultaneously
32. authoritative
33. nonverbal
34. mixed
35. language
36. telling
37. listening
38. perception
39. screen
40. filter
41. interpretations
42. accuracy
43. stereotypes
44. halo
45. perceptions
46. projections
47. stereotype
48. halo
49. individual
50. selective
51. jobs
52. self-awareness
53. decision
54. empathetic
55. perceptions
56. distortions
57. organizational
58. formal
59. informal
60. grapevine
61. incorrect
62. downward
63. subordinates
64. problems
65. improvements
66. subordinates
67. lateral
68. role
69. ambiguity
70. conflict
71. expectations
72. expectations
73. attitudes
74. performance
75. content
76. feelings
77. feel
78. ideas
79. purpose
80. human
81. consult
82. message
83. help
84. communication
85. tomorrow
86. words
87. listener

Testing Your Knowledge

True and False	Multiple Choice	Matching
1. F	1. E	1. F
2. T	2. D	2. E
3. T	3. E	3. J
4. T	4. D	4. D
5. F	5. D	5. C
6. T	6. C	6. A
7. F	7. E	7. I
8. F	8. C	8. H
9. F	9. E	9. B
10. F	10. E	10. G

CHAPTER 12

Programmed Learning

1. try
2. motivation
3. level
4. direction
5. persistence
6. environment
7. rewards
8. reward
9. attention
10. well
11. content
12. process
13. reinforcement
14. needs
15. tensions
16. physiological
17. safety
18. social
19. self-actualization
20. deficit
21. hierarchy
22. deficit
23. progression
24. growth
25. power
26. affiliation
27. goals
28. power
29. process
30. inequity
31. rewards
32. unequal
33. inputs
34. rewards
35. leave
36. points
37. distort
38. effort-performances
39. outcomes
40. expectancy
41. instrumentality
42. valence
43. high
44. positive
45. environmental
46. thought
47. external
48. consequences
49. repeated
50. positive
51. negative
52. punishment
53. extinction
54. punishment
55. contingent
56. immediate
57. continuous
58. intermittent
59. punishment
60. people
61. behavior
62. ability
63. effort
64. support

Testing Your Knowledge

True and False

1. F
2. F
3. F
4. T
5. T
6. T
7. T
8. T
9. T
10. F

Multiple Choice

1. A
2. C
3. D
4. C
5. E
6. D
7. B
8. C
9. C
10. E

Matching

1. B
2. F
3. G
4. A
5. H
6. C
7. J
8. E
9. I
10. D

CHAPTER 13

Programmed Learning

1. group	33. outputs	65. behavior
2. authority	34. process	66. effort
3. resource	35. inputs	67. performance
4. outputs	36. inadequate	68. cohesiveness
5. networks	37. inappropriate	69. membership
6. interconnected	38. organizational	70. relationships
7. integrate	39. task	71. activities
8. task	40. membership	72. achievements
9. members	41. forming	73. memberships
10. goals	42. storming	74. loyalty
11. leader	43. integration	75. security
12. progress	44. total	76. self-esteem
13. informal	45. behavior	77. conformity
14. needs	46. task	78. norms
15. social	47. tension	79. interrelate
16. security	48. integration	80. groupthink
17. identification	49. working	81. task
18. psychological	50. integration	82. maintenance
19. leaders	51. dynamics	83. task
20. members	52. inputs	84. maintenance
21. synergy	53. performance	85. task
22. individual	54. maintenance	86. maintenance
23. expert	55. required	87. leadership
24. labor	56. psychological	88. inter-group
25. creative	57. activities	89. competition
26. interactions	58. sentiments	90. cooperation
27. fulfillments	59. interactions	91. coordination
28. maintenance	60. complement	92. enemy
29. social	61. support	93. goal
30. performance	62. harmonious	94. negotiation
31. maintenance	63. effectiveness	95. skills
32. inputs	64. norms	96. team

Testing Your Knowledge

True and False	Multiple Choice	Matching
1. T	1. E	1. D
2. T	2. E	2. F
3. F	3. D	3. E
4. T	4. D	4. A
5. T	5. D	5. G
6. F	6. B	6. H
7. F	7. A	7. I
8. F	8. D	8. J
9. T	9. E	9. B
10. T	10. D	10. C

CHAPTER 14

Programmed Learning

1. controlling
2. plans
3. performance
4. intentions
5. what
6. when
7. way
8. uncertainty
9. complexity
10. limitations
11. delegation
12. monitoring
13. objectives
14. prevent
15. correct
16. opportunities
17. cybernetic
18. self-controlled
19. objectives
20. performance
21. objectives
22. necessary
23. results
24. deviations
25. problems
26. opportunities
27. internal
28. external
29. precontrols
30. steering
31. yes/no
32. steering
33. postaction
34. performance
35. behaviors
36. result
37. policies
38. procedures
39. selection
40. job
41. authority
42. power
43. authority
44. performance
45. performance
46. evaluation
47. development
48. judgmental
49. counseling
50. relevant
51. unbiased
52. significant
53. rating
54. scale
55. critical
56. behaviorally
57. rank
58. paired
59. forced
60. individuals
61. organization
62. once
63. separately
64. attract
65. effort
66. performance
67. control
68. performance
69. job
70. control
71. benefit
72. discipline
73. progressive
74. objectives
75. objective
76. objectives
77. plans
78. standards
79. procedures
80. performance
81. measurement
82. defensiveness
83. performance
84. results
85. information
86. complexity
87. exception
88. understand
89. flex
90. structure
91. self
92. positive
93. objective

Testing Your Knowledge

True and False

1. T
2. T
3. F
4. T
5. F
6. T
7. F
8. F
9. T
10. F

Multiple Choice

1. C
2. E
3. E
4. D
5. D
6. C
7. C
8. D
9. E
10. E

Matching

1. F
2. G
3. B
4. H
5. A
6. C
7. D
8. E
9. I
10. J
11. K

CHAPTER 15

Programmed Learning

1. information
2. time
3. people
4. budgeting
5. resource
6. results
7. information
8. objectives
9. standards
10. performance
11. deviations
12. actions
13. activities
14. monetary
15. commitment
16. proposals
17. conditions
18. centers
19. revenue
20. cost
21. profit
22. investment
23. critically
24. future
25. planning
26. fixed
27. flexible
28. operating
29. master
30. long-term
31. zero-based
32. objectives
33. resource
34. evaluating
35. monitoring
36. on-going
37. master
38. demand
39. cost
40. costs
41. operating
42. budget
43. budget
44. budget
45. responsibility
46. profit
47. operating
48. cash
49. financial
50. break-even
51. revenue
52. costs
53. results
54. information
55. understandable
56. exception
57. flexible
58. controllable
59. objective
60. self-control
61. data
62. information
63. information
64. external
65. internal
66. information
67. system
68. hardware
69. software
70. processing
71. people
72. objectives
73. behavioral
74. used
75. information
76. information
77. improve
78. communication
79. understand
80. everything

Testing Your Knowledge

True and False	Multiple Choice	Matching
1. T	1. D	1. C
2. T	2. E	2. D
3. T	3. E	3. A
4. F	4. E	4. E
5. T	5. E	5. B
6. T	6. E	6. F
7. T	7. E	7. I
8. F	8. D	8. G
9. F	9. B	9. H
10. F	10. D	10. J

CHAPTER 16

Programmed Learning

1. people
2. equipment
3. material
4. people
5. equipment
6. finished
7. raw
8. people
9. continuous
10. intermittent
11. demand
12. production
13. services
14. working
15. deviations
16. inventories
17. schedules
18. demand
19. extrapolating
20. analysis
21. trend
22. seasonal
23. cyclical
24. moving
25. recent
26. recent
27. random
28. exponential
29. random
30. seasonal
31. trend
32. cyclical
33. short
34. forecast
35. independent
36. regression
37. least-squares
38. product/operations
39. things
40. time
41. people
42. aggregate
43. scheduling
44. goods
45. logistics
46. factory
47. capacity
48. machine
49. material
50. production
51. material-requirements
52. capacity
53. time
54. capacity
55. resource
56. efficiency
57. effectiveness
58. utilization
59. routing
60. capacity
61. Guntt
62. PERT
63. dependent
64. independent
65. ordering
66. holding
67. ordering
68. holding
69. equal
70. economic
71. inventory
72. lot-by-lot
73. Kanban
74. just-in-time
75. quality
76. statistics
77. defects
78. avoid
79. quality
80. circle
81. computer
82. production/operations

Testing Your Knowledge

True and False	Multiple Choice	Matching
1. T	1. E	1. C
2. T	2. C	2. A
3. F	3. E	3. F
4. F	4. E	4. E
5. T	5. C	5. D
6. F	6. B	6. B
7. F	7. C	7. G
8. T	8. D	8. H
9. F	9. C	9. J
10. T	10. D	10. I

CHAPTER 17

Programmed Learning

1. survive
2. criticism
3. suggestions
4. ideas
5. creativity
6. innovation
7. innovation
8. ideas
9. needs
10. implement
11. goals
12. resources
13. rewards
14. emotional
15. destructive
16. creativity
17. innovation
18. effort
19. cohesion
20. tension
21. individual
22. interpersonal
23. intergroup
24. interorganizational
25. approach-approach
26. avoidance-avoidance
27. approach-avoidance
28. double
29. substantive
30. emotional
31. competition
32. intensity
33. managed
34. facts
35. methods
36. goals
37. values
38. antecedent
39. felt
40. manifest
41. resolution
42. aftermath
43. ambiguities
44. resources
45. interdependencies
46. barriers
47. tension
48. discomfort
49. manifest
50. antecedent
51. nonattention
52. suppression
53. resolution
54. underlying
55. cooperativeness
56. assertiveness
57. avoidance
58. competition
59. accommodation
60. compromise
61. collaboration
62. desires
63. win-lose
64. confrontation
65. problem solving
66. problem solving
67. collaboration
68. superordinate
69. resources
70. human
71. structural
72. change
73. performance
74. organizational
75. objectives
76. strategy
77. technology
78. people
79. unfreezing
80. changing
81. refreezing
82. force-coercion
83. empirical-rational
84. normative-reeducative
85. threatened
86. communication
87. participation
88. support
89. agreement
90. diagnosis
91. intervention
92. reinforcement
93. interventions
94. sensitivity
95. role
96. redesign
97. career
98. team building
99. process-consultation
100. team building

Testing Your Knowledge

True and False
1. T
2. T
3. T
4. F
5. T
6. T
7. T
8. F
9. T
10. T

Multiple Choice
1. D
2. D
3. A
4. E
5. A
6. A
7. E
8. A
9. E
10. D

Matching
1. B
2. D
3. F
4. A
5. G
6. H
7. C
8. E
9. I
10. J

CHAPTER 18

Programmed Learning

1. union
2. labor-management
3. bargaining
4. 1800
5. 1930s
6. class
7. immigrants
8. high
9. resistance
10. industry
11. manufacturing
12. immigration
13. economic
14. legal
15. structural
16. characteristics
17. react
18. economic
19. capitalistic
20. representation
21. trades
22. craft
23. industrial
24. national
25. international
26. AFL-CIO
27. association
28. political
29. autonomy
30. local
31. stewards
32. crime
33. centralization
34. Wagner
35. National Labor Relations
36. Taft-Hartley
37. crimes
38. investigates
39. remedial
40. refrain
41. employees
42. worth
43. expansion
44. inflation
45. expansion
46. satisfaction
47. intrinsic
48. extrinsic
49. power
50. conditions
51. employment
52. communication
53. personnel
54. participation
55. compensation
56. security
57. within
58. petition
59. interest
60. majority
61. bargaining
62. security
63. rights
64. benefits
65. job
66. position
67. grievance
68. contract
69. arbitration
70. mediation
71. decision making
72. compensation
73. measures
74. seniority
75. jurisdictional
76. subcontract
77. just
78. displacement
79. adversarial
80. cooperation
81. communication
82. labor
83. grievance
84. "team"

Testing Your Knowledge

True and False

1. F
2. T
3. T
4. F
5. F
6. F
7. F
8. T
9. T
10. T

Multiple Choice

1. C
2. E
3. C
4. B
5. A
6. C
7. D
8. D
9. B
10. E

Matching

1. F
2. B
3. D
4. A
5. G
6. C
7. H
8. E
9. I
10. J

CHAPTER 19

Programmed Learning

1. international	29. corrupt	56. language
2. profits	30. intentions	57. etiquette
3. expanded	31. standards	58. external
4. raw	32. marketing	59. weaknesses
5. financial	33. general	60. worldwide
6. lower	34. cultural	61. forecasts
7. grow	35. economic	62. political
8. importation/exportation	36. legal-political	63. investment
9. licensing	37. educational	64. instability
10. management	38. constraints	65. conflict
11. ventures	39. life	66. governmental
12. foreign	40. deficiencies	67. economic
13. multinational corporation	41. shortages	68. environment
14. global	42. economic	69. context
15. adverse	43. free	70. geographic
16. complement	44. centralized	71. product
17. profits	45. western	72. decentralization
18. domestic	46. supply	73. flexibility
19. personnel	47. demand	74. staff
20. technologies	48. centralized	75. foreign
21. customs	49. culture	76. management
22. economy	50. power	77. centralization
23. government	51. uncertainty	78. formalization
24. politics	52. individualism-collectivism	79. lifetime
25. economic	53. masculinity	80. rotation
26. jobs	54. tailored	81. collective
27. capital	55. theories	82. circles
28. needs		

Testing Your Knowledge

True and False	Multiple Choice	Matching
1. T	1. E	1. A
2. T	2. E	2. F
3. T	3. B	3. B
4. T	4. E	4. C
5. T	5. E	5. E
6. T or F (contingent upon the situation)	6. B	6. D
7. F	7. C	7. I
8. T	8. D	8. G
9. T	9. E	9. H
10. F	10. C	10. J

CHAPTER 20

Programmed Learning

1. morals
2. standards
3. legality
4. moral
5. norms
6. values
7. norms
8. values
9. standards
10. principles
11. social
12. superiors
13. customers
14. employees
15. communication
16. advertising
17. kickbacks
18. person
19. employing
20. external
21. command
22. cohesiveness
23. ambiguous
24. superiors
25. moral
26. expectations
27. goals
28. expectations
29. codes
30. freedom
31. enforce
32. reasonable
33. safe
34. environmental
35. consumer
36. needs
37. relations
38. relations
39. economic
40. obligation
41. responsibility
42. responsiveness
43. responsiveness
44. profit
45. cost
46. skills
47. purpose
48. power
49. accountability
50. support
51. expectations
52. viability
53. image
54. environment
55. regulation
56. responsibility
57. try
58. resources
59. profits
60. curing
61. interests
62. life
63. interpersonal
64. campaigns
65. lobbying
66. candidate
67. illegal
68. values
69. profit
70. trusteeship
71. life
72. planning
73. organizing
74. controlling

Testing Your Knowledge

True and False

1. T
2. T
3. F
4. T
5. T
6. F
7. T
8. T
9. T
10. T

Multiple Choice

1. E
2. E
3. D
4. A
5. E
6. E
7. C
8. C
9. C
10. E

Matching

1. C
2. F
3. A
4. G
5. H
6. B
7. D
8. I
9. E
10. J

CHAPTER 21

Programmed Learning

1. express
2. leadership
3. broad
4. courage
5. service
6. determination
7. rights
8. security
9. life
10. technology
11. computer
12. electronic
13. robot
14. money
15. fear
16. financially
17. promotions
18. flexibility
19. centralize
20. decentralize
21. participation
22. scientific
23. unemployment
24. transition
25. stress
26. task
27. role
28. interpersonal
29. career
30. achievement
31. personalities
32. constructive
33. effort
34. creativity
35. diligence
36. destructive
37. disease
38. illness
39. humanitarianism
40. productivity
41. creativity
42. investment
43. productivity
44. prevent
45. cope
46. conflict
47. ambiguity
48. wellness
49. ambiguities
50. others
51. pace
52. relax
53. wellness
54. career
55. career
56. planning
57. self-awareness
58. work
59. performance
60. early adulthood
61. midlife
62. late adulthood
63. plateau
64. personal
65. ability
66. opportunity
67. perform
68. visible
69. move
70. mentor
71. career
72. education
73. skills
74. functions
75. roles

Testing Your Knowledge

True and False

1. F
2. F
3. T
4. T
5. T
6. F
7. T
8. F
9. F
10. T

Multiple Choice

1. E
2. E
3. C
4. D
5. D
6. E
7. A
8. E
9. C

Matching

1. C
2. D
3. B
4. A
5. G
6. E
7. H
8. F
9. J
10. I

NOTES